Black Religion / Womanist Thought / Social Justice
Series Editors Dwight N. Hopkins and Linda E. Thomas
Published by Palgrave Macmillan

"How Long this Road": Race, Religion, and the Legacy of C. Eric Lincoln
Edited by Alton B. Pollard, III and Love Henry Whelchel, Jr.

African American Humanist Principles: Living and Thinking Like
the Children of Nimrod
By Anthony B. Pinn

White Theology: Outing Supremacy in Modernity
By James W. Perkinson

The Myth of Ham in Nineteenth-Century American Christianity: Race,
Heathens, and the People of God
By Sylvester Johnson

Loving the Body: Black Religious Studies and the Erotic
Edited by Anthony B. Pinn and Dwight N. Hopkins

Transformative Pastoral Leadership in the Black Church
By Jeffery L. Tribble, Sr.

Shamanism, Racism, and Hip Hop Culture: Essays on White Supremacy
and Black Subversion
By James W. Perkinson

Women, Ethics, and Inequality in U.S. Healthcare: "To Count Among the Living"
By Aana Marie Vigen

Black Theology in Transatlantic Dialogue: Inside Looking Out, Outside Looking In
By Anthony G. Reddie

Womanist Ethics and the Cultural Production of Evil
By Emilie M. Townes

Whiteness and Morality: Pursuing Racial Justice through Reparations and Sovereignty
By Jennifer Harvey

Black Theology and Pedagogy
By Noel Leo Erskine

The Theology of Martin Luther King, Jr. and Desmond Mpilo Tutu
By Johnny B. Hill

Representations of Homosexuality

Black Liberation Theology and Cultural Criticism

Roger A. Sneed

REPRESENTATIONS OF HOMOSEXUALITY
Copyright © Roger A. Sneed, 2010.

First published in 2010 by
PALGRAVE MACMILLAN®
in the United States—a division of St. Martin's Press LLC,
175 Fifth Avenue, New York, NY 10010.

Where this book is distributed in the UK, Europe and the rest of the world,
this is by Palgrave Macmillan, a division of Macmillan Publishers Limited,
registered in England, company number 785998, of Houndmills,
Basingstoke, Hampshire RG21 6XS.

Palgrave Macmillan is the global academic imprint of the above companies
and has companies and representatives throughout the world.

Palgrave® and Macmillan® are registered trademarks in the United States,
the United Kingdom, Europe and other countries.

ISBN: 978–0–230–60824–5

Library of Congress Cataloging-in-Publication Data

Sneed, Roger A.
    Representations of homosexuality : black liberation theology and
cultural criticism / Roger A. Sneed.
        p. cm. — (Black religion/womanist thought/social justice)
    Includes bibliographical references and index.
    ISBN 978–0–230–60824–5
    1. African American gays. 2. African Americans—Attitudes.
3. Black theology. 4. Liberation theology—United States. I. Title.

HQ76.3.U6S64 2010
277.3'08308664—dc22   2009041348

A catalogue record of the book is available from the British Library.

Design by Newgen Imaging Systems (P) Ltd., Chennai, India.

First edition: March 2010

10 9 8 7 6 5 4 3 2 1

Printed in the United States of America.

To Grandmother

Contents

Series Editors' Preface

After Horace Griffin's *Their Own Receive Them Not: African American Lesbians and Gays in Black Churches* (2006), Roger Sneed now becomes the second major self-identified and African American gay Christian leader to produce a scholarly work on black liberation theology, culture, and black religion. And Sneed achieves his textual goal masterfully.

Sneed broaches core issues in the debate about same-gender loving couples—notions that, in reality, are heterosexual obsessions about their own sexual identities. For Sneed, the fundamental contentious presuppositions are: (1) The Bible is the authoritative voice of God concerning homosexuality, the Bible explicitly prohibits homosexual behavior; (2) Homosexual expression is neither physiologically viable nor safe; and (3) A person who identifies himself or herself as gay or same-gender loving always knows that they are and will automatically identify himself or herself as such to others. And his voice rings with clear insight and compelling evidence in the book's central argument: Black gay men's literature gives profound resources for deepening African American religious and culture critical theory, particularly in the discussions of sexual differences. Moreover, he surfaces a trenchant critique of black theology of liberation and womanist theology for egregious dereliction. The latter two conceptual disciplines and ways of life continually fall short by not building foundations upon which black gays can exercise their full human and religious identities.

Yet Sneed's work is not dry itemization of a thesis. The work does offer the reader the academic astute insight of a professor whom the church and the academy need to watch for future publications. For instance, he surfaces these questions: "What has black theology to say about the black gay man? What has the black gay man to say about his experiences, religious and otherwise?" He deploys bodies of knowledge and methodological insights from religious studies, black liberation theology, philosophical sensibilities, racial representations, and cultural criticism, among others.

At the same time, exhibiting conceptual clarity, *Representations of Homosexuality* gifts the reader with an almost autobiographical quality. Thus, we hold in our hands a book that uses narrative techniques of stories with interdisciplinary approaches, wrapped in deep faith. Sneed shares his life, one of struggling to come to terms with being black and gay. He was born and raised in Tulsa, Oklahoma, which is not known as a major Mecca for black people's creative and dominant self-creation space. Consequently, Sneed did not pursue his full open self. Moving to Atlanta for his Master's of Divinity degree, he encounters black gay preachers, community organizers, poets, literati, and other public figures. But some of his most challenging experiences take place in his seminary classes and within the black church. Sneed's path to embracing all of his identity dimensions reeks with struggle, tribulation, and periodic successes within the larger black community. However, it is telling the story of his proudly hugging both aspects of his being—black and gay—within the African American church that rivets the reader to the unfolding journey we undertake in this book.

At the end, Sneed's work suggests the universal notion of an ethics of openness. All of humanity would benefit in building the common good with such a move toward the realization of all as part of the whole.

Representations of homosexuality, black liberation theology, and cultural criticism represent one definite dimension of the black religion/womanist thought/social justice series' pioneering conceptual work and boundary-pushing effort. The series will publish both authored and edited manuscripts that have depth, breadth, and theoretical edge and will address both academic and nonspecialist audiences. It will produce works engaging any dimension of black religion or womanist thought as they pertain to social justice. Womanist thought is a new approach in the study of African American women's perspectives. The series will include a variety of African American religious expressions. By this we mean traditions such as Protestant and Catholic Christianity, Islam, Judaism, Humanism, African diasporic practices, religion and gender, religion and black gays/lesbians, ecological justice issues, African American religiosity and its relation to African religions, new black religious movements (for example, Daddy Grace, Father Divine, or the Nation of Islam), or religious dimensions in African American "secular" experiences (such as the spiritual aspects of aesthetic efforts like the Harlem Renaissance and literary giants

such as James Baldwin, or the religious fervor of the black consciousness movement, or the religion of compassion in the black women's
club movement).

DWIGHT N. HOPKINS
LINDA E. THOMAS

Acknowledgments

The process of writing a book is a very intense, personal, and often lonely endeavor. It involves hours of reading, writing, rereading, deleting and rewriting. However, I have been lucky to have friends, family, and colleagues who have been willing to listen to me "thinking out loud," or vent my frustrations during my occasional bouts with writer's block.

I am deeply indebted to the faculty, staff, and students of Furman University for their support. I owe a great debt to Victor Anderson. This book could not have been completed without his keen insight. He has been an exemplary mentor, teacher, and friend. I am forever indebted to him for the many discussions and debates that led to this book. I owe an equally great debt to Dwight Hopkins, who offered substantive critiques when this was a dissertation project and encouraged me to submit this manuscript for inclusion in this series. I am also eternally grateful for the support of my friends; Meredith Hammons, Heather McMurray, Charles Bowie, Patrick Bahls, Maggie Hoop, Kevin Happell and Suzanne Schier-Happell, Rima Abunasser, Darin Bradley, and Srdjan Smajic are true friends who provided both emotional and intellectual support. I must also thank Craig Johnson for being one of the best friends a person could have and for understanding when I would tell him to not ask me about my progress on "the D-word" back when this was a dissertation and then, simply, "The Book" as I was doing the work of revising and rewriting. Finally, I am extremely grateful for the support of my family, especially my sisters, Kim Peigne and Petronella Sneed. Through our almost weekly telephone calls and Internet chats, I have come to appreciate the women they have become, and I hope they have come to appreciate their sometimes-overbearing brother. Last, and certainly not least, I dedicate this book to my grandmother, Petronella Sneed. Without her unconditional love, quiet confidence, and patience, I do not know where I would be. Without her, I would not have known what an ethics of openness looks like.

Introduction

This book finds its genesis in an argument I had with a former friend of mine. On Wednesday evening, November 26, 1997, during my Thanksgiving break in Tulsa, I had occasion to visit one of my college fraternity brothers. As we chatted, the subject of homosexuality came up. More specifically, the subject of my homosexuality came up. For over two hours we argued about my rejection of what I consider to be homophobic interpretations of Scripture, what my standard for Christian living is if it is not the Bible, the physiological viability of male-to-male sexual intercourse, and, finally, whether or not I had fully thought out my decision to live my life as an open and proud same-gender-loving person.[1]

I was very angry for days following the conversation. For my friend, my fraternity brother, a person who had known me for more than six years, to tell me that I am not gay and that I was somehow confused was insulting to me. I fumed, wondering how I could answer his questions and counter his assumptions about homosexuality. As I sat at a breakfast counter at a Denny's restaurant outside of Memphis, the answer came to me: write an open letter and refute his assumptions in a systematic and controlled manner.

There were three major assumptions that surfaced during our debate:

1. The Bible is the authoritative voice of God concerning homosexuality. The Bible explicitly prohibits homosexual behavior;
2. Homosexual expression is neither physiologically viable nor safe;
3. A person who identifies himself or herself as gay or same-gender loving always knows that he or she is, and will automatically identify himself or herself as such to others.

These assumptions enjoy a prominent status in contemporary Christian beliefs regarding persons of homosexual orientation. The church has promulgated the first two assumptions in various ways, from the casual comment that "God made Adam and Eve, not Adam and Steve," to the less benign belief that homosexual persons are demon-possessed.

This letter found its focal point in black theology. Both my former friend and I were children of the black church and I assumed I could graft onto black liberation theology a "gay component" that would speak to the alienation I experienced as both a black person and a homosexual person. At that point, I was a seminarian at Candler School of Theology at Emory University in Atlanta, Georgia. I had begun to read the work of James Cone, Dwight Hopkins, Katie Cannon, and Emilie Townes. Their work influenced my response to my fraternity brother. It was my argument that it is imperative that we not separate our experiences as African Americans from our sexual identities.

The letter that I wrote to my fraternity brother and the subsequent paper that I submitted to my Christian ethics class were the products of a seminarian who was still attempting to come to terms with the intersections of race, religion, and sexuality. I drew on my understandings of biblical canon formation, African American history, and, primarily, black liberation theology. I argued that God and Jesus Christ stood for and with the oppressed. I wrote:

> You asked me what I choose to live by, implying an "either-or" dichotomy. You have attempted to back me into a corner with a "live it or leave it" ideology. Such an ideology is, for me, incompatible with the witness of Jesus Christ. If you must have a standard, then here it is: my standard is the witness of the life of Jesus Christ. Christ's life was a life lived with, around, and among the outcasts of society. From his opening mission statement in the fourth chapter of Luke to his death outside Jerusalem as a convicted outcast himself, Jesus stood for and with people whom society cast off. Those who society shunned, Jesus affirmed.
>
> I appeal to the Jesus of the oppressed. No, I do not appeal to Paul. Do I reject Paul? Do I reject the validity of the Bible? By no means, but to adapt a statement by Martin Luther King, Jr., an unjust interpretation of scripture is not an interpretation at all. I do not appeal to Pauline writings in either affirming or rejecting my own sexual orientation. To put it bluntly, Paul has nothing to do with my relationship with God and my sexuality. Jesus is my standard. Jesus is the mediator who has stood, stands, and will stand with me. The word of God was and is embodied in Jesus.
>
> The gospel of Jesus Christ does not condemn or exclude gays or lesbians. The gospel of Jesus Christ accepts and affirms us by the Great

Commandment: "'You shall love the Lord your God with all your heart, and with all your soul, and with all your mind.' This is the greatest and first commandment. And a second is like it: 'You shall love your neighbor as yourself.' On these two commandments hang all the law and the prophets." What was Jesus' standard? His standard was love. The love that Jesus allowed—no, propelled him to experience the companionship of people whom society had ignored, enslaved, and oppressed. Jesus, the living Word, gave us the standard by which we live and have our being: that standard is love grounded in mutual respect for and with the Other.

As I reread that letter (which I submitted as a final paper for my Christian Ethics course at Candler School of Theology) some ten years later, I find parts of it quaint and overbearingly naïve. I find other parts of it sermonic and syrupy, without much intellectual heft. Further, it represents a theologically limited viewpoint, one that I now critique. At that time in the late 1990s, I had attempted to graft onto black liberation and womanist theologies another level of experience in African American life. As I advanced in my graduate studies, I always questioned where and when sexual orientation would enter into discussions of black life. This line of questioning was the result of my own experiences both as a college student in my hometown of Tulsa, Oklahoma, and as a seminarian in Atlanta, Georgia.

Atlanta seemed to be a quantum leap away from my formative years in Tulsa. Here was a metropolis, a city bursting with pride and excitement, a black Mecca. I moved there two weeks after the conclusion of the 1996 Summer Olympics. The possibilities seemed endless. Atlanta offered a class of black professionals, a growing black upper-class, and social and professional opportunities that I could not have dreamed possible back in Oklahoma. It also offered a class of African American gay men who were out, proud, and productive. When I wasn't in class arguing with the professors and students, I was writing poetry with a group of poets, engaging in heated discussions with social activists, participating in marches, and attending book signings and readings.

By the end of my first month in Atlanta, I had joined a discussion group called Second Sunday. This was a discussion group for black gay and bisexual men. We would discuss a range of issues, from the question of religion and homosexuality to classism among gay men. I had encountered people like Malik Williams, Duncan Teague, and Tony Daniels, a trio of men who formed a spoken-word and performance group named Adodi Muse. They were political activists and performance artists who were audacious and transgressive. These were not men who were being spoken for. They were doing the speaking. They were not being signified upon by others. Instead, this group of out, socially and politically active black gay men were doing the work of signifying.

In addition to the political activity of black gay men, there was the aspect of their mere presence. Black gay men were everywhere. Of all shapes, sizes, ages, and colors, I could rest knowing that I was not alone. I would spend my Friday evenings at Loretta's, a legendary black gay club in Midtown Atlanta, and my Saturday evenings at Traxx, a club that specialized in house music. House music was where I discovered the liberation of the body through music—as Tony put it, "I got my life" through dancing for hours, as the disc jockey exhorted the crowd. There were Saturday nights in which the DJ morphed into a Baptist preacher. I can still hear the DJ saying, "Some of you shouldn't be here! You know someone who isn't here!" The implication of that exhortation was that many of us knew someone who had died, or, as he later put it, "wasn't in their right mind," and we should be happy that we were among those who yet lived. Occasionally, I would dance with another man, and discovered that dancing could be even more rapturous.

I had no qualms about being "out of the closet," or, open about my sexual orientation. When I came out in Oklahoma, I had to contend with people who had known me for most of my life. Some people expressed shock, others dismay, others simply said, "We were waiting for you to figure it out." I encountered other black gay men in Tulsa, but none were willing to be out. None were willing to take the chance, to risk being ostracized by a community that was deeply rooted in conservative Protestantism. However, in Atlanta, I found churches where I could not only be open about my sexual orientation, but could participate in the life of the church without having to separate my sexual self. I did not have to apologize for being gay. Being black, gay, and out was far easier in Atlanta than it had been in Tulsa.

Thus, it would perturb me when I would encounter other African Americans who espoused antigay sentiments. "How could someone living in a metropolis like Atlanta say or think such things?" I would wonder. I still find it ironic that Atlanta is known as both a Mecca for black gays and lesbians and yet is also known for being home to virulently antigay preachers like New Birth Missionary Church pastor Bishop Eddie L. Long.[2] My attempts to engage people (often my classmates at Candler) in discussion about issues of sexual orientation often degenerated almost into shouting matches. I am reminded of a particularly contentious class session in my Black Theology and Ethics course. We were tasked with forming groups and addressing a particular theological or moral issue. I chose to participate in the group dealing with homosexuality. The presentation itself was contentious, with a group member nearly sabotaging the group with a virulently homophobic screed. However, the question-and-answer session proved far more problematic when a cross-registered student from another local seminary bluntly stated, "When you pull down your pants, I'm sure you'll find you have a penis and not a vagina!"

I would also engage in debates with my classmates concerning the authenticity of biblical texts—especially those that were repeatedly referenced in relation to homosexuality. However, by my final year at Candler, I had decided that I would remain silent. I had spent the previous two years arguing with professors and students about sexuality and religion and had decided that I would be a "good" student and leave the arguing to others. After all, I reasoned, I had graduate school applications to complete and the Graduate Record Examination to prepare for. I would comfort myself with the notion that after the working week was over I could retreat into my busy black, gay world. I would not bother with engaging my classmates in yet another argument over biblical interpretation and its relevance to African Americans. However, in a class called "The Black Church As A Social Institution," Dr. Alton Pollard asked us about our views of the Bible. I decided that I would not say a word. Other students replied that they thought it was the inerrant word of God. Dr. Pollard looked around the class and, smiling, asked if anyone thought differently. Again, I remained silent. Eventually, the silence wore on, and then I raised my hand. I said that I perceived the Bible as a collection of texts that documented people's encounters with that which they considered to be the divine. Dr. Pollard then asked me if that meant I did not take the Bible as the inerrant word of God, to which I replied that I did not. Other students reacted viscerally to the statement and led to a spirited exchange about the Bible and the black church.

The church to which my colleagues repeatedly referred and appealed was a heteronormative black church. My fellow students acknowledged the existence of black gays and lesbians—there were a few of us at Candler who would continually remind them of such. However, the manner in which they constructed the presence of black gays and lesbians was vis-à-vis heterosexual experience and description of gays and lesbians. In other words, the presence of black gays and lesbians was always circumscribed and mitigated by stereotype. We were choir directors and choir members, but we were never the pastor or the deaconess, despite the reality that there were black gay pastors in Atlanta.

I sought out and found black churches that affirmed sexual difference. They were diverse, usually small religious communities. They usually patterned themselves after larger denominational churches, except with one major difference. These churches reconfigured God so that God was open and not closed to queer identities. They spoke of God as a god who loves all and refuses none. Some of the pastors who preached messages of universal love based their sermons on black liberation theology, as I had when I wrote my open letter.

However, I found that in black churches that explicitly affirmed sexual difference, black liberation theology had not progressed much beyond simplistic statements such as "God Loves You." My debates in that world often centered on the problematic questions of what God is and what that God requires of human beings. God was often described as an entity who not only stands on the side of the oppressed but loves the outcast. The standard refrain of "God Loves You" that permeated these churches was an attempt to combat the sentiment in other churches that God does not sanction homosexual identity or behavior. Further, black gays and lesbians who attended "open and affirming" churches such as Unity Fellowship Church and were active in the community attempted to reconfigure God. For example, at Unity, the motto was "God is love and love is for everyone." The motto is reflective of the denomination's approach to God as an entity who does not withhold love from anyone. The denomination's Web site offers a glimpse into their theological approach in the "About Us" section:

> We are the Unity Fellowship Church Movement ("UFCM"), a movement of churches across the United States whose primary work is to proclaim the sacredness of all life, focusing on empowering those who have been oppressed and made to feel excluded and ashamed. UFCM brings the message of God's unconditional love and the principles of liberation theology to often ostracized communities. UFCM opens its doors to all of God's people, especially those fighting for social justice. The churches within our movement offer those seeking to worship God, in spirit and truth, a place to come just as they are.[3]

Having attended these churches and been active in black gay organizations, I found that black gays and lesbians reconfigured themselves as much as they attempted to reconfigure God. In an attempt to divest themselves of what they perceived to be a racially loaded designation, some black gays and lesbians rejected the term "gay" and adopted "same-gender loving." This shift reflected activist Cleo Manago's argument that "same-gender loving" (SGL) was a more appropriate way of describing African American homosexuals. What black homosexuals sought was a way to articulate both the manner in which "gay" had come to signify white privilege and a new consciousness among African American gays and lesbians. It signified an attempt to come to terms with seemingly disparate and incommensurate identities.

The concern over conflicting identities stretched beyond the intersections of race and sexual orientation. Sometimes, when I would reveal to people that I was in seminary, I would be asked, "How can you be gay and study religion?" That may appear as a naïve or silly question, but there was a certain logic behind the question—albeit, that logic was rooted in a particular reading of religion and human sexuality. In other words, the problem of the intersections of race and sexuality was not limited to black heterosexuals, as the aforementioned question often came from other black gays and lesbians. As I interpreted that question, it appeared to me that many black gays and lesbians whom I encountered also failed to imagine a world wherein sexual difference was not antithetical to religious experience or the academic study of the said experience.

Further, the logic behind the question was that if one identifies himself or herself as gay, he or she has already assumed a subject position. To describe oneself as gay (or any of its satellite markers, like transgender or bisexual) is to locate that self (especially the body) within a position that is not constructed by the person disclosing his or her sexual orientation. The action of "coming out" is made possible by this construction of sexual difference, particularly the notion that nonheterosexual orientations are deviant. Coming out is made possible by the very binaries and dualisms (heterosexuality and homosexuality, gay and straight) that revelations of sexual difference might appear to destabilize. Rather than destabilizing these dualisms, the notion of "coming out" appears to reify those distinctions.

As I begin this project, I am reminded of several conversations I had with my mentor Victor Anderson, who said that once one identifies himself or herself as gay or lesbian, then it allows the audience to marginalize or trivialize his or her work as that "gay" or "lesbian" work. He questioned the necessity and efficacy of self-identification in relation to academic scholarship. Further, our conversations often turned to both the job market and my audience for my writing. These conversations were, in turn, influenced by a conversation I once had with Anthony Pinn, wherein he pointedly asked me, "Who's your audience?" The linkage between Pinn's question and Anderson's concerns about an autobiographical turn is compelling.

As I continue to ponder Pinn's question of audience, I think that it is a problematic one. As a scholar, I write of my own particular intellectual interests. In other words, there is a question or series of questions that I am trying to make sense of. Nevertheless, academic writing is an intensely personal endeavor, as many of the questions to which I try to bring a response are influenced by what occurs in the world around me. In the case of this book, I ask the questions, "What has black theology to say about the black gay man? What has the black gay man to say about his experiences, religious and otherwise?" Insofar as a potential audience, I cannot say anything. I would like to suggest that everyone should read this book. However, given the nature of academic writing, it is likely that my fellow academicians as well as a number of students will read this work.

In a sense, Anderson's argument makes sense, from a Foucauldian perspective. In "confessing" one's sexual orientation, the work then risks taking a therapeutic turn as opposed to a scholarly tone. By this I mean that the writer can then be "diagnosed" by his or her readers as writing out of a particular impulse that may need to be remedied or mediated. Further, the confession itself might reify the heteronormative categories that govern academic discourse concerning sexual orientation, as heterosexual scholars do not tend to have their arguments concerning sexual ethics and the like reduced to the sexuality of the author. As Anderson notes in *Creative Exchange: A Constructive Theology of African American Religious Experience* (2008), the Western tradition of philosophical and religious argumentation emphasizes the argument itself, instead of the social location of the writer.[4] Further, an autobiographical turn occasions the possibility of having one's argument dismissed or trivialized.

However, this book foregrounds the necessity of speaking to the worlds of difference that constitute the intersections of race, sexuality, and religion. If late twentieth-century African American theology is concerned with addressing African American experiences as a way of understanding the ways in which human beings approach that which they consider to be the divine, such theologies are impoverished if they only consider those experiences that are palatable to only a particular segment of the potential readership. Thus, I think it fitting that I begin this book with a reflection on previous attempts to address the intersection of race, sexuality, and religious experience.

As I reflected on that letter as a representation of the time I spent in Atlanta, I found myself critical of my own desire to forge out of black liberation theology a more atomized or reductivist black *gay* liberation theology. At the time, I was critical only of black liberation theology's failure to speak to the diversity of black experiences. I had not at the time considered that black liberation and womanist theologies were reifying anything other than a heteronormative conception of black identity. It was out of the particularity of black liberation theology that I sought a more particular theological emphasis on sexuality and sexual difference. While the questions and concerns that led me to write that letter may remain, my conclusions have changed. When I wrote that letter and when I wrote the dissertation upon which this book is based, I was concerned with the intersections of race, religion, and sexual difference. Simply put, I wanted to uncover when and where the black homosexual enters into African American religious dialogue. In seminary and graduate school, I had grown weary of seeing black gays entering into discussions only as victims of plague or predators who sought out putatively heterosexual married men. I had simultaneously grown tired of seeing black gays presented in the larger culture as a threat to the integrity of the black body politic. The late 1990s saw the birth of the black cultural obsession with the "down low" or closeted black gay (male). The threat of the HIV/AIDS virus served as the impetus behind this cultural obsession in the popular media and, later, among black theologians. However, such a focus on HIV/AIDS only reinforced the presentation of black gays as social pariahs, outcasts, and objects of scorn or pity. It seemed that the only way to gain an audience among black heterosexuals was to present gay experience and existence through the lens of victimization.

What I sought at that time was visibility. This might appear odd or poorly stated, as I have already mentioned that black gays were not invisible to the larger world. I sought the same kind of visibility in African American religious life that I saw in African American gay life in Atlanta. Reflecting on what Essex Hemphill (or was it Joseph Beam) said about going into a library and not once being able to find a book that accurately reflected the struggles of being a black gay or black lesbian youth, I found it more and more difficult to find anything that reflected my existence as an African American gay man that did not rise above the trivial or the tragic. When coming out, I encountered much in the way of "sympathy" from supposedly well-meaning black Christians. However, that sympathy often took the form of concern over whether or not I was practicing "safe sex" and the real possibility that I might contract HIV/AIDS (as though that possibility was somehow not part of their particular existence). As I reflect on what I sought, I did not seek mere visibility. In other words, simply being presented or acknowledged as existing was not enough. I had grown tired of seeing sexual difference in African American life presented, at best, as a "cause" that could highlight the problematic nature of white supremacy (in chapter 2 I discuss the manner in which black liberation theologians and cultural critics attempt to link negative attitudes toward sexual difference in African American life to white supremacy), or, at worst, as a problem to be regulated through trivialization or demonization.

I can point to "In Living Color's" Blaine and Antoine and the figure of "the down low brother" as examples of the problematic ways in which black gays were presented in the 1990s and into the twenty-first century. The characters of Blaine and Antoine were caricatures that were every bit as stereotypical and offensive as Mammy, Jezebel, or the Black Brute. Blaine and Antoine were mincing queens who were apparently obsessed with seducing and having sex with popular Hollywood actors. As played by Damon Wayans and David Allen Grier, their respective characters Blaine and Antoine were overtly effeminate and played for laughs. Through the stereotypical gaze of heterosexual blacks, Blaine and Antoine were the late twentieth-century equivalent of Sambo. While Blaine and Antoine executed various double entendres (I am reminded of one of their fake sponsors for their movie review segment, "Nuts N' Honey"), spoke in high pitched voices, and dressed flamboyantly, they were nevertheless rendered harmless. These gays never interacted with other characters. In essence, they were contained, sequestered away from the other characters and skits so as not to contaminate them with their homosexuality.

In addition, their sexuality was presented as a choice, an intentional deviation from the more correct black heteronormative masculinity. In an infamous skit, Blaine is accidentally hit on the head by a stage prop and knocked unconscious. After Blaine regains consciousness, the audience recognizes a dramatic shift in Blaine's character. His speech is no longer affected with a lisp; rather, it is now deep and commanding. Blaine notices his clothing and shows discomfort at wearing a blouse. Of course, the audience realizes that Blaine has suffered amnesia as a result of the accident and cannot remember that his former persona was a gay man. Blaine's amnesia and Antoine's dismay at his partner's change is played for laughs, until Blaine is again hit over the head and his homosexuality is "restored."

In this manner of representation, one might argue that "black homosexuals" are not invisible. However, *black homosexuals* are not visible either. "In Living Color's" Blaine and Antoine are comical figures that can be dismissed. Their homosexuality is denatured, played for laughs and rendered innocuous and nonthreatening. Further, there is a reason I bracket the term "black homosexuals" first by indexical marks and later by italics in the above sentences. When speaking of "black homosexuals," particularly in the case of Blaine and Antoine from "In Living Color," I am speaking of heterosexuals playing as homosexuals. The playing as a homosexual almost usually involves some kind of stereotype, often exaggerated beyond itself to the point of parody, slapstick, and absurdity. Thus, black homosexuals—those who are gay, lesbian, bisexual, and the like—and their concrete realities are dismissed.

In the middle of this spectrum is the virtual erasure of black gays and lesbians from allegedly "black" concerns. Tavis Smiley's *The Covenant With Black America* (2006) serves as a prime example of this near-total erasure of black gay and lesbian existence. Smiley's publication came about in the aftermath of the 2004 presidential election that saw George W. Bush elected to a second term and the strengthening of a right-wing agenda that was perceived as dangerous to African American political interests. Also, according to the Web site designed to disseminate information about the *Covenant*,

> Americans are deeply divided between race, class, gender, political ideology and moral values. A divide so extreme, that in order to bridge it, we must speak openly, freely, without judgment and work together. It is imperative that we take this opportunity to consider the issues of particular interest to African Americans and to establish a national plan of action to address them. No longer can we sit back and expect one political party, one segment of the population or one religious denomination to speak for us or to act on our behalf. It is our responsibility as an entire community to no longer be left behind politically, socially, or economically and to bridge the economic and social divides ourselves, by encouraging a conversation and a commitment that will inevitably benefit all Americans.[5]

What Smiley and others see in contemporary America is an ongoing crisis that threatens the integrity of African American life. While the

Covenant speaks to political, economic, medical, and justice issues that affect African Americans, I can find nothing in the *Covenant* that addresses the problems of heteronormativity and homophobia in African American public life. As far as the *Covenant* is concerned, black gays and lesbians simply do not exist.

On the other end of the stereotypical spectrum lay the "down low brother," the black man who has sex with other men and "passes" for heterosexual to the larger black community. Instead of being a joke, the down low (DL) brother now exists as a threat to the integrity of a putatively heterosexual black community. However, the down low brother is still a phantasm, a ghost who haunts the black community. In neither case are black gays visible. In other words, the picture of black gays available to black communities in the late twentieth century was painted not by black queers themselves, but by black heterosexuals. However, those examples from popular culture raised the question of what kind of visibility did black gays and lesbians have? What I sought was visibility beyond the problems of homophobia and HIV/AIDS. Further, as I became more involved in organizations specifically for black gays and lesbians, I sought a wider discourse that was facilitated by black gays and lesbians. At the same time, I sought descriptions of God that were amenable to black homosexual experiences.

I proceeded from the same assumption as black liberation and womanist theologians: God stood for and with the oppressed. As I understood sexual difference as a category of oppression, it was simple for me to argue that God would also exercise a preferential option for gays and lesbians of color. Again, borrowing from both Gustavo Gutierrez, the father of Latin American liberation theology, and James Cone, the father of black liberation theology, I linked the struggles of black gays with the larger struggle of African Americans and, influenced by early readings of Jürgen Moltmann, contended that God would break into history and, through the activity of human beings, bring about liberation of black gays in particular from the yoke of homophobia. As I continued to read black theology, I encountered what I now consider to be a critical error. Though important in its endeavor to craft a liberation theology that speaks to the experiences of black peoples, black liberation theology first appeared to ignore and then later downplay the roles of black lesbians and gays in the black church. This oversight is not unexpected, however. Many disciplines that concern themselves with black life and thought have either disregarded the contributions of gay and lesbian people or ignored their sexuality altogether.

Only recently has homosexuality even begun to be discussed within black theology. However, African American gays and lesbians are still marginalized, relegated to a subset of womanist ethics. Womanist theology and ethics is admirable in that it seeks to address homophobia with an even hand and treats it as a grievous sin, at par with racism and white supremacy. Thanks to scholars like Renee Hill and Kelly Brown Douglas, discussions of sexual difference as part of black theology have gained greater attention. Nevertheless, this implied linkage of homosexuality with womanist ethics feminizes and marginalizes black gay men. The continued stereotyping of black gay men as feminine or of womanist theological concern by the largely male black theological leadership allows that leadership the ability to view black gay men as insignificant or secondary. My early attempts to intellectually come to terms with the intersection of black life and sexual difference adopted a strategy of victimization.

It is that strategy of victimization (and implied victimizing) that undergirds contemporary discussions of sexual difference in African American life. As I mentioned before, the "problem" of the "down low" (or DL) had become a topic of much conversation in black communities. The first years of the twenty-first century have seen a number of black media outlets dissecting and obsessing about African American men who have sex with other men. However, they have not been concerned with black men who are proud of their sexual orientation. Rather, these outlets have been inordinately concerned with those who appear to be not only ashamed of or embarrassed by their sexual orientation, but work diligently to cover it up. This prurient interest in these so-called "DL" men had nearly spawned a cottage industry of literature (as evidenced by the books written by J.L. King), "special" episodes of television series, and "very special" episodes of daytime talk television. Black men "on the DL" had become inextricably linked with the alarming rise of HIV-infection rates among heterosexual black women. As scapegoats, black men on the DL served as the entry point for attempting to "discuss" issues of homosexuality in African American life.

However, as talk shows presented "shocking exposes" about men on the DL and magazines targeted toward African American heterosexual women continued to present black men who have sex with other men as a dangerous, yet utterly fascinating, curiosity, black gay men who did not characterize themselves as being on the DL or display any fear or shame about their sexual orientation receded further and further into the background. Black scholars such as Cornel West and bell hooks continually wrote about the evils of homophobia and attempted to link homophobia with white supremacy. However, they never seemed able to actually speak about homosexuality—what or who was this black homosexual about whom they spoke? Womanist theologians wrote eloquently about the problem of heteronormativity in African American life. They spoke to the need for black communities to become communities that would look like Martin Luther King's "beloved community." Nevertheless, they never allowed black gays to speak for themselves. As they wrote about homophobia and heterosexism, they appeared to assume that their readers knew just who this "black gay" was. However, to borrow from Marlon Riggs, could the queen speak? It appears as though the queen had been silenced, or, effectively policed and circumscribed, so that their utterances disappear into a vacuum.

Plan of the Book

As I have approached this book, the question of whether or not sexual orientation is acceptable in God's sight is not a central concern. Indeed, I wonder whether appeals to a deity for "tolerance" of sexual difference are efficacious. I have read and examined theological arguments proffered by gay theologians, both black and white. Their arguments, such as can be found in Robert Goss' *Jesus Acted Up* (1993) or Richard Cleaver's *Know My Name* (1995), contend that God stands in solidarity with gays and lesbians.[6] These theologians argue that the Christian church cannot be the true church of Christ so long as it continues to support the disenfranchisement of its gay and lesbian members. For example, Father John McNeill's book, *The Church and the Homosexual* (1993), takes the Catholic Church to task for a moral theology that explicitly excludes homosexual Christians. He argues that the church's moral theology forces homosexuals into marriages in order to "escape detection," which further undermines marriage.[7]

This book represents an attempt to move away from representing black sexual difference under the rubric of victimization. Thus, attempting to refute homophobic assertions of the abnormality of homosexuality would be counterproductive. It would be counterproductive in that, again, the black queer would recede into the background. In other words, it would be yet another book engaging in special pleading with black heterosexuals to accept this nebulous, amorphous black homosexual. There are a plethora of intellectual

resources available that have explored the question of sexual orientation and biblical texts and have dealt with the problem of heteronormativity. From Daniel Helminiak's *What The Bible Really Says About
Homosexuality* (2000) to Kelly Brown Douglas's critique of the ways
in which African American churches use the Bible to justify antigay
sentiments to John Boswell's seminal *Christianity, Social Tolerance
and Homosexuality* (1980), religious scholars have conducted exhaustive examinations of ancient proscriptions of sexual difference. What
I am concerned about is how black liberation theologians and African
American cultural critics approach sexual difference in black communities. Further, I am interested in presenting an alternative to viewing
black gays as a "problem people." Thus, the approach in this book
is fairly straightforward. The central argument of this book is that
there are rich sources in black gay men's writings that can and should
inform and help reshape the manner in which black religious scholars
and cultural critics approach sexual difference in African American
religious and cultural life. A secondary, though no less important,
argument is that black liberation and womanist theologies have failed
to provide a substantive ground upon which black gays can reconstruct their sexual experiences and orientations.

Chapter 1 introduces the major themes that lead to both the development of black theologies of liberation and also precipitate particular responses to black sexuality (including homosexuality) in black
theologies and African American cultural criticism. This chapter is an
overview of the development of black liberation and womanist theologies. The emergence of black liberation and womanist theologies
is but two of many responses to the problem of racism and white
supremacy in American society. They are by no means the sole theological responses to white supremacy in America; however, in the
late twentieth century, they have been the most insistent. Further, for
nearly thirty years, black liberation and womanist theologies have
been the most strident and critical academic theological discourses
concerning African American life and experience. Thus, the first
chapter will outline the major influences that led to the development
of these theological movements. Further, this chapter will address the
manner in which black theologians approached sexuality in African
American life.

Chapter 2 will present an inquiry into the manner in which homosexuality enters into black liberationist discourse, namely, the black
power movement. This interrogation is important, as it is the black
power movement that supplies black liberation theology with its

rhetorical force, and the development of feminism and the sexual revolution formed the background conditions that led to the emergence of womanist theology. This chapter will pose the question, "When and how does homosexuality enter into black liberation and womanist theologies and African American cultural criticism?" This book does not assume that homosexuality is completely absent from the entirety of black theological discourse. Discussions of sexual difference do not appear in James Cone's formulation of a black theology, nor do they appear in the works of any of his critics until Elias Farajaje-Jones and Renee Hill presented their challenges, which appear in the second volume of *Black Theology: A Documentary Witness*. Chapter 2 will take up the questions that Farajaje-Jones and Hill posed, as well as Cheryl Sanders' response and Kelly Brown Douglas' examination of black sexuality in *Sexuality and the Black Church* and *What's Faith Got To Do With It?* What I am concerned about and what this chapter addresses is the manner in which these theologians present sexual difference in African American life.

Chapter 3 is a return to black theology. However, it is not a return to black theology as written by black heterosexuals. This chapter will focus on the theological responses to the question of black queer existence and experiences as presented by Horace Griffin, Elias Farajaje-Jones, and Victor Anderson. As Dwight Hopkins noted in *Introducing Black Theology of Liberation* (1999), there are theologians who are working to bring black queer experiences from the margins of black theological discourse. This chapter will examine how these theologians present God in the light of black queer experience. In other words, a series of questions constitute the framework of this chapter. What do black queer theologians have to say concerning black queer experience and theological reflection? How do they construe the figure of God in relation to black homosexuals? How do they take hold of African American religious and intellectual life vis-à-vis black sexual difference?

Chapters 4 and 5 present a shift as I turn to the literary expressions of African American gay men. I recognize that readers may question my specific use of black gay men's literature and be concerned that I am replicating the same hegemonic discourse I claim to be critiquing. However, this book is not intended to present an exhaustive examination of black gay literature. Indeed, this book does not purport to present a complete assessment of all black gay men's literature. Such a task would take years to write and, because new literature is always forthcoming, would never be complete. What I intend to do in this book is to take a representative sample of black gay men's literature and pose two questions.

These chapters may be read as the crux of my argument. If black liberation and womanist theologies purport to speak for marginalized black folk and claim the utterances of the folk as sources for doing theology, then it appears to be vitally important for this critique to turn to the voices of black gay men. Again, I return to a guiding question: what is it that black gay men have to say about themselves and their religious experiences? This question is not easily answered, for we first have to contend with deciding which voices will enter into the discussion.

During the writing of this book, I engaged in several conversations concerning the efficacy of using writers like E. Lynn Harris alongside Langston Hughes and Randall Kenan. The assumptions and concerns behind the conversations addressed the potential problem of classifying Harris's works of fiction alongside those of Hughes and Kenan. I was told that, by examining Harris's novels and subjecting them critical analysis, I was taking Harris too seriously and giving him too much credit. A criticism might arise that I am favoring popular writers and assigning to them an undeserved critical status. My response is that I do not wish to replicate the same mistakes that I criticize black liberation and womanist theologians of making. If this book characterizes or construes the fictions of E. Lynn Harris as less worthy of critical attention than the fictions of Randall Kenan, then I have developed a rigid canon based on a subjective account of black gay men's writings that is rooted in a "high versus low culture" dichotomy.

The first question is, "What do black gay male writers have to say about themselves and their experiences?" As I noted earlier, the prior chapters examine what black theologians and cultural critics (who are largely self-identified heterosexuals) have said about sexual difference in black communities. Thus, it is only logical to turn to the subject itself and, as Marlon Riggs put it, "let the queen speak." Bringing black queer voices forward is important, as these voices speaking for themselves and about their experiences enrich our descriptions of black life.

In chapter 4, I ask a different yet similar question, "What do black gay male writers have to say about their religious experiences?" A reviewer for an essay I wrote for *Black Theology: An International Journal* pointedly asked if the writers I examined presented their own theology or if they followed the same theology of black liberation and womanist theologians. In response to that query, I replied that black queer writers do not explicitly present a theology. Rather, they call for black religious communities to revise the ways they approach sexual orientation and God. Here, I intend to expand upon that evaluation and examine the religious orientations of black gay male writers. It is my contention that black gay male writers have remained focused on the black body and the replication of power upon black gay bodies. In other words, black queer writers are concerned with the ways in which black heterosexuals try to limit or proscribe the black gay body. Thus, their writings are focused on a this-worldly freedom. When they approach the black church, thy approach it as a human institution filled with black bodies, erotic, hypocritical, passionate, and, ultimately, human.

These chapters will not serve as an uncritical valorization of black gay men's writings. In other words, I do not presume to argue that black gay men's literature is a perfect, unified whole and offers black theologians a ready-made wellspring from which to construct a black and gay theology of liberation. Indeed, these chapters will be quite critical of the ways in which black queer writers address the inter-section of religion and spirituality and queer experience. In many of these writings by black gay men, the concept of God is quite nebulous. For example, E. Lynn Harris's novels mention God, but his characters (usually his protagonists) who invoke God do so in such a weak and unsustained fashion that it appears that there would be no substantive difference had they not mentioned or invoked God in the first place.

Chapter 6 and the Conclusion are constructive moves that offer different responses to sexual difference in African American life. Chapter 6 represents an attempt at a constructive move. Much of the book is concerned with the presentation and re-presentation of black gay men's identities. Consequently, I offer my own argument con-cerning the reconstruction of black gay men's identities beyond the problem of plague and homophobia. This chapter is a return to black gay men's voices and the ways in which they construe their identities. However, I turn not to literature, but, rather, to the Internet. The task of this chapter is not to find some "perfect" black gay male. Rather, the task is to examine how black gay men construe their sexual selves vis-à-vis personal advertisements. It is the contention in this chapter that black gay men use the medium of the Internet in order to present pictures of black gay identity that conforms to particular notions of masculinity. While HIV/AIDS and social stigmas concerning being "out" affect the ways in which users of Internet "social networking" or "hooking up" sites configure their profiles, I do not think that those issues are wholly determinant. Further, I offer an examination of Internet dating/hooking-up profiles as an example of black gay men constructing themselves and their experiences in and through their bodies.

The final chapter is a synthesis of the previous chapters and concludes the book. It is an examination of the previous six chapters and presents my own constructive ethical move. As I have suggested in this introduction, black liberation and womanist theology is concerned primarily with God's activity on the behalf of the oppressed, namely, African Americans. Thus, it turns to black experience as a controlling category. Far from suggesting a black and gay brand of black theology that seeks to reproduce the theological orientation of black liberationist discourse, the constructive move in this final chapter draws on the work of Anthony Pinn as I argue for a turn toward humanism in black religious scholarship concerning black queer experience. It is my contention that part of the intellectual problem with black liberationist discourse when it encounters sexual difference is its allegiance to particular conceptions of God in relationship to humankind. This chapter offers a prologue to a humanist ethics of openness, the contours of which are shaped around two controlling themes of honesty and openness. As I will articulate in greater detail, this humanist ethics of openness is neither predicated upon a nostalgic reading of race nor a heroic reading of sexual difference in African American life. Further, this ethics is predicated upon a serious consideration of sexual difference in African American life and a strong revision of the ways in which we as African American academic theologians and cultural critics take hold of discourses concerning sexual difference. In essence, this final chapter is an attempt to move beyond allowing others to not only speak for black gays but to also distort those experiences in order to further a particular intellectual agenda and to move toward an ethics that is consciously based upon an examination of human activity and aimed toward human flourishing. Thus, this ethics of openness is not bound to previous presentations of God's activity on behalf of oppressed peoples, as is articulated in black liberationist discourse. I contend that reliance upon a theistic underpinning for reflection on human activity limits us. In the particular case of black theological reflection on African American life, I argue that black liberation theology's insistence upon a god who stands for and with the oppressed does very little except to frame black life in terms of crisis, struggle, and enduring oppression. Worse, when black liberation theology addresses sexual difference in African American life, black theologians' insistence upon such a theological construction renders black gays themselves virtually invisible.

This book is a critique of the presentation of black homosexuals as problems and to offer some ways in which black religious discourse can move beyond essentialism with regard to African American homosexuals. It is an attempt to bring forward the voices and experiences of a group of African Americans that often is framed in the context of heterosexuality and white supremacy. I realize that there is a potential methodological problem with the book, one that becomes clear in chapters 3 and 4. In the survey of black gay literature that forms the core of these chapters, I focus exclusively on black gay men's writings. This may appear to readers as a methodological blind spot or, even worse, a deliberate marginalization of black lesbian experiences.

This book does not represent an attempt to marginalize black lesbian experiences or privilege black gay men's experiences as superior or more important than those of black lesbians. My reasons for focusing on the writings of black gay men are twofold. First, I am using black gay men's writings as a tool by which black religious scholars may approach difference in African American life. Having read the writings of black lesbians such as Barbara Smith, Audre Lorde, and April Sinclair, I believe those writers are also approaching differences in African American life. However, my reading of those writers has not been as deep or sustained as my readings of the writings of black gay men. That lack of depth perhaps betrays a gendered privilege. That said, the second reason I focus on the writings of black gay men is related to that previous statement. I do not wish to replicate the mistake of black theologians in merely mentioning black lesbians as though a few sprinkled token references to black lesbian writings can sufficiently address the varied and diverse literatures that they have contributed to the African American literary and cultural canon.

A second criticism or concern that can be leveled (and one that probably deserves its own treatment) is the selectivity of sources. As I note in chapter 3, what finds itself as part of a black gay literary canon is problematic. In short, a reader may ask, "Why would Sneed include the popular novels of E. Lynn Harris alongside the more critical writings of Essex Hemphill?" It was a question that came up when this book was a dissertation, and it has occasionally come up in conversations that I have had with people concerning the project.

As I will discuss in greater detail, Harris' novels (especially *Invisible Life* and *Just As I Am*) appeared at a time when the visibility of black gay men was at a low. His strategy for selling his books created a fan base of primarily heterosexual black women and contributed to the popular mythology surrounding the down low. However, that same strategy garnered the attention of a major publisher and catapulted him—as well as the subject of black homosexuality—into a larger spotlight. I am not attempting to evaluate the relative worth of Harris's novels versus the writings of Essex Hemphill or Marlon Riggs. If I privilege Hemphill over Harris, then I am concerned that I am reproducing a "high" versus "low" culture distinction within black gay men's writings. Further, that is not the task that I undertake in chapters 4 and 5. The task of those chapters is to find out what black gay men's literature reveals about themselves, their experiences, and how they construe their religious experiences.

Indeed, the task of this book is to bring forward the voices of black gay men and make them relevant in African American religious discourse. As I see it, it is not enough to merely invoke the presence of black gay men. That phantasmic existence of black gay men on the periphery of African American religious and cultural discourses is problematic in that it reifies the primacy of heterosexuality and the deviance of homosexuality. Even more problematic is the manner in which these discourses attempt to promote theologies that would accommodate this problematic deviation from the sexual norm. If black liberation and womanist theologies are to be theologies that can express the diversity that is African American life, I think it is imperative that they focus on those narratives that reveal such diversity.

I

Black Liberation Theology, Cultural Criticism, and the Problem of Homosexuality

Introducing Black Liberation Theology

The birth of black liberation and womanist theologies in the United States should not have been unexpected. The theological discourse oriented around liberation arose during a period in which African Americans were wrestling with the question of identity and culture in a society that seemed intractable in its racism, classism, and sexism. This discourse arose in a period when new voices in black life were emerging and not only critiquing and challenging racism and white supremacy but also providing active leadership that challenged the entrenched power structures that supported racism and white supremacy. Further, the emergence of a black theology of liberation was made possible by the nascent critiques of blackness coming out of the black power movement.

Black liberation theology and African American cultural criticism are two critical discourses in the academic study of black life in the United States. These discourses are oriented toward expanding descriptions of and the possibilities for black existence. James Cone's *Black Theology and Black Power* (1969), *A Black Theology of Liberation* (1970), and *God of the Oppressed* (1975) issued scathing indictments of white supremacy and called for a theology forged from the experiences of black people. He argued that white supremacy had poisoned white Christianity and rendered it incapable of speaking to and for the oppressed and downtrodden. Cone argued that theology is relevant only when it is drawn from the experiences of the people whom it addresses and when it can speak positively to those experiences. Reading Cone's theology, I found his descriptions of black life and his call for a revision of God as a God who liberates the oppressed provocative and compelling.

His argument concerning God's identification with the most despised of the earth prompted me to begin interrogating black liberation theology concerning what I saw as an omission, namely, the silence regarding sexuality and sexual difference in black communities. This omission led me to the work of womanist theologians such as Emilie Townes, Katie G. Cannon, and Kelly Brown Douglas; and black cultural critics such as Michael Eric Dyson, Cornel West, and bell hooks. In contrast to the first wave of black liberation theology, I found womanist theologians and black cultural critics to be indeed open to discussions about sexuality in black life.

Womanist theologians and black cultural critics decry sexism in black communities, characterizing oppression of black women as part of the destructive nature of white supremacy. Further, these critics condemn heterosexism and homophobia in black life, claiming that these attitudes assist in the oppression of black people. What these critics seek is the physical, spiritual, and social emancipation of blacks from what Cornel West calls "a market culture dominated by gangster mentalities and self-destructive wantonness."[1] This second wave of theologians and cultural critics contend that an emphasis on ruthless profit-making and acquisition of wealth; a political system that pits whites against blacks, men against women, and gays against straights; and popular film, music, and television that reinforce rather than dismantle racial and gender stereotypes exacerbate racial crisis in America. These critics contend that this market culture thrives on reductivist and negative portrayals of black people. They contend that the promotion of sexist images of black women, the promulgation of images of bestial black men, and the widening gap between the black middle class and the black poor are all part of an enduring racial crisis that threatens black well-being and flourishing.

Womanists and black cultural critics alike oppose sexism, classism, and homophobia by turning to and actively critiquing black cultural productions. Through African American literary theory and cultural criticism, these critics seek to retrieve black cinema, music, and literary productions from the margins of American life. The goal of this strategy of retrieval is to defeat monolithic presentations of black life and experience. It is this goal that drew me to the work of womanist theologians and black cultural critics.

After reading these critics who had previously turned to black literature, film, and television as a means of expanding descriptions of black life, I began to question the ways in which they approached discussions of sexual difference in black communities. Unlike Cone's theology that led me to question if and when black homosexuals entered into black liberation theology, black cultural critics and the second wave of black theologians prompted me to ask how black homosexuals were portrayed in contemporary African American cultural criticism. That, however, is a concern that will be addressed in the following chapter. In this chapter, I am going to outline and detail the emergence of a black liberation theology. Also, this chapter will articulate the cultural milieu in which black liberation theology is birthed and how that cultural milieu addresses issues of sexuality and difference in African American life.

The Civil Rights Movement and Black Power: The Antecedents to Black Liberation Theology

To understand the development of black liberation theology, it is necessary to understand the conditions that made such a theological discourse possible.[2] During the late 1960s, writers and activists challenged racism in American society as part of a growing black consciousness movement. Building upon the critiques of American society offered by the civil rights movement and also upon the larger postcolonial movements taking place on the African continent, African Americans argued that American society could no longer afford to deny black citizens the political, economic, and social rights enjoyed by white citizens. Further, black writers and activists called upon black people to think and act critically. Martin Luther King Jr. and Malcolm X are often recognized as the two most influential and powerful figures in what we now call the civil rights movement.

Indeed, there has been some discussion among African American religious scholars as to whether King should be considered a "black theologian." James Cone regards Martin Luther King Jr. as a spiritual predecessor to black liberation theology. Delivering the plenary address at the Society for the Study of Black Religion in March of 2007, Cone stated that it was King who supplied black liberation theology with its Christian character. His essay on Martin Luther King and black theology in *Risks of Faith* (1999) suggests that while he differs from King in many respects, he acknowledges that both he and King derive their theological perspectives from one source: the black church:

> With that community (the Black Church) in mind, one can then under-
> stand both the similarities and differences between King's theology
> and my own perspective on black theology. Although our differences
> on violence versus nonviolence, love and reconciliation and the possi-
> bility of change in the white community are real, they are differences
> between two persons who are deeply committed to the same faith of
> the Black Church.[3]

Here Cone is presenting a clear demarcation between himself and King. However, it might not be the kind of demarcation that he intends. While he contends that he receives his theological orientation from the black church, it appears that Cone's outlook regarding the possibility of racial reconciliation are different not only from King but also the church. For Cone, reconciliation may occur—if whites renounce racism and "become" black. I will return to this concept later in the chapter.

Cone's self-described divergence from Martin Luther King was shaped primarily by his early project of relating the black power movement to black Christianity. The emergence of the black power movement occasioned a change in the tenor of discussions about race. The black power movement did not characterize itself as a movement of reconciliation, for reconciliation meant that it would be black folks who would concede power while whites would maintain a status quo. The black power movement was a movement concerned with black self-consciousness, self-reliance, and complete liberation from depen-dence upon whites. Influenced heavily by the rhetoric of the Nation of Islam and, more importantly, Malcolm X, the black power move-ment challenged the civil rights movement's assumed primacy among African Americans. As articulated by Stokely Carmichael, black power was a logical extension of the civil rights movement. It was logical, Carmichael argued, for black people to wish to be in control of their own institutions.

Carmichael begins with the question of power. His October 1966 speech at the University of California at Berkeley outlined the basic tenets of the burgeoning black power movement:

> And in order to get out of that oppression one must wield the group
> power that one has, not the individual power which this country then
> sets the criteria under which a man may come into it. That is what is

called in this country as integration: "You do what I tell you to do and then we'll let you sit at the table with us." And that we are saying that we have to be opposed to that. We must now set up criteria and that if there's going to be any integration, it's going to be a two-way thing. If you believe in integration, you can come live in Watts. You can send your children to the ghetto schools. Let's talk about that. If you believe in integration, then we're going to start adopting us some white people to live in our neighborhood.[4]

Carmichael's call for black power was clearly nothing like Martin Luther King's calls for peaceful resistance and integrationism. Indeed, Carmichael viewed such tactics as the tools of the weak. For Carmichael, to adopt integration was to adopt a weakened status. Integration, for Carmichael and other proponents of black power, was nothing more than a tool used by whites in order to control blacks. Taking their cue from Malcolm X's strident critique of integration and previous nationalist movements, proponents of black power sought ways in which African Americans could determine their own political, economic, and social lives.

Carmichael's and others' calls for black power displeased Martin Luther King, Jr. and other leaders of the civil rights movement. King believed that the rhetoric of black power was emotional and potentially divisive and could work against the multiracial coalition he was working to build. Although he strongly criticized it, he did not openly condemn black power. The Southern Christian Leadership Conference as well as other civil rights organizations openly condemned black power.[5]

Nevertheless, black power flourished among younger African Americans. The naked brutality of Southern whites against blacks galvanized members of the Student Nonviolent Coordinating Committee (SNCC). Further, the rhetoric of Malcolm X deeply impressed and inspired members of the organization who had grown tired of the integrationist rhetoric of the SCLC, the NAACP, and the Urban League.[6] The divisions within the core civil rights organizations widened because of Congress for Racial Equality's (CORE) and SNCC's leanings toward black power. Jeffrey Ogbar's assessment of black power's growing influence, in *Black Power* (2004), is worth quoting at length:

Black people all across the country…continued to gravitate to new levels of racial consciousness and militancy as Black Power took shape and gave rise to its own movement…[T]he call for Black Power by

[Willie] Ricks and Carmichael was a reaction to and acknowledgment of this new and emerging consciousness. Despite the denunciations made by most black leaders, the appeal of Black Power grew in virtually all segments of black America...[7]

African American clergy were pressed to respond to the burgeoning black power movement. Roy Wilkins' denunciation of black power could not stem interest in the movement, nor did it ease the minds of a generation of African Americans who saw nonviolent resistance as little more than cooperation with a deeply racist and corrupt power structure.

Black Liberation Theology as a Response to Crisis

The development of black liberation theology is as much a theological response to three statements that came out during the 1960s as it is a response to the general racial climate in the United States. The first of these statements, titled "Black Power," was released on July 31, 1966 by the National Committee of Negro Churchmen (NCBC) and appeared as a full-page advertisement in the *New York Times*. The statement itself was a response to the burgeoning black power movement, spearheaded by the SNCC. According to Gayraud Wilmore, this statement was designed to "vindicate the young civil rights workers laboring in the rural south...[and to] galvanize the left wing of the Southern-based civil rights movement and reassemble it within the province of black Christians who lived in the urban North."[8] In short, black clergy in the North sought to mediate the growing division between Martin Luther King, Jr.'s nonviolent philosophy and SNCC's strident call for active black resistance to white oppression.

The NCBC's affirmation of black power set in motion a series of moves by black academics and laid the groundwork for a black theology of liberation. A Detroit conference held in 1967 and organized by black grassroots organizers addressed the role of churches and synagogues in alleviating the problems of the urban poor. From this conference, the "Black Manifesto" was released. This manifesto outlined economic grievances held by black Americans. The presenters of this manifesto demanded that white Christian churches and Jewish synagogues, as "part and parcel of the system of capitalism," pay reparations to black Americans in the form of $500,000,000. These reparations would be used in order to establish independent economic, social, and educational institutions for black Americans.

Further, the manifesto called on black Americans to avail themselves of "whatever means necessary" in pressuring white churches and synagogues to acquiesce to the half-billion dollar demand.[9] According to the manifesto, it was the churches and synagogues that not only possessed the majority of wealth in the United States, but also profited from the slave trade and continued to exploit black people.[10]

Joseph Washington's *Black Religion* is the third statement that influenced the development of black liberation theology. Washington asserted that the theology of black religion was inadequate. For Washington, black religion was only a "folk" religion and lacking fundamental qualities necessary to be considered "true" religion. In the preface to *Black Religion*, Washington makes his beliefs concerning black religion plain: "...I believe, the religion of the Negro lacks the following: a sense of the historic Church, authentic roots in the Christian tradition, a meaningful theological frame of reference, a search for renewal, an ecumenical spirit, and a commitment to an inclusive Church."[11] Washington argues that Christianity in black communities is "pseudo-Christianity," a folk religion committed more to the emancipation of black people than establishing itself as a non-folk religion.[12] Perhaps his most damning charge is that the folk religion of black people is "dysfunctional." While black folk religion is dynamic and energetic, it is not particularly creative, nor does it contribute anything to larger Christendom. Because of segregation, repression, and the like, black folk religion has concentrated solely on the enfranchisement of black people and, thus, has not created congregations that are more than "amusement centers."[13]

Washington's charges that the black church is not a church "in the theological sense" and that black religion lacks a theology are as damning as white claims of black inferiority and cultural deficiency. As is noted in the first volume of *Black Theology, A Documentary History* and is shown in a review included in a later edition of *Black Religion*, white scholars hailed Washington's work as groundbreaking. For example, Martin Marty's review asserts that *Black Religion* "succeeds in involving all of us, all who live in and profit from and hope for Western culture."[14] Marty agrees with Washington: black folk religion has no tradition, no theology. It is a religion predicated solely on race. The solution to this problem is assimilation into dominant Protestant Christianity.[15] According to Washington:

> Assimilation is a mediating concept—more realistic than integration and less provocative than miscegenation. If Negroes and whites are

to the "one as the hand in all things essential to mutual progress," a heightened sense of assimilation beyond integration is the conscious process toward this objective. It is visionary to place confidence in integration, for the realization of the Negro as integrant will hardly lead to the desired end of assimilation. As an integrant the Negro perpetuates compartmentalization, and in the specific area of faith this means a continuance of a heritage without roots in the Christian tradition, cut off from the Protestant perspective.[16]

By assimilating into dominant Protestant Christianity, African Americans will be able to abandon the separatism engendered by black folk religion. For Washington, the only way for both black and white people to be faithful to the Gospel is to abandon "separate but equal" religious accommodations. Washington's call to abandon such religious accommodations and to embrace assimilation assumes that, as per him, black folk religion is bereft of genuine theological roots in Protestantism.

The implications of Washington's arguments would have a profound effect on the development of a black theology of liberation. Taken together with later criticism of the black power movement, Cone's theology had a twofold task: first, a black theology of liberation has to reconcile the black power movement with a Christian Gospel. Second, this theology has to show that the black church that Washington dismisses as a black folk religion that has no authentic theological roots does indeed have a distinct theology.

Martin, Malcolm, and Black Theology

James Cone's development of a black theology of liberation is both an attempt to reconcile black power with the church and a critique of theology. At it's core, the development of a black theology of liberation is Cone's attempt to reconcile his anger, his leanings toward black power, his existential angst with his Christian identity. This is not a criticism. Rather, it is an explanation of how Cone pays heed to Paul Tillich's argument that theology "makes an analysis of the human situation out of which the existential questions arise, and it demonstrates that the symbols used in the Christian message are the answers to those questions."[17] For Cone, the struggle is to connect academic theology with the existential crises facing black peoples in the United States. In *Risks of Faith* (1999), Cone describes his contention with the prevailing theologies of his time, and is worth quoting at length here.

After I completed the Ph.D. in systematic theology in the fall of 1964, I returned to Arkansas to teach at Philander Smith College in Little Rock...I turned my attention to the rage I had repressed during six years of graduate education. Martin Luther King, Jr., and the Civil Rights movement helped me to take another look at the theological meaning of racism and the black struggle for justice. My seminary education was nearly worthless in this regard, except as a negative stimulant. My mostly neo-orthodox professors talked incessantly about the "mighty acts of God" in biblical history. But they objected to any effort to link God's righteousness with the political struggles of the poor today, especially among the black poor fighting for justice in the United States. God's righteousness, they repeatedly said, can never be identified with any human project. The secular and death-of-God theologians were not much better. They proclaimed God's death with glee and published God's obituary in *Time* magazine. But they ignored the theological significance of Martin King's proclamation of God's righteous presence in the black freedom struggle.[18]

Cone's concern here is how to relate academic theology to the existential concerns of African Americans. By recounting his experiences in seminary and in graduate school, Cone is setting up a dichotomy between academic theology and the experiences of black folk, wherein the experiences of African Americans are more connected to the power of divine action than are the ruminations of "neo-orthodox" white professors whose intellectual ruminations were so completely divorced from reality, they were virtually useless.

For Cone, Martin Luther King, Jr. and Malcolm X loom large in his theology. As mentioned above, Cone acknowledges that it is Martin Luther King who supplies his theology with its Christian character, but it is Malcolm X who provides black liberation theology with its radical critique of white supremacy. This may appear to be somewhat simplistic. However, Cone's argument is an attempt to present a synthesis where previous attempts at understanding both King and Malcolm have presented both men as dichotomous and diametrically opposed to one another. He notes in his reflections on black liberation theology that both King and Malcolm have been distorted in order to present King as palatable to white elites.[19] King and Malcolm are focal points in Cone's theology because these two men represent the spirit of black liberation and black liberation theology. By reclaiming both men, one a Christian and the other an ardent critic of Christianity, Cone is able to posit his theology as an organic extension and synthesis of their thought.

Foregrounding Black Experience

Given that Cone formulates his theology in the years following the assassinations of Malcolm X, Martin Luther King, Jr., and Robert F. Kennedy and during the tumultuous years during and after the civil rights movement, and the manner in which black power foregrounds the black experience of white supremacy and the need for rebellion against any and all forms of white supremacist thought, it is not surprising that Cone would also foreground experience in this theology. The argument that undergirds African American critical, political, and religious thought during this period is the marginalization of African American experiences. However, black power argues that it is not enough to merely acknowledge the existence of African American experience. Centering black experience and securing black autonomy and self-determination are centerpieces of black power and, by extension, black liberation theology.

Black liberation theology depicts black existence as being fraught with turmoil, imposed by the forces of white supremacy. According to Cone, black theology is a "passionate theology" that rejects an unemotional theological discourse that fails to take seriously human experience. Cone contends that any theology that does not spring from the experiences of humans is an alienated, abstract discourse that cannot defeat evil in the world.[20] He indicts American theology for failing to speak with passion. This dispassionate theology has also failed to speak prophetically against white supremacy. I will quote Cone at length concerning the use of black experience as a controlling theme for black theology:

> There can be no black theology which does not take seriously the black experience—a life of humiliation and suffering. This must be the point of departure of all God-talk which seeks to be black-talk. This means that black theology realizes that it is humans who speak of God, and when those human beings are black, they speak of God only in the light of the black experience. It is not that black theology denies the importance of God's revelation in Christ, but blacks want to know what Jesus Christ means when they are confronted with the brutality of white racism.[21]

Black experience is fraught with misery and travail. The existential horrors of the Atlantic slave trade, chattel slavery, and lynching prompt black people to ask what Jesus Christ has to offer them. Cornel West argues that black people have, since the first encounter with chattel slavery, struggled against nihilism. Indeed, for West and other critics, the "nihilistic threat" posed by white supremacy is a "loss of hope and absence of meaning."[22] Black theologians and cultural critics recognize that humans in general and black people in particular cannot speak of God without reflecting upon their own experiences. Cultural critics like West, Michael Eric Dyson, and bell hooks agree with Cone in noting that speaking about black life and black religion requires a passionate love and respect for black experience. Indeed, hooks' latest works have focused on the issue of love in black communities. In *Salvation*, she contends that "doing the work of love" will "ensure our survival and our triumph over the forces of evil and destruction."[23]

According to black liberation theology and black cultural criticism, black experience is laden with a history of struggle against the powerful forces of white supremacy. It is black people being subjected to a system that dehumanizes black people. The black experience according to black theology is black peoples' heroic responses to attempts by whites to dehumanize black people. Black religious critics turn to such cultural productions as music and literature to show that black people employ creative tools in resisting white racism and affirming black identity and experience.[24]

For these critics, black culture grows organically from black experience. The experiences of slavery, degradation, sorrow and loss of family members at the hands of white racists, living in dilapidated tenements, joblessness, and poverty have forged among black people creative, innovative ways of singing and writing these experiences. That which Cone calls "black soul" emerges out of black cultural forms such as music, art, and literature. These cultural forms serve a heroic function in black life, as is clear when Cone refers to Don Lee's assertion that "black art will elevate and enlighten our people and lead them toward an awareness of self, i.e., their blackness."[25]

In their use of black literature, black liberation theologians form a theological interpretation of black culture. However, black religious critics do not rely solely on black literature as a source for interpreting black culture. Both Cone and Dwight Hopkins argue that this cultural genius appears in the black church in the form of spirituals, the blues, and in the form of slave narratives. These narratives are exemplars of the black soul that Cone alludes to in *A Black Theology of Liberation*. The black soul that emanates from black culture in black theology is a direct product of the black arts movement. The black soul, as Cone argues, is James Brown's "I'm Black and I'm Proud" and Aretha Franklin's "RESPECT."[26] These hallmarks of black cultural genius are theological resources for constructing a black identity that defies white cultural supremacy.

Cornel West also speaks of black culture as that which contains black genius. He, like Cone, presents black cultural genius in and through the cultural productions emanating from the black church. I will quote West at length:

> Rhythmic singing, swaying, dancing, preaching, talking and walking—all features of black life—are weapons of struggle and survival. They not only release pressures and desperation, they also constitute bonds of solidarity and sources for individuality...The heartfelt groans acknowledge the deplorable plight of a downtrodden people. The cathartic acts provide emotional and physical relief from the daily scars of humiliation and degradation. The individual stylistic vocals assert the sense of "somebodiness" in a situation that denies one's humanity.[27]

Echoing W.E.B. DuBois, the music of the black church stands alongside European classical music in its ability to provoke the listener's awareness of the human condition. For West and other black religious critics, this elevation of black music as a cultural production to the status of genius is a call for a revised approach to black cultural productions. When West likens the black spirituals to Shakespeare's *Hamlet* or poet Fyodor Tyutchev, and when Cone says that Aretha Franklin's "Respect" and other forms of black expressive culture contain a "mythic power" that aids the "present revolution against white racism," they do not seek a paternalistic tolerance of black culture. They want a repositioning of black cultural productions that echoes W.E.B. DuBois' arguments concerning black life and culture in *Souls of Black Folk*. Instead of a bemused pity and thinly veiled contemptuous attitude toward black culture, these religious critics seek an appreciation of black culture and the black church.

Black cultural critics and black liberation theologians also take seriously forms of popular cultural productions and seek to place them in discussion with black religion. When speaking of black popular culture, I am following John Fiske's description of popular culture that refers to those cultural productions (literature, art, music, film, television) that are mass-produced but selected by people according to "socially located criteria of relevance."[28] I agree with Stuart Hall when he contends that black popular culture involves those cultural productions that draw their strength from black communities.[29] When I speak of black popular culture, I am speaking of those mass-produced productions of literature, art, music, film, and television that have relevance for and draw their meanings (both overt and covert) from the experiences within black communities. For example, James Cone's *Spirituals and the Blues* is an attempt to reposition black spirituals and blues as theological sources for doing black liberation theology. In *The Spirituals and the Blues*, Cone gives a theological defense of forms of black folk music. For Cone, the spirituals and blues music represent an important moment in black religious life. He dismisses the idea that the spirituals were concerned solely with achieving relief in an otherworldly afterlife. Rather, he argues that the spirituals were intimately concerned with black existence on Earth and that God too was concerned with black existence and black flourishing. The spirituals are the expression of black people's sufferings and yearnings for freedom and self-determination:

> The spiritual, then, is the spirit of the people struggling to be free; it is their religion, their source of strength in a time of trouble. And if one does not know what trouble is, then the spiritual cannot be understood...Trouble is inseparable from the black religious experience...The spiritual is the people's response to the societal contradictions. It is the people facing trouble and affirming, "I ain't tired yet."[30]

Here, Cone not only places the spirituals as reflections on black existence, he makes a categorical judgment about black existence. Black existence is an existence bound by trouble. The spirituals that arise out of this troubled existence bear witness to black perseverance in the face of such overwhelming odds. Further, Cone argues that the spirituals contain a prototypical black theology of liberation. He contends that the spirituals that African Methodist Episcopal bishop Daniel Alexander Payne once dismissed as heathenish are, in fact, part of a distinctly black form of resistance to slavery and white supremacy.[31] These spirituals "affirmed their somebodiness" and presented a God who was intimately concerned with the suffering of blacks.[32]

Cone notes his intellectual debt to Albert Camus and Jean Paul-Sartre in his defense of black power:

> Black Power is analogous to Albert Camus's understanding of the rebel. The rebel says No and Yes. He says no to conditions considered intolerable, and Yes to that "something within him which 'is worthwhile'...and which must be taken into consideration." To say No means

that the oppressor has overstepped his bounds...To say No means that death is preferable to life, if the latter is devoid of freedom.

Therefore, freedom cannot be taken for granted. A life of freedom is not the easy or happy way of life. That is why Sartre says man "is condemned to freedom." Freedom is not a trivial birthday remembrance but, in the words of Dostoeyvsky's Grand Inquisitor, "a terrible gift."[33]

Black liberation theology is also hermeneutical theology that is concerned with describing the conditions in black communities that would (and should) give rise to a theology of liberation. As a hermeneutical theology, black liberation theology is concerned with interpreting the existential conditions of black life in and through revised approaches to biblical texts and by retrieving black voices from the margins of American society. Further, this theology is concerned with relating intellectual reflections on God's existence and activity with the existential conditions of black life.

God in Black Liberation Theology

The God of black liberation theology is configured so that God is not only intimately concerned with the well-being of blacks, but also intends the liberation of blacks in this world. For Cone and other black liberation theologians, God and Jesus Christ are virtually one and the same. Jesus Christ is presented as the physical manifestation of God's activity on behalf of the oppressed. As such, both Jesus and God are intimately connected to those who are oppressed and downtrodden by racist (and, later, classist and sexist) societies.

The God of black liberation theology is presented as an ontological reality that moves in and through history. Relying on the Exodus motif, Cone and other black liberation theologians argue that God cannot help but support and provide succor for those who have been enslaved and who have suffered the effects of an immoral social structure. As an ontological reality, God is an entity concerned with justice. The God of white Christianity is emphatically not the God of the oppressed. As such, God is black.[34]

God's blackness and identification with the oppressed creates certain obligations for humanity. What Cone is setting up in his descriptions of God as black is an ethical argument. If white people claim to love God, then they are bound by a duty to live faithfully according to divine will. Part of that will, then, is to act decisively on the side of the oppressed. God is not neutral; as such, neither can human beings be neutral, nor can they favor a love that places no moral obligation upon its adherents.[35] Those who would continue to support a political and social structure that does not allow for blacks to experience human flourishing are characterized as oppressors. Those who seek human flourishing and advancement of black interests (namely, freedom from oppression) are those who are on God's side. Thus, black liberation theology is the theological expression of God's love on behalf of blackness.[36]

While God in black liberation theology is connected to and concerned with black experience, this assumed connection raises two questions. What constitutes liberation for blacks? Whose experience counts when doing black liberation theology? When Cone speaks about liberation, he is not clear about what liberation for black people would look like. He argues that blacks in the United States must be freed from economic and social oppression. However, if black experience is constituted by poverty and suffering, then it would appear that those blacks who belong to the middle class are not black. Cone attempts to ameliorate this possible contradiction by arguing, in *Risks of Faith* (1999), that "it is not that poverty is a precondition for entrance into the Kingdom." In the next sentence, Cone claims that "those who recognize their utter dependence on God and wait on him despite the miserable absurdity of life are usually poor, according to our Lord."[37] As part of a black theology of liberation, Cone cannot and does not separate blackness from poverty. Thus, liberation for blacks entails some form of economic improvement. However, when Cone argues that the Kingdom of God "breaks through even now like a ray of light upon the darkness of the oppressed," he is not clear about what that metaphor means. If God breaks into history only occasionally and brings hope to oppressed blacks, it appears that this relief might manifest itself in the form of class mobility. Second, Cone's theology assumes that black people in the United States have a unified, singular experience. When he speaks of black experience as being an experience of ghettos, poorly maintained tenements, and rats in *A Black Theology of Liberation*, he is speaking about an urban Northern setting. However, Cone does not allow for any descriptions of black experience that are not framed by living in abject poverty and misery. While Cone positions Aretha Franklin's "Respect" as a nationalist anthem that proclaims black resistance to white oppression, it is also possible to read that song as a declaration of independence from male oppression. Cone says in a 1971 interview in the

Christian Century, "I cannot be free until all men are free. And if in some distant future I am no longer oppressed because of blackness, then I must take upon myself whatever form of human oppression exists in the society, affirming my identity with the victims."[38] However, if Cone recognizes that he cannot be free until all are free, and argues that all blacks suffer from oppressive conditions, then it is surprising that this first wave of black liberation theology fails to acknowledge sexism as a problem. It is all the more evident that there is a gap in black liberation theology's appraisal of black life and experience given black women's response to Stokeley Carmichael's assertion in 1964 that the only position for women in SNCC was "prone," and Eldridge Cleaver's statements in *Soul on Ice* that he "practiced" rape on black women before perfecting the crime upon white women.[39] If black liberation theology is predicated upon a theological reflection of black power, as is indicated by Cone's *Black Theology and Black Power*, then black liberation theology must, in some way, respond to the problematic positioning of black women vis-à-vis black men. To borrow from Paula Giddings, where, when, and how do black women enter into black theological discourse? Who is God for black women?

Womanist Theology

As black liberation theology grew into an academic discourse, it encountered sharp critiques. One such critique was from black women who challenged the manner in which black liberation theology failed to speak to their concerns. These women critiqued the lack of presence of black women in religious and cultural studies. They critiqued the blatant sexism within the civil rights and black power movements. These women scholars acknowledge and affirm black male critics' concerns with racism, black experience, and black religion. During the 1970s and 1980s, African American women began openly countering what they perceived to be the blatant racism and classism of the feminist movement as well as the blatant sexism and misogyny of academic black theology and the institutional black church.

Delores S. Williams notes in *Sisters in the Wilderness* (1993) that she recognized a distinct lack of black women's experience in "*all* Christian theology" (emphasis author's).[40] Jacquelyn Grant argues Williams's point more forcefully: "In examining Black Theology it is necessary to make one of two assumptions: (1) either Black women have no place in the enterprise, or (2) Black men are capable of speaking for us."[41] She immediately dismisses both assertions as artifacts of gendered power relations. If black women have no place in black theology, then it is a counterfeit theology that cannot be a theology of liberation. Also, if black men are speaking for black women, then the theology replicates a set of power relations that have governed the interactions between whites and blacks, namely, the white person speaking for blacks. In other words, black women theologians sought not only visibility, but agency. Grant's and Williams's concerns are echoed by other theologians like Emilie Townes and Katie Cannon.

They began to call themselves womanists, after a trope in Alice Walker's *In Search of Our Mothers' Gardens: Womanist Prose* (1983), which describes "womanist" as "A black feminist or feminist of color."[42] The trope ends by describing a womanist as related to feminism. According to Cannon, the development of a womanist theological discourse using Walker's definition as a starting point was meant to challenge (and dismantle) intellectual traditions that had reified "androcentric patriarchy."[43] Part of challenging the androcentric patriarchy that privileged the voices of men over women involved drawing on the voices of those who had been marginalized by the dominant discourse. Womanist theologians, like the black male liberation theologians who preceded them, saw revision of the theological tradition as their task.

Prior to the development of womanist theology, black women had been relegated to the periphery of African American political and religious life. Black women had to conform to standards of "proper" womanhood both inside and outside black communities. Outside of black communities, black women were characterized as licentious beings whose very presence could arouse an uncontrollable lust in white men. Winthrop Jordan's *White Over Black* cites a 1777 poem that includes the lines "These sooty dames, well vers'd in Venus' school, Make love an art, and boast they kiss by rule."[44] In *Introducing Womanist Theology* (2002), Stephanie Mitchem outlines the dilemma that faced black women:

> The belief that black women must conform to a certain standard of being women, being real "ladies," was and is enforced within communities in many ways. One place of enforcement can be black churches, where the way a woman is dressed is a code for the way she is to be treated by the members of the church...Too often, black women are given the message that they are just not good enough unless they *earn* respect and prove their communal worth, often by emulating white women. Black women are told through many means, from families to

churches to schools, that they must conform to standards, that their reputations as women are open for public discussion, and that their own communities may stand in judgment. African American women can adopt these attitudes and enter the trap. They are then caught in the need to prove themselves, feeling the need to do more and to be best in any situation. (emphasis author's)[45]

As Mitchem outlines the dilemma in which black women find themselves, she draws on the problematic relationship between white feminists (who exercise white supremacist discourse) and black women as well as the problematic relationships between black men (who exercise sexist discourse) and black women.

The development of womanist theology both affirms and critiques the liberation project begun by Cone.[46] For example, in her essay "Womanist Theology: Black Women's Experience as a Source for Doing Theology, With Special Reference to Christology," Jacquelyn Grant acknowledges the damage white supremacy has done to black communities. However, she shifts the critical gaze from black men to black women. Grant, bell hooks, Angela Davis and other black women critics address what they perceive to be the omission of black female presence and voice in black cultural criticism, black theological discourse, and in the life of the black church. According to Grant, womanist scholarship takes seriously black liberation theology's claim that black people are oppressed by white supremacy. Further, they take seriously the use of black people's experiences as a point of departure from traditional white Christian theology. However, womanist scholars begin their project by questioning the replication of black male hegemony in black theology. They have developed a critique of the male chauvinism within black theology and the black church. Womanist theologians did not call themselves feminists, claiming that feminism was primarily a movement promulgated by white, middle-class women who failed to acknowledge and criticize their own participation in racist oppression of black women.[47] Instead, black female theologians chose to call themselves "womanist," following Alice Walker's definition of the term in a trope contained in *In Search of Our Mothers' Gardens: Womanist Prose*. Delores Williams outlines the efficacy of the term in an essay, "Womanist Theology: Black Women's Voices:"

What then is a womanist? Her origins are in the black folk expression "You acting womanish," meaning, according to Walker, "wanting to know more and in greater depth than is good for one...outrageous, audacious, courageous and willful behavior." A womanist is also "responsible, in charge, serious." She can walk to Canada and take others with her. She loves, she is committed, she is a universalist by temperament.[48]

Here, Williams turns to black women's literature as a source for theological reflection. Using Walker's trope, she rejects individualism in favor of communalism. By repositioning black women as the center of theological discourse, womanist theologians highlight black women's heroic qualities. It is the black woman who is committed to the spiritual and social emancipation of black folk. It is her universalist temperament that allows her to act on behalf of the entire black community.

Womanist theologians do not differ significantly in their appropriation of the major themes that shape black liberation theology and black cultural criticism. However, they want to take seriously women's roles in the black church and in black religious life. In addressing black women in the church, they seek to expand black theological and cultural discourse concerning black life. For example, the anthology *Embracing the Spirit: Womanist Perspectives on Hope, Salvation, and Transformation* contains several essays by womanist scholars that address black women's existence, their spirituality, and how that spirituality sustains and renews the black community. Rosetta Ross' 2003 book *Witnessing and Testifying: Black Women, Religion and Civil Rights* examines the ways in which black women's faith and spirituality sustained the civil rights movement.

As black women have traditionally been excluded from the positions of power within the church, womanist religious critics locate black women's experience in the church in ways that cannot be easily quantified. Indeed, Delores Williams argues that the black church "escapes precise definition."[49] She locates the black church in the experiences of black women:

> The black church is invisible, but we know it when we see it: our daughters and sons rising up from death and addiction recovering and recovered; our mothers in poverty raising their children alone, with God's help, making a way out of no way and succeeding; Harriet Tubman leading hundreds of slaves into freedom; Isabel, the former African-American slave, with God's help, transforming destiny to become Sojourner Truth, affirming the close relation between God and woman; Mary McLeod Bethune's college starting on a garbage heap with one dollar and fifty cents growing into a multimillion dollar

enterprise; Rosa Parks sitting down so Martin Luther King, Jr., could stand up.[50]

In presenting this litany of black women's activity on behalf of black people, Williams shows that the black church is ever present, an institution that is not located solely in brick buildings and led by black men. By moving the black church from neat, concrete definitions to a more abstract, universal set of actions, Williams is able to foreground black women's experience and narratives. For womanist critics, the foregrounding of black women's experience combats the marginalization of black women's experiences by white people and black men.[51]

Womanist religious scholars find rich resources in African American women's literature. From the beginning of this discourse, in which scholars like Cannon located religious meanings within black women's literature, womanist scholars have turned to the cultural productions of black women. Indeed, black women and black female sexualities, religious experiences, and the like shared experiences similar to that of black gays and lesbians. Whether in the form of black male nationalists speaking of "our women," or in the form of denominational refusal to ordain black women for the ministry, black religious and cultural scholarship rendered black women as spoken for, rather than the women doing the speaking. Even in the project of retrieving black innovators and activists from racialized obscurity, black women, such as Sojourner Truth, Harriet Tubman, and others, tended to be presented as heroic but secondary to black men as advancing the causes of African Americans. The task then for womanist scholars is to retrieve the voices of black women from the margins of African American life and bring them to the center, as womanist theologians identify black women as the most oppressed of the oppressed.[52]

By turning to black women's cultural productions, womanist theologians argue that black women have borne the burden of protecting and nourishing black communities. Emilie Townes examines the development of black women's clubs in *In A Blaze of Glory* (1995). These clubs function as a public manifestation of black women's "intense personal experience of the divine in their lives."[53] Townes is careful to note that the reform movement by black women in the nineteenth century was not an individualistic movement, but a communal one:

> Their spirituality, which at first viewing resembles a self-centered piety with little relation to the larger context, is an excellent example of the

linking of personal and social transformation to effect salvation and thereby bring in the new heaven and new earth. These women sought perfection and advocated social reform in the framework of a spirituality that valued life and took seriously the responsibility to help create and maintain a just and moral social order. These women of the nineteenth century lived their spirituality.[54]

The religious experiences of black women in the nineteenth century affirms black women as they serve as co-laborers in the work of resisting white supremacy. The life-affirming experiences of black women led them to engage in social activism oriented toward transformation. Townes rejects a possible interpretation of black women's spirituality as an individual otherworldly project. Rather, she wants to show that black women were able to make their personal spiritual development relevant to ongoing reform projects that would benefit black communities.

Sexuality and Sexual Difference in Black Liberation Theology and Black Cultural Criticism

Part of bringing black women's experiences to the foreground of theology involves addressing the hurtful, damaging, and destructive ways in which black women's bodies and sexualities have been presented. Some womanist critics argue that black liberation theology and black cultural criticism fail to take black sexuality seriously. Indeed, womanist scholars recognized that it would be impossible to speak of black women's experiences and ignore black women's sexualities. Their arguments are not unfounded, as a perusal of the major works in black theology shows a dearth of substantial references to sexuality. For example, there are no references to sexuality in general in either *Black Power and Black Theology* or *A Black Theology of Liberation*. Cone's latest book *Risks of Faith*, which traces the emergence and impact of black theology, fails to even mention homosexuality as a reality within black communities. The chapter "New Roles in the Ministry" is an example of the lack of attention to sexual difference in black liberation theology. In it, Cone calls attention to the problem of sexism within the black church and argues that black men will have to combat their sexism. He notes that the status of black women in the ministry "is not acceptable," and that if the black church is to be consistent with Christian theology and with liberation, it must find ways to defeat oppression.[55]

However, Cone does not mention sexuality. As presented by Cone, the primary concern for any incarnation of black theology is the survival of black people and the heroic resistance to white racism. As such, oppression of black women runs counter to the interests of black communities. The purpose of challenging the roles of black women in ministry is to show that both black men and women are engaged in a valiant struggle against white supremacy. Nevertheless, Cone does not address issues of sexual difference and appears to have left it to others to address issues of sexuality.

A recent sociological study of the effects of religion in the lives of black folk also fails to yield any references to sexuality in black life. *Religion in the Lives of African Americans: Social, Psychological, and Health Perspectives* (2004) is a sociological study that seeks to contribute to "scholarly discourse on the nature, antecedents, and consequences of religious involvement among African Americans."[56] The authors of this study acknowledge criticisms of prior portrayals of black religious life as failing to take "social class, region, gender, and socioeconomic status" into account.[57] While the authors make space for understanding the intersections of gender and religion in the lives of black people, sexuality, however, enters nowhere in this study.

Womanist religious critics respond to what they perceive to be a crisis in black life that rivals the issue of race. Womanist theologians point to teenage pregnancy rates, the increase of HIV/AIDS infection in black women, and continued and consistently negative portrayals of black women in popular culture as indicative of an ongoing crisis concerning black sexuality. Black women's sexualities were historically cast as subordinate to both black and white men. As such, black women had historically not been in control of their reproductive or sexual selves. As chattel slaves, black women could not defend themselves or object to becoming sexual objects for use by white slaveholders However, black men would not only use black women's bodies but also deny them the ability to name their own sexual experiences. Further, black women and their sexualities had been cast as problematic. In *Womanist Ethics and the Cultural Production of Evil* (2006), Emilie Townes mentions the myriad ways in which black women's bodies and their sexualities are packaged and presented:

> ...the ultimate mammy, the emasculating bitch, the tragic mulatta, the castrating matriarch, and the pickaninny continue to ooze from the pores of videos and magazines and television and radio and music and the pulpit.[58]

The multiple negative ways in which black women's bodies are presented in popular culture as well as other areas of African American life are clearly problematic for Townes and must be deconstructed and "understood for the awful impact they have on how a stereotype is shaped into 'truth' in memory and in history."[59] Thus, a task for Townes, as well as other womanist scholars, is resistance to dehumanizing depictions and descriptions of black women's sexuality.

While not a womanist theologian, bell hooks' concerns about the presentation of black women's sexuality is important to consider, as many womanist theologians share her concerns. hooks discusses the representations of black women's sexuality in both white and black popular culture. In her 1992 essay "Selling Hot Pussy," hooks calls attention to contemporary black culture's often stereotypical portrayals of black women's bodies. She perceives the portrayal of black women as "mammy or slut, and occasionally a combination of the two" as a moment of crisis in black life.[60] For hooks, black women cannot rely on black or white men to speak positively about black women's sexuality, for they are too bound by historical racist and sexist presuppositions about black women's bodies. Her response to this crisis of representation in black life is for black women to speak for themselves in popular culture. She argues that black women producing images of black female sexuality produce imagery "outside a context of domination and exploitation."[61]

While hooks seeks to foreground black women's sexuality in and through black popular culture, Renee Hill's essay "Who Are We for Each Other?" argues that black religious critics, including womanist scholars, have failed to address black people's sexuality. For Hill, black sexuality should advance to the foreground in womanist scholarship. Taking her theological and ethical cue from Alice Walker's trope, Hill argues that black men have marginalized black women's sexuality and that acknowledging and affirming the diversity of black women's sexuality and, by extension, the sexuality of black people as a whole helps combat white racism. Hill argues that

> Sexuality is an issue for Christian womanist theologians. It is not any less or any more important than community or survival. It simply is a part of community and survival. Sexuality (and male dominance) must be addressed in the Black community. Only then will we be able to begin to address subjects like rape, the AIDS epidemic, as well as sexual orientation in the Black community.[62]

Hill presents sexuality as a problem in black life that needs to be addressed, as black male critics before her presented race and black experience as a problem that needed to be addressed. However, the question that confronts Hill and other womanists is: why does sexuality in black life recede into the background in black theological and ethical discourse? Kelly Brown Douglas believes that black people have been reluctant to speak about sexuality owing to a fear of affirming white racist views of black sexuality. Indeed, negative accounts of black sexuality are prevalent in white descriptions of African peoples. According to Winthrop Jordan, Europeans described African peoples as lustful and lascivious.[63] Patricia Hill Collins notes that, for centuries, black people in general and black women in particular have been subjected to invidious stereotypes regarding their sexuality. I will quote her at length:

> From the display of Sarah Bartmann as a sexual "freak" of nature in the early nineteenth century to Josephine Baker dancing bare-breasted for Parisian society to the animal-skin bikinis worn by "bootylicious" Destiny's Child to the fascination with Jennifer Lopez's buttocks, women of African descent have been associated with an animalistic, "wild" sexuality...Black men have their own variety of racial difference, also constructed from ideas about violence and dangerous sexuality.[64]

In her introduction to *Sexuality and the Black Church*, Douglas echoes Collins and bell hooks when she argues that whites have displayed a peculiar and curious fascination with black sexuality. Douglas recognizes that black people were burdened with responding to this torturous fusion of race and sexuality. Black Christians responded to this ongoing stereotype by adopting a set of responses that presented black men and women as being sexually chaste.

Although womanist religious critics have opened up black liberation theology and black cultural criticism to discussions concerning black sexuality, those discussions have not been limited to womanist scholars. For example, Michael Eric Dyson has contributed significantly to discussions of black sexuality. For example, when discussing the O.J. Simpson trial in his book *Between God and Gangsta Rap*, Dyson contends that sexuality stands alongside race as problems in analyzing the case. He voices what tended to recede into the background. That is, Dyson examines how race and sexuality are intertwined when speaking of domestic violence. He argues, "the male sexual ownership of women, the presumption of male discretion over women's bodies that feeds obsession and domination, must simply desist."[65] Dyson charges that allowing sexual oppression within black communities to continue vitiates the possibilities for black flourishing. By categorizing domestic violence as a form of sexual oppression and labeling it an "epidemic," Dyson seeks to call to attention a destructive approach to masculinity and femininity.

Black theologians and cultural critics have created and sustained a critical movement that has been responsible for critiquing race, class, and gender in black life. These critical discourses argue that racial and class conflicts divide black communities and vitiate the possibilities of cultural and economic freedom. Black theologians and cultural critics address what they perceive to be a nihilism and sense of hopelessness in black communities that is rooted in American racism. Black religious critics have, through exploring black experience, black culture, and black religion, resisted negative imagery of black people. What black religious critics seek in their discussions regarding black life in America is a revised hermeneutical approach to black folk. That is, they seek a different, more positive interpretation of black life in America. As black religious critics approach sexuality in black life, they contend that distorted views of black people's sexuality are part of the enduring crisis of race in the United States.

However, in the discussion concerning black sexuality, I question when and where black homosexuality enters. As I noted at the beginning of this chapter, I approached black liberation theology and black cultural criticism with an assumption that the presence of black homosexuals is erased from religious and cultural descriptions of black life. Horace Griffin argues that black homosexuals are absent in black liberation theology and black cultural criticism as well. In his essay "Their Own Received Them Not: African American Lesbians and Gays in Black Churches," Griffin states that black clergypersons and theologians either ignore or condemn outright black gay and lesbian experience.[66] However, that categorical judgment belies the fact that not all black clergypersons ignore or condemn black homosexuality. Indeed, if we read the black church as a location where religious criticism takes place, we may also read the church as being intimately concerned with sexuality in general and homosexuality in particular. Griffin is more correct in his assertion that the black church condemns homosexuality. For example, a study by the Human Rights Campaign that examined organized religion and gay people found that the major African American Christian denominations (African Methodist Episcopal, National Baptist Convention, and Church of

God in Christ) categorized homosexual sexual activity as outside divinely acceptable sexual behavior.[67]

Victor Anderson is correct when he refutes the assertion that the black church is silent regarding homosexuality.[68] The church is quite vocal when it addresses sexual difference in black communities, as evidenced by some of the sermonic moments in black religious life. Operationrebirth.com is a Web site that tracks and critiques major black religious leaders' sermons regarding homosexuality. Nationally recognized black preachers, like Bishop Eddie Long of New Birth Missionary Baptist Church in Atlanta, Georgia, and Bishop Frank M. Reid III of Bethel African Methodist Episcopal Church in Philadelphia, Pennsylvania, have preached sermons that characterize homosexuality as a "lifestyle" that is incompatible with a Christian identity. That does not mean that all black preachers are categorically opposed to and vitriolic concerning homosexuality. Jeremiah Wright, former pastor of Trinity United Church of Christ in Chicago, Illinois, is a notable example of black clergypersons who does not ignore black gay people. In a collection of sermons entitled *Good News: Sermons of Hope For Today's Families*, Wright contends that gay people have access to the same God as heterosexuals. Wright argues that, theologically, God stands for the outcast. For Wright, God's love "is greater than your love and my love, wider than our love could ever be and deeper than we could ever comprehend."[69] Thus, "homophobes," or, those hypocritical preachers who would condemn gay people, cannot prevent them from accessing God's love.[70]

However, black theologians have been slow to acknowledge and attend to the issue of sexual difference in African American religious life. Dwight N. Hopkins' *Introducing Black Theology of Liberation* yields few references to gays and lesbians. The sparse references to black gays and lesbians present them as a problematic situation facing black theology. The introduction to *Introducing Black Theology of Liberation* presents sexual difference as a challenge to black theology that must be resolved. As Hopkins traces the stages of development of black liberation theology, he approaches sexual difference as standing outside black liberation theology and black cultural criticism:

> Finally, a small group of black Christian educators and ministers are openly establishing their lesbian and gay identities as gifts from God and are, therefore, directly challenging the black church and black theological beliefs about liberation.[71]

In this brief introduction of the intersection of black gay sexuality and black liberation theology and black cultural criticism, Hopkins sets up a confrontational space in black life. As black gays and lesbians exist to confront black liberation theology and black cultural criticism, they exist on the periphery of black experience. Gays and lesbians appear again at the "Conclusion" of the book, and then, only in two paragraphs. In these two paragraphs, Hopkins argues that black heterosexuals have some form of "agreement to oppress and discriminate against African American lesbians and gays in the church, the family, and the community."[72] He also contends that black heterosexuals use the Bible in order to "hold black lesbians and gays down."[73] Further, Hopkins accuses the black church with clinging to a patriarchal worldview that ignores those "poor African American lesbians and gays" that "are struggling to build stable families and raise their children."[74]

What is curious about both Wright and Hopkins' discussions of black homosexuality is that it is not at all clear about what is distinct about black homosexuals. Apparently, this group of poor black folk is struggling with the same problems as poor black heterosexuals. However, the two short paragraphs about black homosexuals in *Introducing Black Theology of Liberation* reveals very little about black homosexuals other than that they are poor and downtrodden, just like every other black person. Hopkins' argument implies that the black church is wrong for oppressing black homosexuals, but since these black homosexuals are faceless and are mute in these paragraphs, it appears as if these poor black homosexuals are merely an incidental and problematic afterthought that requires attention before continuing to engage weightier matters in black life.

While Wright's sermon is provocative in that he calls attention to questions of biological determinism and psychology, it appears as if gay sexual expression remains problematic. Wright's sermon is even more problematic in the way it correlates black gay identity with death and oppression. As he cites Mary Borhek's book *My Son Eric* and quotes her assertion that "God is confronting the church with the present crisis over homosexuality," Wright reinforces that assertion by admonishing his audience to realize that "AIDS is everybody's concern."[75] This statement, appended to the Borhek quote, seems to imply that the issue of sexuality, sexual difference, and black religious life is centered on the problem of plague. The study-questions at the end of the sermon present a peculiar ambivalence when speaking about gay sexuality. One question asks, "Should the church challenge sexual practices between consenting adult homosexuals? Are these practices any better or worse than illicit sexual practices among consenting heterosexuals, such as fornication and adultery?"[76] It is interesting to note that the sermonic moment does not mention sexual relations between persons of the same gender. The question presupposes that sexual relations between people of the same sex are equivalent to "illicit" sexual practices like fornication and adultery. Neither this question nor the other questions posed presents the possibility that homosexual sex could be anything but illicit.

Both Hopkins and Wright are examples of the trend within black liberation theology and black cultural criticism of reducing black gay experience to a problem characterized by plague and oppression. What is it that accounts for these discussions about black gays and lesbians in black theology? What is at stake for black liberation theology and black cultural criticism is not solely the representation of sexual difference. As this chapter has discussed, black liberation theology and black cultural criticism is concerned primarily with refuting negative claims about black identity. Black liberation theology and black cultural criticism's account of black experience and existence leads to a monolithic account of black communities. As this chapter has shown, black liberation theology and black cultural criticism, whether in the form of black liberation theology or general black cultural criticism, asserts that God is a real entity with real interests in black life and survival. Cone frankly states that God stands for and with the oppressed of the earth. Because the God of African American Christianity is a god of justice, God cannot help but align Godself with poor black people as they struggle against white supremacy. As Victor Anderson points out in *Beyond Ontological Blackness*, the DuBoisian "double consciousness" finds expression in black liberation theology and black cultural criticism, in that black thinkers are concerned primarily with addressing the "dialectic of race and citizenship."[77] The masculinist, crisis-based orientation of black liberation theology and black cultural criticism prevents it from taking into account multiple representations of black life in America. As such, black homosexuality enters into black liberation theology and black cultural criticism as one of many problems to be fixed in order to combat white supremacy.

Conclusion

As I read black liberation theology and black cultural criticism, I understand it to be hermeneutical in orientation. That is, it takes seriously the stories within black life and considers attention to black narratives necessary in approaching black religious and cultural life. Black liberation theology and black cultural criticism concerns itself with what it perceives to be major problems within black life, namely, the problem of white supremacy. As black liberation theology and black cultural criticism seek to address black existence and white racism, it focuses on providing critical analyses and interpretations of black experience.

In keeping with its hermeneutical orientation, black religious critics have endeavored to include and speak about black sexuality as an important part of black experience. Although black male religious critics initially did not include issues of black sexuality in their writings, black women religious critics quickly corrected this oversight. Sexuality, or, more specifically, sexism, advanced to the fore in womanist discourse concerning black religious life in the United States. Womanist religious critics have been instrumental in broaching the subject of sexual difference in black life. They have argued that homophobia and sexism were damaging to black life, as both homophobia and sexism prevent black people from living the type of socially engaged, loving black Christian life necessary for continued struggle against white supremacy.

I will devote the next chapter to presenting detailed analyses of representations of sexual difference in representative texts in black liberation theology and black cultural criticism. I will use Kelly Brown Douglas' exploration of homosexuality in *Sexuality and the Black Church: A Womanist Perspective* as a representative text in black liberation theology's minimal attempt to deal with sexual difference among African Americans. Her book is the most coherent work on sexuality and black people produced by the black theological academy. Her analysis of sexuality and the black church crystallizes the themes that other womanist scholars have hinted at in their works. While I find Douglas' exploration of sexual difference in black communities lacking, I acknowledge and appreciate that Douglas' work in the field has opened black theology up to dialogue regarding homosexuality and black peoples.

I will also turn to both bell hooks and Michael Eric Dyson's respective chapters dealing with issues of sexuality and sexual difference in two of their books. Of the two, hooks has written more on the subject of sexual difference among black people. In *Talking Back*, she includes a chapter on homophobia. I will not focus on that chapter, as her essay entitled "Embracing Gayness" in *Salvation: Black People and Love* is a more recent and detailed exploration of the subject. Although Dyson does not devote an entire chapter of *Race Rules* to a discussion of sexual difference and black people, he uses a good portion of his chapter on the black church and sex to examine sexual orientation and the black church. Dyson argues that the black church needs a theology that can accommodate same-sex sexual practices. It is my argument that this theology is only hinted at, rather than fully explicated. Further, I will argue that black liberation theology's and black cultural criticism's focus on homophobia obscures the subject of homophobia, the black homosexual. Also, I will further expand my argument that black liberation theology and black cultural criticism's approaches toward sexual difference in black communities remain rooted in a presentation of black homosexuality as bound by plague and prejudice.

2

Black Religious Criticism and Representations of Homosexuality

Introduction

At the conclusion of chapter 1, I outlined the logic of both black liberation and womanist theology and African American cultural criticism. I analyzed the ways in which these two areas of critical thought construct racial identity and difference. While black theology is clear that the primary criterion for its theological analysis is race, black cultural criticism seeks to move beyond racial essentialism as a primary category for doing the work of exploring black existence. In the previous chapter, I sought the presence of black homosexuals in black religious criticism. I found that in the work of womanist scholars and contemporary black cultural critics, sexual difference is mentioned as a problem to be solved. As I noted in chapter 1, both black and womanist theologies and black cultural criticism fail to adequately explore the reality of sexual difference in black communities. In the previous chapter, I put forward a hypothesis that the black liberation theology and African American cultural criticism marginalize homosexuality in black communities because of a preoccupation with dismantling white supremacy.

A number of questions lay in the background of this chapter. At the close of the first chapter, I asked, "When and where does the black homosexual enter into black religious criticism?" In this chapter, I ask, "How does the black homosexual enter into black religious criticism?" This chapter will explore my aforementioned hypothesis that black theology and African American cultural criticism marginalize homosexuality and focus primarily on homophobia through a critical analysis of the ways in which sexual difference is represented in both black theology and black cultural criticism. Here, I will use representative figures of both black theology and black cultural criticism to disclose detailed representations of black gay people. To that end, I will look closely at Kelly Brown Douglas's exploration of homosexuality and the black church in her book *Sexuality and the Black Church: A Womanist Perspective*, as well as Elias Farajaje-Jones' essay "Breaking Silence" in the second volume of *Black Theology: A Documentary History, 1980–1992*. After examining their representations of sexual difference, I will turn to the African American cultural critics.

Heretofore, my examination of where and when homosexuality enters into black religious thought has centered largely around black liberation and womanist theology. However, these theologians participate in a larger field of discourse surrounding African American cultural and religious criticism. In the previous chapter, I mentioned thinkers such as Cornel West, Michael Eric Dyson, and bell hooks specifically because their projects are also concerned with the emancipation of African Americans from white supremacy. West and Dyson expressly address African American religious life and theology, though not as extensively as black liberation and womanist scholars. Conversely, theologians such as Kelly Brown Douglas and Katie Cannon draw on Dyson, West, and hooks as they take up African American culture. I think it prudent and necessary to examine the ways in which both black theology and cultural criticism attend to sexual difference in African American cultural and religious life. Here, Michael Eric Dyson's chapter on the black church and sex in *Race Rules* as well as bell hooks's chapter in *Salvation: Black People and Love* will serve as the representative texts within black cultural criticism's analysis of homosexuality.

Also, this chapter will address what is happening in black religious criticism's discussions of black homosexuality. I contend that black religious criticism deploys a rhetoric of tolerance. Such rhetoric allows for these critics to speak about black gay people affirmatively in that black communities should tolerate the existence of black gay people, as such tolerance is a defiant act against white supremacy. However, I believe that such tolerance leads to limited descriptions of black gay existence that are framed by death and prejudice.

The contours of this chapter are different from previous discussions of sexual orientation and religious thought. Prior discussions of sexual orientation have, by necessity, engaged in a discussion and interpretation of biblical injunctions against homosexual practices. I will not replicate those studies in this chapter, as that discussion does not fall under the scope of this book. The purpose of this book in general is not to present a biblical defense of homosexuality, but to enlarge the categories of discourse in black religious criticism through the literary utterances of black gay men. As I noted in the previous chapter, both black liberation theologians and African American cultural critics utilize black literature as a lens for interpreting black experience. As such, that method will be used in this study as well.

Currently, debates surrounding homosexuality have turned away from the ways in which heterosexuals perceive gays and toward securing equal rights, namely, the right to marry. However, the gay marriage debate cannot completely escape the question of what is considered natural. Opponents of gay marriage contend that allowing homosexuals to marry degrades the "natural" institution of marriage. William Bennett argues that legalizing same-sex marriage would

> ... shatter the conventional definition of marriage, change the rules which govern behavior, endorse practices which are completely antithetical to the tenets of all of the world's major religions, send conflicting signals about marriage and sexuality, particularly to the young, and obscure marriage's enormously consequential function—procreation and child rearing.[1]

Here, Bennett inscribes moral function upon marriage. Marriage in Bennett's view provides the necessary model for sexual interaction. Gay marriage in his view would legitimate in illegitimate constellation of sexual behaviors. However, proponents of gay marriage argue that marriage is a right that ought to extend to gay people. The pro–gay marriage argument contends that homosexual identity and behavior is "not something one chooses, it is something one is."[2] By claiming sexuality as innate and immutable, gay activists argue that denying gays the same rights that pertain to heterosexuals is as immoral as the denial of equal rights to African Americans.

The aforementioned analogy of civil rights for African Americans and civil rights for homosexuals is fraught with controversy. In his book *One More River To Cross*, Keith Boykin outlines the conceptual differences that black people raise concerning the comparison of gay rights with civil rights for African Americans:

> Many blacks, understandably hesitant after years of struggle against racist oppression, are reluctant to be compared and "reduced" to the

level of an even more disfavored group in society. "I don't want to be put in that bag," a forty-seven-year-old black carpenter told the Wall Street Journal in October 1994. Homosexuality is different from blackness, he said, because homosexuality is wrong.[3]

An assumption regarding the nature of both identities is implicit in this man's desire not to have his racial identity compared to homosexuality. When this man declares homosexuality is wrong, he is implicitly arguing that homosexuality is a choice, while a person's racial identity is something fixed, natural, and, thus, socially acceptable. This unnamed man's opinion regarding homosexuality is not significantly different from the views about homosexuality presented by Frances Cress Welsing or Molefi Asante. While Boykin does not explicitly define homophobia, he does assume that negative discourse concerning homosexuality constitutes homophobia.

Addressing the assertion that African Americans are more homophobic than whites could itself comprise a stand-alone book, and, as such, I will attend to that only very briefly. Scholars who address homosexuality in America tend to assume that black people are "more" homophobic than whites, or that homophobia in black communities is more virulent and problematic than in white communities. For example, Horace Griffin's *Their Own Receive Them Not* (2006) addresses at length the antipathy black churches bear regarding homosexuality. He treats antigay sentiment among African Americans as qualitatively different than among whites.[4] This, however, is not a problem unique to Griffin. Kelly Brown Douglas takes care to not assert that African Americans are more homophobic than whites; however, she notes that it appears that blacks are more homophobic due to what she describes as the "white cultural attack" on African American life. Thus, she qualifies homophobia in black culture as being "more passionate, trenchant, and unyielding" than in white culture.[5] Her assertions here are a bit confusing. She claims that blacks are not more homophobic than whites, but her subsequent argument concerning black homophobia and black biblical interpretation appears to argue the opposite. While she places the "blame" for black responses to homosexuality on white culture, that is not a refutation of what she calls "hyperhomophobia" in black communities.

The Pew Forum on Religion and Public Life conducted a study concerning American attitudes toward homosexuality that seems to contradict an assumption of black hyperhomophobia. Among the whites surveyed, 50 percent held unfavorable views of gays and lesbians. Among the blacks surveyed, 60 percent held unfavorable views of gays and lesbians.[6] This does not indicate a marked difference between whites and blacks concerning negative views toward gays. Rather, this statistic, derived from black respondents who claimed a Christian religious orientation, shows that black people interpret the Bible as proscribing homosexual sexual behavior.

Despite a narrow statistical difference between white and black Christian attitudes concerning homosexuality, news items frequently highlight black churches' negative views of homosexuality. In 2007, *The Washington Post* ran a piece entitled, "Rift Over Gay Unions Reflects Battle New to Black Churches."[7] The article implies that African American churches have not dealt with the question of blessing same-sex unions, but notes that the National Baptist Convention USA, Incorporated, and the African Methodist Episcopal Church both "forbid clergy from officiating at ceremonies for same-sex couples."[8] The presumption in this article is similar to that of black theologians in that African American congregations have somehow been completely silent concerning sexual difference in black life. The article notes that predominantly white denominations have struggled with the issue of homosexuality in ways that predominantly black denominations have not. The article is correct in that black churches have not issued proclamations concerning the status of homosexuals in their congregations. However, that is not to say that black churches have been silent concerning sexual morality. Black churches have been rather outspoken (though not to the point of making official policy) concerning the moral status of homosexuality, and it is that outspokenness that black religious scholars are responding to.

Black Theologians and Homosexuality

Black intellectuals' perception of the intersections of race and sexual orientation are framed around the crisis of homophobia, or heterosexuals' negative perceptions of sexual difference. As I will discuss later, black religious critics structure their discussions of black homosexuals not around the subject but around homophobic representations of sexual difference. Black religious scholars labor and write under the assumption that antigay sentiments within black communities are substantively different and more virulent than in larger "mainstream" America. Thus, their approaches to the recipients of such sentiments tend to also be substantively different. They argue that intolerance of sexual difference threatens the flourishing of black people in America.

Such scholars argue that tolerance toward homosexuals is in keeping with a liberationist message to all black people. According to Dwight Hopkins, black gays and lesbians who speak about their oppression constitute "a small group of black Christian educators and ministers [who] are openly establishing their lesbian and gay identities as gifts from God and are, therefore, directly challenging the black church and black theological beliefs about liberation."[9] For Hopkins, liberation for gays and lesbians is less about gays themselves and more concerned with the ways in which black heterosexuals should combat homophobia. Of paramount concern for Hopkins are the ways in which discourse concerning black gays and lesbians can fit into black liberationist thought.

That said, scholars such as Elias Farajaje-Jones and Renee Hill represent early attempts to foreground black homosexual experiences and relate them to black liberation and womanist theologies. However, what they often promote is a gay gloss on black liberation theology. In other words, they adopt the theological, ethical, and rhetorical structures that have come to characterize black liberation and womanist thought. Their constructions of black homosexuals are framed and bound by narratives of disease and homophobia. Thus, they construe black homosexuals as the most despised of the despised and therefore represent them as a kind of chosen people with whom God identifies.

Elias Farajaje-Jones' "Breaking Silence: Toward an In-The-Life Theology" is one of the first attempts to graft categories of sexual difference onto black liberation theology. Farajaje-Jones begins his essay with a discussion of homophobia and biphobia. He acknowledges that a theology of liberation for gay and lesbian African Americans must address the oppression that they experience from not only whites but also black heterosexuals. He contends that black Christianity forces black gays to remain secretive about their sexuality. His allegations are worth quoting at length, as they are repeated later in Kelly Brown Douglas' and Michael Eric Dyson's respective works. Farajaje-Jones says:

> Religion, especially African-American Judeo-Christian religion, is still being used to persecute and oppress people who are in-the-life. It forces people to remain closeted. Perhaps one of the worst things about it is that it is used to destroy people's self-esteem and to augment their self-hatred. Religiously-inspired homophobia and biphobia are actually killing people. It is one of the main reasons that the United States is not more aggressive in dealing with AIDS; it serves as an inspiration

for violent crimes against lesbian/gay/bisexual/transgender people, in much the same way that inflammatory anti-Jewish preaching often leads to pogroms...The white religious right is trying to co-opt the Black Church into supporting its homophobia/biphobia. Some of us need to articulate theologies for the Black Church that teach that we are inclusive, not exclusive; that we are about life and not about death. This is my struggle.[10]

Farajaje-Jones presents themes that will become constitutive of black theological discourse concerning sexual difference in black communities. When he speaks of black gays being forced to hide their sexuality, he is insisting that black gays are estranged from their communities. For Farajaje-Jones, the black church should be a place that welcomes all African Americans. Instead of serving as a haven for black gays, it is hostile to them. This hostility presents a dilemma for black gays. Either they affirm their sexual identity and risk being marginalized or vilified in the black church, or they hide their sexual identity and exist within the confines of a lie. The black church encourages the development of heterosexual relationships by providing rituals that solemnize commitments, provide legitimacy for sexual activity, and honor these relationships as part of the church, the family, and the community. For black gays, however, none of the aforementioned support is available. Farajaje-Jones indicts the black church for refusing to support black gays and aiding and abetting the negative attitudes toward black gays that subsequently force them to engage in clandestine sexual encounters and relationships lest they be figuratively (and, sometimes, literally) cast out of the church and the community.

Farajaje-Jones seeks to resolve such estrangement through the development of a theological discourse that resolves alienation and estrangement within black communities. In Farajaje-Jones' view, any orientation that estranges black people from one another should not be tolerated. Homophobia must be vigorously opposed, as it alienates black gays and leads them to engage in self-destructive behaviors that, in turn, lead to the spread of HIV/AIDS. Further, African Americans must vigorously oppose homophobia as it is the product of a European worldview that stigmatizes sex in general and homosexuality in particular.[11] Again, this is a theme that finds expression often in Kelly Brown Douglas's work.

Farajaje-Jones' talk of an "in the life" theology draws on Joseph Beam's anthology and use of the term "in the life" as a way of describing black gay experience. He contends that the use of in-the-life is inclusive of the wide range of sexual identities open to blacks and, according to Farajaje-Jones, "has been used in our African-American tradition for generations."[12] Beam's anthology contains the following description of the term:

> In the life, a phrase used to describe "street life" (the lifestyle of pimps, prostitutes, hustlers, and drug dealers) is also the phrase used to describe the "gay life" (the lives of Black homosexual men and women). Street life and gay life, at times, embrace and entwine, yet at other times, are precise opposites. In this context, in the life refers to Black gay men.[13]

If Farajaje-Jones wants to take in-the-life seriously, he has to contend with the negative associations that this term entails. He argues that in-the-life is a term that is inclusive of all and that it grows out of the suffering and struggles of all oppressed peoples. However, if Beam's presentation of in-the-life is to be taken seriously, then the black gay men indicated in this term stand alongside the pimp, prostitute, hustler, and drug dealer as unsavory elements in black life.

Perhaps Farajaje-Jones is engaging in a "transvaluation of value." That is to say, if the term "in-the-life" had been traditionally used in order to refer to unsavory elements within black life, then he may be attempting to retrieve this term from such readings. As black homosexuals were lumped into this group of seedy persons, and this term evolved to later refer only to black homosexuals yet never lost the connotation of unsavoriness, then Bishop Beam and Farajaje-Jone's use of the term is an attempt to turn that which once denoted something objectionable into something that is positive and affirming.

Farajaje-Jones does recognize that, according to black heterosexuals, black people who are "in-the-life" are undesirable. He combats the perception of black queers as unacceptable by reminding the reader that black queers are victims of a pernicious system of heterosexism and homophobia.[14] Heterosexism functions as compulsory heterosexuality, or the assumption that all black people are (and should) be heterosexual. Compulsory heterosexuality leads to homophobia in that those who are heterosexual label those blacks who are gay, lesbian, or bisexual as deviant, depraved, and contradictory to black interests.

Farajaje-Jones does not limit his critique of homophobia and heterosexism to the black church. Like Renee Hill, he indicts black liberation theology for failing to discuss homosexuality. He contends that what is unacceptable is not the presence of black queers, but the presence of homophobia. Farajaje-Jones implicates black liberation theology in aiding and abetting the perpetuation of homophobia because of its silence regarding black queer sexuality.

Farajaje-Jones adopts the method of black liberation and womanist theologians by turning to the experiences of black peoples as a hermeneutical lens. Of course, as he is attempting to construct a black theology for black homosexuals, he points to black queer experience as the hermeneutical lens that informs a theology of liberation. In his hermeneutical approach to black queers, those who are in-the-life are the most despised. He points out that black queers are oppressed on multiple levels. Black queers are oppressed by the black church because of their sexuality, by whites because of their race, and by heterosexual black men because of their gender. The refusal of the black church to welcome black queers and affirm their relationships exacerbates the HIV/AIDS crisis in black communities. He says, "we often encounter Black gay/bisexual men who have heard all of their lives that they are evil and bad. Many internalize this and then figure that there is no point in their practicing safer sex since they are condemned to be punished anyway."[15] This internalized homophobia demands a theological response. Just as black liberation and womanist theologians combat negative representations of black and female identity, and claim that internalized negative representations do grievous damage to black communities, so too does Farajaje-Jones combat negative representations of sexual difference and internalized homophobia, claiming that these negative representations manifest in ways detrimental to black flourishing.

He situates black gay identity between the problems of plague in the form of HIV/AIDS and prejudicial attitudes and actions toward and against black gays. Further, Farajaje-Jones seeks an "in-the-life" theology that can speak against homophobia in black communities, but the contours and content of this theology remain vague and undefined. By situating black gay life between plague and heterosexual prejudice, Farajaje-Jones presents black gays as at the mercy of two seemingly overpowering forces that are by-products of the other. Black gay life, like black life in general, is a heroic struggle against nihilism.

Kelly Brown Douglas echoes many of Farajaje-Jones's arguments in her book *Sexuality and the Black Church: A Womanist Perspective*(1999). *Sexuality and the Black Church* opened black theology to frank dialogue regarding the representation of sex and sexuality among black Christians. She argues that black people have suppressed sexuality because white people have cast black sexuality as uncontrolled, lascivious, and dangerous. Her text is, as she indicates in her introduction, a response to a challenge laid down by Renee Hill. Her book is also a response to ethicist Cheryl Sanders' critical analysis of womanist thought.

Hill contends that womanist scholars have avoided the issue of sexuality. In her essay "Who Are We For Each Other?: Sexism, Sexuality, and Womanist Theology," Hill charges womanist scholars with failing to "recognize heterosexism and homophobia as points of oppression that need to be resisted if all Black women (straight, lesbian, and bisexual) are to have liberation and a sense of their own power."[16] Hill takes up Alice Walker's trope and focuses on her description of someone who is womanish as being someone who loves women sexually or nonsexually. As a womanist is someone who can love women sexually, this automatically includes the black lesbian. For Hill, any discourse that purports to resist oppression must also acknowledge the existence of sexual difference and oppression based on this difference. Hill articulates why it is important to listen to those who are homosexual:

> By acknowledging the existence of lesbians (and gay men) in the Black community, including the Black church, womanists will confront the denial and invisibility of homosexuality that is a symptom of heterosexist oppression. It would be a way of raising the issue of oppression within the Black community. African Americans need not only theories of resistance and liberation from oppressive forces in the dominant white society, but also those theories which will address oppression *within* the community. (emphasis author's)[17]

Hill does not seek to critique the logic of black and womanist liberation theology. Rather, Hill wants black homosexuality to become part of black liberationist discourse. She appears to agree with black liberation and womanist theologians' presentations of black life. If this theology purports to speak for black peoples, then, in Hill's understanding, it must also speak for and to black homosexuals. She desires that this religious discourse include considerations of sexual difference in black communities. Douglas notes that "at the time of [Hill's] critique, neither I nor any other womanist religious scholar had given any sustained consideration to issues of homophobia/heterosexism or any other issue related to Black sexuality."[18] However, not all black religious scholars uncritically accept the womanist trope as a necessary source for doing black theology.

In the essay "Christian Ethics and Theology in Womanist Per-spective," Cheryl Sanders argues that the appropriation of womanist thought must be done critically and must not lose sight of Christian ethics and values. She is concerned that uncritical adoption of wom-anist discourse leads to an ethical orientation that accepts homosexu-ality as a morally commendable practice. She contends that what is at stake for black communities is the development of healthy and stable black families. Homosexual practices threaten the stability of black families. Sanders is explicit about her concerns regarding womanist thought and unequivocal affirmation of sexual difference:

> In my view there is a fundamental discrepancy between the woman-ist criteria that would affirm and/or advocate homosexual practice, and the ethical norms the black church might employ to promote the survival and wholeness of black families. It is problematic for those of us who claim connectedness to and concern for the black family and church to engage the criteria authoritatively and/or uncritically in the formation of theological-ethical discourse for these two insti-tutions…There is a great need for the black churches to promote a positive sexual ethics within the black community as one means of responding to the growing normalization of the single-parent family, and the attendant increases in poverty, welfare dependency, and a host of other problems. Moreover, it is indisputably in the best interests of black children for the church not only to strengthen and support existing families, but also to educate them ethically for marriage and parenthood. The womanist nomenclature, however, conveys a sexual ethics that is ambivalent at best with respect to the value of heterosex-ual monogamy within the black community.[19]

In Sanders' view, the ethical norms of the black church include a com-mitment to a sexual morality that fosters stable black families. Her negative position on homosexual practice is borne out of a concern for the well-being and sustenance of black nuclear families. For Sanders, the ethical norms of the black church and the interests of stable fam-ilies are linked, and the "uncritical acceptance" of womanist criteria is not in keeping with those norms. She does not favor an interpreta-tion of womanist thought that allows for homosexual practice, as she believes that such practice runs counter to the ethics and theology of the black church. In *Saints in Exile* (1996), Sanders points out that the ethics of the Holiness tradition place an "emphasis on personal morality and ascetic lifestyles" and prohibits drinking, smoking, the use of addictive drugs, "extramarital sex, gambling, secular dancing and the like."[20] This emphasis on personal morality is important, for it is part of a program of Christian formation and transformation that Sanders believes is necessary for maintaining black families and communities living in the margins of American society.

Sanders contends that if academic black theology is to be hermeneutically faithful to the church from which it claims to have sprung, then it cannot equivocate on the matter of homosexuality. Sanders explores her commitment to the moral standards of the Holiness tradition and rejection of homosexual practice as a form of legitimate sexual activity more fully in her essay "Sexual Orientation and Human Rights Discourse in the African-American Churches." For Sanders, homosexual acts do not lead to the formation of healthy black families. Rather, the promotion of same-sex marriage as a means of legitimating homosexual practice may lead to the disintegration of extended familial relationships.[21] In order to promote a positive sexual ethics among African Americans, the black theological project must promote heterosexual monogamy instead of homosexual practice.

Douglas' response to Sanders is simple and direct. Any discourse in black communities that limits the free expression of sexuality (including homosexuality) "threatens Black well-being instead of protecting it."[22] For Douglas, the white cultural attack, the exploitation and totalization of black sexuality, has negatively affected all black people, including black gays and lesbians.[23] This white cultural attack, along with the desire of black people to weather this attack, prompts black people to adopt an intolerant approach toward homosexuality. As shown in her introductory discussion of her experiences with black seminary students' reactions to homosexuality, Douglas characterizes these negative critiques as homophobia and heterosexism. Her section regarding homosexuality deals less with black gays and lesbians themselves and more with attitudes of black heterosexuals with regard to same-sex sexual practices. Black attitudes regarding homosexuality stem from black attitudes regarding sexuality in general. Douglas argues that black people derive their views of homosexuality from both the Bible and from particular cultural concerns.[24] For black people, the Bible serves as a primary source for ethical and moral reflection. Douglas cites both Vincent Wimbush and Renita Weems as she presents the argument that black interpretation of the Bible with regard to homosexuality is part of the way in which black people have traditionally appealed to the Bible's themes of justice, freedom, and self-worth in the eyes of God. Douglas comments on African American interpretations of the Bible, arguing that blacks have shaped an oral/aural biblical tradition. This tradition allows for blacks to draw on particular stories (such as the Exodus story) as wellsprings for black faith. According to Douglas, black people have uncritically accepted biblical injunctions against homosexuality. This uncritical acceptance of certain interpretations of homosexuality formed the basis for much of the homophobia present in black communities. Douglas does not find the use of the Bible to legitimize anti-gay sentiments in black communities persuasive. Rather, she finds the interpretations of biblical pronouncements regarding homosexuality to be harmful for the flourishing of black communities.[25] She suggests a wider discussion of homosexuality in black communities that "must take place within the wider context of Black people's own struggle for life and wholeness."[26] By presenting this suggestion, Douglas seeks to move discussions about sexuality away from questions about the moral life of blacks and toward larger questions of black oppression and resistance to oppression.

Douglas argues that black people's use of the Bible to support a position against homosexuality is understandable "in light of their history of oppression."[27] The history of white supremacy is replete with examples of white denigration and demonization of black sexuality, as Winthrop Jordan's study shows. In the initial contacts between Europeans and Africans, Englishmen first hypothesized that Africans "had sprung from the generation of ape-kind or that apes were themselves the offspring of [Africans] and some unknown African beast."[28] By associating apes with Africans vis-à-vis sexual union, whites "were able to give vent to their feelings that [Africans] were a lewd, lascivious, and wanton people."[29] The association of Africans with wanton, uncontrollable sexuality and savagery led to the formation and perpetuation of sexual stereotypes. Douglas highlights the development of the stereotypes of the Jezebel, the Mammy, and the Violent Buck. The Jezebel and the Violent Buck are both sexual deviants and are governed by their lusts. She notes that black people have fought these representations of deviant black sexuality by rejecting forms of sexual expression that might be considered aberrant.[30]

Douglas' argument mirrors Michael Eric Dyson's argument in *Race Rules* (1996) that blacks have constructed a black Christian sexual identity that demonizes the sexual body. The rhetoric that Douglas displays in her argument is centered around a notion that blacks have, since the beginning of slavery, resisted white supremacist descriptions of black bodies. However, this resistance to oppression led to the rejection of any kind of sexual expression that did not lead to procreation or might confirm white suspicions about black sexual deviance. Thus, blacks cast homosexuality (and also bisexuality, transgenderism, as well as other sexual practices) as a "white thing," and not part of black sexual experience.

Douglas acknowledges Cheryl Sanders' concerns and freely admits that black people consider homosexuality a threat to the well-being of black families. In short, Douglas accepts the position held by many black religious critics that black people are in an existential crisis. She tacitly accepts Sanders' position that black families are in crisis. However, she contends homophobia exacerbates the black existential crisis rather than resolves it. Douglas turns to the statistical evidence surrounding HIV/AIDS in black communities. The alarming rate of HIV infection among African Americans in general and black women in particular should have elicited a swift response by the black church. Instead, the black church (via black preachers) equated HIV with homosexuality. Douglas argues that, despite the devastating effect the HIV/AIDS crisis has had on black communities, the black church has not effectively responded to this crisis. Following Elias Farajaje-Jones' earlier argument, she claims that homophobia within the black church leads to destructive behaviors by gays and lesbians, and it is those destructive behaviors that are responsible for the alarming spread of HIV/AIDS in black communities.[31]

For Douglas, black people need a sexual politics of resistance in order to combat white sexual oppression. Homophobia, as a by-product of the white cultural attack on black sexuality, "mimics White culture in the way it destroys Black lives."[32] This discourse of resistance squarely places homophobia, not homosexuality, as a product of a corrupt white culture that consistently demonizes all forms of black sexuality. Douglas argues that "a sexual discourse of resistance could nurture the kind of discussion that promotes acceptance and appreciation of the rich diversity—*even sexual diversity*—within the Black community" (emphasis mine).[33] Douglas believes that the only way to dismantle black reliance upon interpretations of biblical injunctions regarding homosexuality is to develop a sexual politics of resistance.

As I noted before, *Sexuality and the Black Church* represents the first sustained attempt to critique heterosexism and homophobia via black theology. It is also the first text out of the black theological academy to take black homosexuality seriously. Thus, to borrow from Sylvester Johnson's review, the book represents a "theological watershed."[34] With the exception of a few essays by black religious scholars, sexuality and sexual difference had receded into the background of African American religious scholarship. It appeared as though African American cultural critics were the only black scholars who dared to address sexuality and sexual difference in African American life. Douglas' text serves as the watershed that has prompted a more sustained focus on the intersections of black identity, religious thought, and sexuality.

However, there are a few problems with both Douglas's accounts of homosexuality and her suggestion of a sexual politics of difference. First, her account of homosexuality assumes the validity of certain accounts of black gay sexuality. For example, Douglas, using Keith Boykin's book *One More River to Cross*, assumes that black gay and lesbian lives are bound by disease and hatred. Accepting Boykin's assertion that reducing homophobia would reduce the "risky" sexual behavior that black gay men supposedly engage in reinforces the presumption that black gay men are uniformly promiscuous and are carriers of plague. Although Douglas says that a sexual discourse of resistance would promote acceptance and appreciation of sexual diversity in black communities, her own discourse concerning black gay experiences is thin and does not substantively explore black gay experiences beyond encountering the finitude of either HIV/AIDS or homophobia.

Gays and lesbians are presented as a "problem people." That is, they are both problematic in themselves and bound by problems. Although Douglas seeks to dispel the notion that black gays and lesbians are a threat to black people, she fails to present alternative accounts of black gay and lesbian lives that would counter those negative descriptions. Black gay people exist only though the paradigm of homophobia. Douglas fails to separate black gay sexuality from homophobia. By equating black gay sexuality with homophobia, Douglas renders black gays and lesbians synonymous with the negative attitudes expressed toward them.

With regard to homophobia, Douglas effectively absolves black people and the black church from any moral culpability in the perpetuation of homophobic practices and attitudes.[35] The claim that homophobic attitudes among black peoples are the offspring of white racist attitudes toward black sexuality denies any responsibility black people have in fostering those attitudes. Her assertion that the negative sentiments expressed toward black gays and lesbians are the result of white culture infantilizes the black church. Her contention portrays the black church and community as being incapable of independently formulating responses to human experience.

Finally, Douglas calls for a "sexual discourse of resistance" to combat the white cultural attack responsible for homophobia in black communities. The sexual discourse of resistance is intended to reveal how white culture and racism perpetuates homophobia. It is supposed to show black people that accepting homophobia means complicity in the efforts to destroy black communities. Douglas reinforces the argument that homophobia is not a natural reaction to homosexuality by black people but rather a disruptive force perpetuated by white people by the claim that a sexual discourse of resistance will "disrupt the terrorizing manner in which Black people have used biblical texts in regard to homosexuality."[36] Although she contends that black people have misused the Bible with regard to black gays and lesbians, it is apparent that she believes that this misuse is the result of white oppression. Even if one were to regard Douglas's assignation of blame to white people as true, it is still unclear what a sexual politics of resistance would look like.

Her final chapter, "A Sexual Discourse of Resistance," appears to draw the contours of the discourse of resistance she proposes in her chapter on homophobia. However, the contours of this discourse are still not clear. This discourse seems as if it is intended solely to "help [the black church] understand the role of black sexuality in maintaining the white hegemonic, racist, sexist, classist, and heterosexist structures."[37] If this is the case, then black sexuality exists only to combat white supremacy. Consider what Douglas says regarding the usefulness of a sexual discourse of resistance:

> The Black community needs this discourse to help it to understand the role of Black sexuality in maintaining the White hegemonic, racist, sexist, classist, and heterosexist structures. A sexual discourse of resistance is needed also to help Black men and women recognize how the White cultural exploitation of Black sexuality has corrupted Black people's concepts of themselves, one another, and their God.[38]

According to the quote, black heterosexuals should accept homosexuality in order to fully participate in the titanic struggle between black and white cultures. The difference that sexual difference makes for black communities is constructed vis-à-vis white racism. In other words, black homosexuality ought to be affirmed, not for the sake of promoting and respecting difference in black communities, but for the sake of reifying racial difference. As she positions black folks as heroic, black people must be morally superior to whites. The rejection of homophobia functions as a sign of acceptable morality. As such, her admonition to black communities rests on a moral judgment: those African Americans who espouse antigay sentiments are not acting morally. Indeed, for African Americans to adopt antigay sentiments may be read as participating in the white cultural attack on black sexuality.

Douglas's arguments concerning homophobia bracket sexual difference among black peoples. Black gays and lesbians are either carriers of plague or victims of homophobia. These diseased and oppressed black homosexuals require the salvific gift of black heterosexual tolerance. However, descriptions of black homosexual experience as bound by plague or oppression do not allow for possibilities of transcendence. Douglas so thoroughly grounds black sexual identity in the vicissitudes of white supremacy that it appears as if she is rendering black gay sexuality and responses to it as pathological.

What I have presented is a fairly strong reading of Douglas' exploration of sexuality vis-à-vis womanist theology. However, I by no means intend to give the impression that Douglas is alone in reading, and at times misreading, sexual difference in African American life. I will now turn to contemporary African American cultural critics and their treatments of sexual difference in African American life. The following section will address Michael Eric Dyson and bell hooks as two of the more prolific writers working in African American cultural criticism and how they take hold of homosexuality in black life.

Homosexuality in African American Cultural Criticism

Cornel West's essay "The New Cultural Politics of Difference" sought new ways of understanding black life in America that were not bound to only racial difference. For West, this new cultural politics of difference was a response to the "precise circumstances of our present moment." In other words, this new politics is the product of a postmodernist moment wherein previous modes of cultural and political representation are coming under increasing scrutiny. West writes,

> The new cultural politics of difference is neither simply oppositional in contesting the mainstream (or *male*stream) for inclusion, nor transgressive in the avant-gardist sense of shocking conventional bourgeois audiences. It embraces the distinct articulations of talented (and usually privileged) contributors to culture who desire to align themselves

with demoralized, demobilized, depoliticized and disorganized people in order to empower and enable social action and, if possible, to enlist collective insurgency for the expansion of freedom, democracy and individuality. (emphasis author's)[39]

This new cultural politics seeks coalitions across boundaries of race, class, gender, and sexual orientation in order to secure democracy and freedom of expression for individuals. West sees the "old" politics of difference as being concerned primarily with the difference that race makes. The old politics, as I noted earlier, responds primarily to negative conceptions of racial difference. For example, W.E.B. DuBois' "The Conservation of the Races" or *The Souls of Black Folk* only engages the marker of race as that which differentiates humans. West does not dismiss altogether previous conceptions of cultural criticism that were predicated solely on race. Instead, he seeks to fuse the critical theories of the Frankfurt School, the burgeoning revisionist movement within American history that opens inquiry into the histories of the working class, women, gays and lesbians, and Native Americans, and forms of popular culture into a cultural critique that recognizes and appreciates difference in black communities.[40]

The central argument in "The New Cultural Politics of Difference" is that black cultural politics has assumed the existence of a monolithic black community. This presentation of a unified, singular black folk, while useful in addressing white supremacist notions of black identity, distorts the reality of multiple layers of difference in black communities. The efforts of black people in resisting negative and degrading stereotypes led to cultural judgments that were "moralistic in content and communal in character."[41] These moralistic and communal presentations of black identity "rested upon a homogenizing impulse that assumed that all black people were really alike—hence obliterating differences (class, gender, region, sexual orientation) between black peoples."[42]

For West, instead of relying on a monolithic notion of what constitutes appropriate "black" sources for doing cultural politics, the new cultural politics draws on a wide variety of sources. The canon in the new cultural politics of difference reflects an eclecticism whose intent it is to present more open descriptions of contemporary black life in America:

We listen to Ludwig van Beethoven, Charlie Parker, Luciano Pavarotti, Laurie Anderson, Sarah Vaughn, Stevie Wonder or Kathleen Battle, read William Shakespeare, Anton Chekhov, Ralph Ellison, Doris

Lessing, Thomas Pynchon, Toni Morrison or Gabriel García Márquez, see works of Pablo Picasso, Ingmar Bergman, Le Corbusier, Martin Puryear, Barbara Kruger, Spike Lee, Frank Gehry or Howardena Pindel—not in order to undergird bureaucratic assents or enliven cocktail party discussions, but rather to be summoned by the styles they deploy for their profound insight, pleasures and challenges.[43]

West here is not employing what he calls a "mindless eclecticism" for the sake of appearances. Rather, he argues that this wide array of sources assists cultural critics in fighting enduring problems of racism, classism, sexism, and homophobia. He goes on to say that the homogenizing impulse of racial unity in black cultural criticism was largely driven by "anxiety-ridden, middle-class" black intellectuals who were in a crisis of legitimation.[44] West, like Michael Eric Dyson and others, wants to move beyond this homogenizing impulse and open black cultural criticism up to a multiplicity of difference. West believes that black cultural criticism and the struggle for representation of black peoples must reflect the complex realities of black life in America.

West is not alone in forging this new cultural politics of difference. Michael Eric Dyson and bell hooks are two other major figures in this cultural politics. Dyson's work generally focuses on issues of class, religion, and race, while hook's work emphasizes gender issues in black communities. That is not to say that Dyson's and hooks' works are focused exclusively in those respective areas. Rather, a brief perusal of their collected works shows that while Dyson and hooks both address issues of race, class, sexuality, and religion, they have concerns about black life that are specific to their respective works.

bell hooks is concerned with representations of black people in popular culture. However, she characterizes those concerns as those of a black feminist. She wants to bring black women to the forefront of cultural criticism and reify their voices as a location for doing cultural criticism. While West and Dyson speak strongly against sexism among black people, hooks conducts more detailed and sustained analyses of sexism within black communities.

The new cultural politics of difference combats internal and external representations of black people that appear to be essentialist. However, black cultural criticism often characterizes all negative representations of black people as by-products of white supremacy. For example, when speaking of the movie "Boyz 'N the Hood," bell hooks claims that black reactions to the violence in the movie was a "powerful testimony, revealing that those forms of representation in white supremacist society that teach black folks to internalize racism are so ingrained in our collective consciousness that we can find pleasure in images of our death and destruction."[45]

The goal of the new cultural politics of difference is not completely dissimilar to the goal of the old cultural politics. The new cultural politics of difference is as concerned with the presentation and re-presentation of black people as the old politics were. However, the postmodern black cultural critics such as West, Dyson, and hooks want to bring other mitigating factors into cultural analysis. Returning to hooks' brief analysis of "Boyz 'N the Hood," she contends that black people will not be able to make "radical interventions" that may help alleviate their existential crisis unless they change the ways in which they see themselves. For hooks, movies like "Boyz 'N the Hood" prevent black people from seeing beyond dehumanization and disempowerment.[46]

When Cornel West presented the new cultural politics of difference, he mentioned that sexual orientation is one of those markers of difference that failed to advance to the fore of the old cultural politics of difference. The new cultural politics of difference then aims at broadening representations of black people and demystifying the binary oppositions of race.[47] West argues that the new cultural politics of difference is part of his vision of radical democracy and its transformative possibilities for black people.

The new cultural politics of difference as presented in black cultural criticism seeks to explore the multiple forms of difference that constitute black life in the United States. As noted above, the new cultural politics of difference argues that black life ought not be interpreted solely in terms of race. Class, gender, and sexuality (including sexual difference) stand alongside race in postmodern African American criticism. These scholars are clear when they argue against homophobia in African American communities. As early as the early 1990s, African American cultural critics such as bell hooks were writing against homophobia and urging a revision in the ways in which black cultural discourse approaches black sexuality.[48] In 1993, Cornel West's *Keeping Faith* was published, which contained the aforementioned seminal essay "The New Cultural Politics of Difference." Michael Eric Dyson's incisive and wide-ranging examination of African American culture, *Reflecting Black*, appeared the same year. These scholars working within a new cultural politics of difference are far clearer than many black liberation and womanist theologians. In their approaches to homosexuality, African

American cultural critics argue that black gays and lesbians ought to be able to pursue their happiness unfettered by heteronormativity and homophobia.

However, homosexuality does not receive the same thick descriptions and analyses as race, gender, and class do in the literature of African American cultural critics. Rather, homosexuality recedes into the background. When it does appear in black cultural criticism, homosexuality is presented as a problem. It is often spoken of in terms of homophobia. Michael Eric Dyson's chapter on the black church and sexuality in *Race Rules* and bell hooks's chapter on black gays and lesbians in *Salvation: Black People and Love* serve as illustrative examples of how the new cultural politics of difference fails to adequately take up sexual difference in black cultural criticism.

Dyson's chapter on the black church and sex is a bold chapter. Dyson begins the chapter with an anecdote about a moment in his early preaching days. The scene begins at a revival that Dyson was attending. Dyson describes in great detail the appearance of the unnamed visiting preacher, the "climax" of the sermon, and the orgasmic response of the congregation. It is worth quoting at length:

> The visiting preacher, a brawny brown man with smooth skin and teeth made of pearl, was coming to the close of his sermon, a ritual moment of climax in the black church. It is the inevitable point to which the entire service builds. Its existence is the only justification for the less dramatic rites of the community—greeting visitors, collecting tithes, praying for the sick, reading scripture, and atoning for sins. These rites are a hallway to the sanctuary of zeal and vision formed by the black sermon. The furious splendor of the preacher's rhythmic, almost sung, speech drove the congregation to near madness. His relentless rhetoric stood them on their feet. Their bodies lurched in holy oblivion to space or time. Their hands waved as they shrieked their assent to the gospel lesson he passionately proclaimed. His cadence quickened. Each word swiftly piled on top of the next. The preacher's sweet moan sought to bring to earth the heavenly light of which his words, even at their most brilliant, were but a dim reflection.[49]

Dyson's use of sexual imagery is not accidental. Dyson intends to convey an image of the black church as a complex organization rife with quasi-sexual over- and undertones. In his recounting of the "climax" of the service, Dyson is careful to use language similar to that of a romance novel. The suitor, in this case the visiting preacher, brings his lover, the congregation, to a frenzied pitch. Phrases such as "the preacher's sweet moan" and "they shrieked their assent to the gospel he passionately proclaimed" serve as double signifiers, signifying not only the emotive force of the service itself, but also the erotic components that undergird the experience of the sermon in the black church.

The anecdote is not complete, however. Dyson recounts a conversation that reveals how "dishonest we're sometimes made by the unresolved disputes between our bodies and our beliefs."[50] During the course of the congratulatory meeting of ministers in the pastor's study, the visiting preacher inquired about a woman who he considered attractive. His "shameless lust" stood in stark contrast to his status as a married man.

Dyson asks whether this preacher was acting out of some misguided sense of "black Christian sexuality" that is both repressed and excessive. His question is asked in anticipation of his thesis: black Christians have been sexually repressed by white racism. He claims that white people have labeled black sexuality sinful. His argument regarding the negative status accorded black sexuality vis-à-vis white racism is based on a genealogical reading of the encounter between black people and white people. Dyson argues that white people demeaned black bodies in order to justify enslaving Africans. This demonization of black bodies extended to sexuality. According to Dyson, sexuality for blacks existed only in the service of breeding more black people for slavery.[51]

Dyson goes on to note that the institution of the black church served as a way to protect black bodies from the assaults of white racism and as a channel to "redirect black sexual energies into the sheer passion and emotional explosiveness of its worship services."[52] However, as Dyson further argues, the black church that nurtured black bodies also repressed them in an attempt to present a sexually chaste black Christian. This repression was employed in the service of refuting the myths surrounding black people's sexuality.

Dyson believes that what the black church needs in order to combat repressed black sexuality is a theology of eroticism.[53] This theology of eroticism will free black Christians from the dualism that is a pervasive feature of Christianity. This theology will allow for an embracing of our sensual, erotic selves. However, when speaking of black gays and lesbians, Dyson argues that they require a different theology tailored to accept their form of sexual expression.[54]

His account of black gays and lesbians in *Race Rules* is centered on the theme of sexual dishonesty. This account of gay and lesbian identity presents them as Other, almost wholly separate from an assumed "normal" black people, and forced to live their sexual lives in some sort of Purgatory due to intolerance by heterosexual black people. Dyson's account of black gays and lesbians begins with a stereotypical "scenario of black church life" that "is repeated Sunday after Sunday":

> A black minister will preach a sermon against sexual ills, especially homosexuality. At the close of the sermon, a soloist, who everybody knows is gay, will rise to perform a moving number, as the preacher extends an invitation to visitors to join the church. The soloist is, in effect, being asked to sing, and to sign, his theological death sentence.[55]

Dyson goes on to note that the presence of the gay person in the service serves to negate the preacher's attempt to "deny his legitimacy as a child of God." However, the gay person's presence and performance of ecclesiastical duties serves as a silent approval of the preacher's sermon.

Dyson's section regarding homosexuality and the black church has less to do with sexual relations between black gays and lesbians and more to do with black heterosexuals regarding black gays and lesbians as people of equal worth. For Dyson, vanquishing homophobia frees the black church to carry out its mission of providing comfort to oppressed black people. Eliminating homophobia also has the effect of freeing black gays and lesbians from "destructive behaviors." As an example of the destructive sexual behaviors that are seemingly particular to black gays and lesbians, Dyson notes that James Cleveland died from AIDS, thus indelibly correlating AIDS with homosexual practices. When Dyson presents situations such as gays remaining faithful to their partners, it appears as if he is positing a hypothetical situation rather than a reality.

As a journalist, preacher, and cultural critic, Dyson has perhaps greater access to wider audiences than black liberation and womanist theologians. His books and essays are written to and for larger audiences. However, his appearances on television programs only afford him brief moments in which to get a point across. His television appearances (usually on current affairs programs) are part of the world of news reporting in which conversations are very brief, and "sound bytes" are the order of the day. Further, as his audiences are wider than those of academic theologians, Dyson has to package his arguments so they can be grasped by laypersons. As such, Dyson's presentations of queer issues in African American life suffer from a brevity that tends to render his arguments incomplete. For example, an interview conducted with Dyson in 2002 focused on the Bible, sexual ethics, and homosexuality in African American life. In the interview, published in *Open Mike: Reflections on Philosophy, Race, Sex, Culture and Religion* (2003), Dyson again calls for a "theology of homoeroticism."[56] Dyson's argument here is quite similar to his argument in *Race Rules* and calls for a revised view of theology and the Bible so that African Americans can embrace homosexuals and so that these oppressed gays and lesbians can enjoy full participation in African American cultural life.

As I noted with his section on sexuality in *Race Rules*, his call for a theology of homoeroticism seems to place black gays and lesbians as a different species altogether from other human beings (who are presumably sexual beings, also). Further, his argument for a theology of homoeroticism elevates sexual activity to a higher moral status. He argues that "erotic unions at their best engender the salvific function of intimate contact between God and believer, a relationship often pictured as one between a lover and his beloved."[57] While his argument is designed to counter the Manichean dualism that he contends has led to various forms of sexual repression in African American communities, his desire to claim such a moral status for human sexual contact under a theology of homoeroticism threatens to essentialize homosexuals. He never unpacks why this particular area of human activity should somehow reflect "the salvific function of intimate contact between God and believer." Further, he never articulates how this applies to a specific theology that addresses black homosexuals.

bell hooks' chapter called "Embracing Gayness" is similar to Dyson's arguments concerning black gays and lesbians. That is, her chapter presents gay identity among black people as a problem to be solved. Hooks blames homophobia in black communities on patriarchy. She contends that this patriarchy did not always exist, but arose during the 1960s and 1970s during the black liberation struggle. Hooks claims that there was a time in the black community when the community affirmed sexual difference. I will quote her at length:

> Prior to the sixties, black folks were much more willing to interpret scripture in ways that affirmed loving one another. Growing up in our small Kentucky town, as a family we had the good fortune to live across the street from the Smith family, an elderly couple who lived with their adult son, Mr. Richard, a schoolteacher. In those days everyone used

the word "funny" to describe homosexuals. We learned at school that Mr. Richard was "funny." At home we were taught to respect him, to appreciate the way he cared for his mother and father....in small towns where black people "had known someone all their life," you accepted folks' sexuality because they were "just born that way"— "They couldn't change themselves and you could not change them, so there was no point in trying."[58]

This passage about Mr. Richard is telling. Hooks speaks of the word "funny" as if it is a benign signifier of sexual difference. The term "funny" suggests a difference that is not quite acceptable. As hooks's mother, Rosa Bell later tells her, this difference cannot be changed. However, what she implies is that change would be desirable. It would have been desirable for Mr. Richard to somehow change himself and become respectable to the rest of the community by engaging in the rites of heterosexuality. Clearly, heterosexuality is the "norm" by which Mr. Richard's queer deviance is measured. Because he cannot change, and because no one else in the community can change him, his difference is merely tolerated.

It is also curious that Mr. Richard does not speak for himself. He never enters into the discussion about embracing gayness and embracing it for himself. Instead, hooks leaves it to her friends, relatives, and acquaintances from her "small Kentucky town" to speak for him. It is hooks' relatives (who are presumably heterosexual) who define Mr. Richard as being gay. What is even more interesting is how hooks was taught to "appreciate" Mr. Richard. She says she was taught to "appreciate the way he cared for his mother and father."[59] Although it is commendable that hooks was taught to appreciate Mr. Richard's concern for his parents, it is problematic that what actually constitutes Mr. Richard's alleged difference never surfaces. All the reader has access to are whispered assumptions that fail to acknowledge Mr. Richard as a subject with a voice and an autonomous identity. Hooks even notes that no one in her community had actual evidence that Mr. Richard was gay. Despite the lack of evidence concerning Mr. Richard's sexuality, hooks goes on to use the example of Mr. Richard as proof of the existence and tolerance of black gays and lesbians in pre–civil rights black America.

Hooks presents the black church as the major black institution that taught love and compassion. It is also the major black institution that perpetuates negative stereotypes of black gays and lesbians. Like Dyson, hooks locates the presence of black gay people squarely within the musical activities of churches.[60] However, unlike Dyson, hooks claims that the ministry of music in black churches served as a refuge for black gay men in particular. She continues her analysis of homophobia by reiterating her contention that homophobia is a by-product of the militant patriarchal thinking that arose during the civil rights movement. For hooks, this turn to patriarchy continues to inform "young black heterosexual militants" who claim that homosexuality is an unnatural condition that has no place within black communities. This is a problematic claim. First, hooks simply assumes that the reader clearly understands what she categorizes as homophobia. However, if homophobia is described as negative views about homosexuality, certainly the people in her small town could be considered homophobic, as they called him "funny." Even though the adults encouraged their children to not mistreat Mr. Richard, it is clear that he occupied a different space than the putatively heterosexual people in hooks' childhood town.

In one passage, hooks notes that black gays and lesbians do not require the validation of heterosexuals.[61] However, in order to recover some of the most articulate and powerful black leaders, black people must come to terms with and vanquish homophobic thinking. According to hooks, "judging one another as traitors based on sexual preferences has been the easiest way to discount and dismiss the work of black people who have given or give their all to the black liberation struggle."[62] It seems that for hooks, like Dyson, the only way for black people to struggle against the titanic, nihilistic force of racism is to embrace the "Other." In the case of hooks' *Salvation*, the other is the black homosexual. Thus, it does seem that, in order to defeat white supremacy, black gay people require, at the minimum, a level of tolerance by black heterosexuals.

Hooks characterizes gay identity as one that is framed by crisis and struggle. These crises and struggles that black gay people face are precipitated by the homophobia of black heterosexuals. The crux of her argument in this chapter is that black people who love themselves should also love black people who happen to be gay. She inverts a statement by the late Marlon Riggs that "black men loving black men was the most revolutionary act," transforming it into a psychoanalytic statement that claims that the most revolutionary act involves black men dealing with the traumas of childhood. I will again quote her at length:

When he was alive, Marlon Riggs, activist, scholar, and filmmaker, used to insist in conversations with me and Essex that "black men loving black men was the most revolutionary act." ... He believed that a self-hating individual black male, irrespective of his sexual preference, would never be able to love another black male. While I agree that anyone mired in self-hate cannot love anyone, I used to tell him that the "most revolutionary act" black men could make was to deal psychoanalytically with their childhoods. For it is in childhood that so many black males, gay and straight, come to fear masculinity and manhood. This fear is often based on painful and abusive interaction between fathers and/or male parental caretakers and sons.[63]

If black people, men especially, love themselves and have dealt with their traumatic childhoods, they will be able to love black gay people. Here, it appears that hooks is inextricably linking black male homosexuality and the ways in which it is expressed with childhood traumas and parental relationships. Following hooks' argument, if black people are not able to love gays and lesbians then black people are participating in assaults on the integrity of the entire black community.

As representative figures of the new cultural politics of difference, both Dyson and hooks present examples of what I find problematic within black cultural criticism as it relates to sexual difference among black people. Black religious criticism essentializes black gays, problematizes them, and renders them silent by failing to explore their relationships, sexual and otherwise. These shortcomings make for narrow readings of black gay and lesbian experience and fail to fully open up black cultural criticism to areas of difference in black communities.

As with black liberation and womanist theologies, contemporary African American cultural criticism has, as its primary concern, the survival and flourishing of black people. Black cultural critics such as hooks and Dyson attack homophobia in order to advance a program of racial uplift. However, their truncated accounts of homosexuality undercut their stringent attacks on homophobia. That is to say, while their accounts of the damaging nature of homophobia may be strong, their accounts of gays and lesbians themselves often are thin and laden with stereotypical assumptions about black gay experiences.

In black religious and cultural criticism, black gays and lesbians have been rendered silent and spoken for. Even when black gays or lesbians speak, their words are subverted to advance a program of racial uplift. I return to hooks' subversion of Riggs' assertion that black men loving black men is the revolutionary act. Changing the statement to insist that black men must deal psychoanalytically with their childhoods implies that sexual difference is a problem rooted in some form of childhood psychological trauma. Also, rewording the statement reduces Riggs to a mute figure who can be reconfigured at will. He no longer speaks for himself, and if he does speak, he speaks incorrectly. He requires the assistance of heterosexuals to fully flesh out his own thoughts.

This subversion or syndication of black gay and lesbian utterances is not unique to Dyson and hooks. Henry Louis Gates subverts Audre Lorde in *Loose Canons* (1992). In his effort to include African American literature among the literary canons in the United States, Gates claims that only the master's tools may be used to dismantle the master's house. This claim is a direct inversion of Lorde's famous statement "the master's tools will never dismantle the master's house."[64] Once again, the black homosexual does not speak for herself. She is also considered to be in error regarding her own experience. I will quote Gates at length:

> Maybe the most important thing here is the tension between the imperatives of agency and the rhetoric of dismantlement. An example: Foucault says, and let's take him at his word, that the "homosexual" as life form was invented sometime in the mid-nineteenth century. Now, if there's no such thing as a homosexual, then homophobia, at least as directed toward people rather than acts, loses its rationale. But you can't respond to the discrimination against gay people by saying, "I'm sorry, I don't exist; you've got the wrong guy." The simple historical fact is, Stonewall was necessary, concerted action was necessary to take action against the very structures that, as it were, called the homosexual into being, that subjected certain people to this imaginary identity. *To reverse Audre Lorde*, only the master's tools will ever dismantle the master's house. (emphasis mine)[65]

As Gates wants to point toward the necessity of forming a black literary canon, he simultaneously pushes black gay and lesbian experience to the periphery of black experience. His reversal of Lorde is a selective reversal. Gates merely mentions Lorde without attending to the context that gave rise to the statement.

Further, black religious critics' minimal use of the voices of deceased black gay writers suggests to me a selective reading that situates black gay experience within the context of plague and death. Black religious and cultural critics draw on deceased figures such as Essex Hemphill, Marlon Riggs, and Audre Lorde because their writings emphasize a particular type of protest politics operative in the black community.

As I will discuss in chapter 3, Hemphill's writing adopts the nationalist tone that was prevalent in the late 1960s into the 1990s. His nationalism urges black communities to confront their homophobia and to confront the HIV/AIDS crisis. The angry, strident tone of Hemphill's writings indicts both whites and blacks for rendering the black homosexual invisible. In Hemphill's essays and poems it is evident that gay sexuality is secondary to his identity as a black man in America. Black religious critics then use Hemphill as a gay exemplar of black identity. Black religious critics selectively utilize Hemphill's arguments against white racism and black homophobia in support of their larger project of combating white supremacy.

For black theology and African American cultural criticism, the interests that black gays and lesbians might have are taken up into the generalized interests of "mainstream" black communities.[66] Thus, the sexuality of black gays and lesbians has no distinct identity except as an object of hatred and oppression. By not attending to the "particular of the particulars," black theologians and cultural critics avoid a potential quagmire of attempting to justify or validate homosexual sexual activity.

If, as Douglas and Dyson argue, the black church is a primary site of black homophobia, then the theologians and cultural critics have to attend to the possible reasons for the presence of homophobia. Theologians like Douglas and critics like Dyson and hooks might alienate the black church by speaking at length about black gay and lesbian experience. Instead, black theologians and cultural critics appeal to African Americans' common history of white Christian misappropriation of the Bible in a desire to modify black biblical interpretations of sexuality. Perhaps speaking extensively about black gay and lesbian sexuality would be considered an affirmation of a "lifestyle" that is considered antithetical to Christian living. As can be seen in Cheryl Sanders' critical essay on womanist scholarship, black religious critics are primarily concerned with preserving black heterosexual familial structures and the ways in which white supremacy threatens the integrity of those structures. Kelly Brown Douglas' response to Sanders in both essay and book form do not contradict her assertions about the primacy of the black family. Rather, Douglas presents the black church as a community, a body of black people that is akin to the black family. Black homosexuality in both Sanders' and Douglas' works appears as a problem that needs to be addressed by the larger black family. However, as I have noted before, what constitutes the life-world of black homosexuals is never explicated.

Descriptions of black gay life turn on the categories of problem and prejudice. Addressing the responses to a thinly defined identity and placing those responses as a by-product of white racism works to cement white supremacy as the "real" enemy, not totalized racial discourses in institutions within the black community.

Tolerance in Black Religious Criticism

The aforementioned theological and cultural discourses argue for tolerance of sexual difference in black communities. They contend that tolerance of sexual difference is a necessary activity in that it resists received European notions of sexuality. While both black liberation theology in the form of womanist theology and African American cultural criticism decry homophobia, I find both of these conversations to be silent concerning the black homosexual. Indeed, hooks makes mention of Mr. Richard, the schoolteacher in her town whom her parents and relatives assumed was gay, but does Mr. Richard speak for himself? Hooks argues for black communities to embrace gayness in the same ways in which her Kentucky town appears to have. However, in reading her account of her town, instead of embracing sexual difference, I find a mere toleration of Mr. Richard's unspoken (and unshown) difference. Certainly, the townspeople were tolerant of Mr. Richard, but their tolerance did not require much more than unsupported assumptions about Mr. Richard's identity and personal life.

In my talk of tolerance, I borrow heavily from Janet Jakobsen's discussion of difference both in *Working Alliances and the Politics of Difference* and *Love the Sin: Sexual Regulation and the Limits of Tolerance*. In *Working Alliances*, Jakobsen describes toleration as "accompany[ing] compartmentalization where each part manages its co-existence with the others, precisely by limiting contact and interaction among parts."[67] In other words, the concept of tolerance allows for difference by rigidly maintaining boundaries between particular differences. She argues that tolerance itself is narrow and serves only to reinforce and regulate difference. Jakobsen contends that tolerance "creates an exclusionary, rather than democratic, public" and that it also "sets up a political culture in which extremism, rather than injustice, is the major problem to be addressed in public life."[68] Jakobsen presents the case of Matthew Shepard's murder and the subsequent media coverage as an example of the rhetoric of tolerance in the United States. She examines *Time* magazine's coverage of the Shepard case. Specifically, she scrutinizes the cover caption, "The War Over Gays."[69] Jakobsen argues that the preposition "over" as opposed to "on" "exempts 'ordinary' Americans from any responsibility for hatred or violence."[70] The rhetoric of tolerance absolves those who consider themselves part of the "tolerant middle." For Jakobsen, the rhetoric of tolerance creates three polarized groups: those who hate, those who are the subject of the hatred, and those who purport to tolerate the hated.[71]

As I apply Jakobsen's argument to black religious criticism, homophobia becomes the primary category by which attitudes toward sexual difference are regulated. Black homosexuals become a faceless group constantly acted upon by the malevolent force of homophobia or tolerated by more "accepting" black heterosexuals. This tolerance often finds expression in the form of black heterosexuals speaking for black homosexuals. For black liberation theologians and African American cultural critics, this toleration of homosexuality has less to do with presenting a fuller picture of the lives of black gay people and more to do with absolving black heterosexuals in general and the black church in particular of culpability in homophobic discourse. As a problematic "other," black homosexuals must, at a minimum, be tolerated in order to advance a larger, more important agenda of combating and defeating white supremacy. Thus, it is efficacious for black theologians and cultural critics to attend only to the oppression of black gays by heterosexuals instead of presenting a more complete picture of black sexual difference that is not framed by oppression. By linking homophobia to white supremacy, the black homosexual recedes into the background, while tolerant black heterosexuals advance to the foreground. Further, this form of tolerance maintains stable, recognizable boundaries between black heterosexuals and homosexuals. Tolerance in black religious criticism does not provide space for black gay self-description outside of oppression by intolerant heterosexuals and death by disease.

Conclusion

As I read black religious criticism, I find that black religious criticism relegates black gay people to a problem status. The representative texts highlighted in this chapter show that black gay sexuality as represented by black religious criticism is placed at the margins of black experience. Instead, homophobia is foregrounded in these critical discourses as a way of distinguishing between tolerant and intolerant heterosexual African Americans. Any interests that black gays and lesbians might have are bracketed in order to advance a rhetoric of tolerance in black communities. This rhetoric of tolerance functions within a larger agenda of defeating white supremacy. As black religious critics discuss tolerance within black heterosexual communities, they argue that black heterosexuals who voice antigay sentiments replicate the same dysfunctional attitudes toward sexuality impressed upon black people by white people. However, the rhetoric fails to take seriously the experiences of black homosexuals beyond oppression and plague.

The rhetoric of tolerance within black religious criticism retains stable descriptions of black people by maintaining black heterosexuality as the center of black experiences and keeping black homosexuals at the periphery of black life. By turning only to a constellation of negative attitudes toward homosexuals and categorizing those attitudes as homophobia and then arguing that those attitudes are the by-products of white supremacy, black religious critics fail to substantively attend to the voices of black gays and lesbians. This rhetoric maintains a heteronormative gaze that privileges heterosexuality and makes homosexuality (as well as other forms of sexual difference) dependent upon heterosexual largesse. Further, such tolerance in African American religious criticism is deployed only to subordinate the interests of black homosexuals under the larger interests of black communities, which further perpetuates heteronormativity by placing black heterosexuals (in this case, black heterosexual scholars) as gatekeepers of an African American political and intellectual agenda. As such, the voices of black homosexuals recede into the background of African American intellectual discourse and is retrieved only to serve the interests of the dominant group.

What I propose to do in the succeeding chapters is engage in a "queering" of black religious criticism. By queering, I intend to turn to black gay men's literature and engage in a queer reading of black experiences. First, I turn to the voices of black queer religious scholars Victor Anderson and Horace Griffin. Their respective projects have involved the enlarging of African American religious discourse as it concerns sexual difference. For Griffin, especially, engaging difference in black religious studies has involved the retrieval of black gay men from the periphery of African American history. Anderson is concerned with a larger discourse surrounding "blackness" and how that concept becomes monolithic and exclusionary. The following chapters will operate out of what I call a "black queer hermeneutics of retrieval." Since black religious criticism functions hermeneutically, I ask how black gays have been represented in black religious criticism. As I have argued that black gay voices have receded into the background in black religious discourse, careful attention to the literary utterances of black gay men destabilizes the centrality of black heterosexuality in black religious criticism.

3

Black Theology and Homosexuality Revisited: Black Queer Theologians Respond

Introduction

This book has heretofore focused on black liberation theologians speaking about homosexuals and black queer writers speaking about themselves and how they take hold of their religious or spiritual orientations. It might appear as though the preceding chapters commit the same kinds of hermeneutical divisions that I have been critiquing. This book so far might appear to suggest there are no black queer theologians or religious scholars who are, as Marlon Riggs put it, "letting the queen speak." As I began writing this book, I realized that I had not taken Horace Griffin's or Victor Anderson's works into account. In hindsight, it was a grave mistake when this book was in dissertation form. I think that to not treat their responses would be an obvious attempt at setting black liberation theology up as a "straw man" in order to claim that it wholly ignores black queer voices. This chapter will focus on the ways in which African American gay male theologians and religious critics take hold of sexual difference in African American life.

I focus primarily on Griffin and Anderson as they have been most prolific in their responses to the black theological academy concerning black homosexuality, religious studies, and black churches. Horace Griffin's *Their Own Receive Them Not: African American Lesbians and Gays in Black Churches* (2006), and Victor Anderson's *Beyond Ontological Blackness: An Essay in African American Religious Thought* (1995) and subsequent essay "Deadly

Silence: Reflections on Homosexuality and Human Rights in the African American Community" as well as his latest book, *Creative Exchange: A Constructive Theology of African American Religious Experience* (2008) represent two theological responses to the question of black queer visibility in black theological discourse. Their writing represents far more than a minimal response to the issue of homosexuality in black religious thought. What these writers seek are expanded understandings and an appreciation of sexual difference in African American life. This chapter's central concern is the manner in which these theologians understand and represent sexual difference in their work.

Horace Griffin

Griffin's *Their Own Receive Them* Not is a more detailed restatement of his earlier essay, "Their Own Received Them Not," where Griffin lays out a grievance against the black church's intransigence concerning black homosexuals. The subsequent book is aimed squarely at the black church and has two tasks. First, this text represents an attempt to craft a pastoral theology that can participate in the liberation of black gays and lesbians. Further, Griffin wants this pastoral theology to overturn what he perceives to be a heteronormative, heterosexist orientation in the church.

Griffin presents the work as a practical test of contemporary black theology's slant toward liberation. The book is an attempt to critically evaluate both the black church and black liberation theology's claims of justice and liberation. He argues that black Christians have failed to live the liberating message of the Christian Gospel concerning black gays and lesbians. Thus, the black church does not promote a "true" liberation theology.[1]

He is quite clear from the outset of the book that African American churches have taken on a virulent form of homophobic discourse that prevents it from being the truly prophetic and energetic institution that it could be. He at first appears to differ from Kelly Brown Douglas in that he does not want to lay the blame for homophobia in black communities at the doorstep of whites. According to Griffin, homophobia in African American communities and churches cannot be blamed solely on white supremacy.[2]

However, Griffin spends a great deal of time outlining cultural and historical views on homosexuality. By the end of the first chapter, it is clear that he wants to position the situation of black gays and lesbians alongside that of white gays and lesbians and the church. Griffin's treatment of African American homosexuals and the black church shows that he clearly finds homosexuality and homophobia in black churches to be substantively different than for whites. From the introduction, Griffin is clear about the status of black gays and lesbians in the black church. They are cast as victims. They are victims of homophobia and of HIV/AIDS. For Griffin, black homosexuals exist in parallel worlds. They exist in black worlds and white worlds, gay worlds and straight worlds. In essence, they are always strangers in strange lands.

For Griffin, it is the "making of black Christians" as a result of chattel slavery in the United States that forms the background conditions for homophobic discourse in black religious communities. This might appear to be a contradiction of his earlier caveat that the blame for homophobia in black communities cannot be assigned to white supremacy and racist discourse. However, he relies heavily on Kelly Brown Douglas' description of racial and sexual bigotry. In doing so, he affirms that it is indeed the legacy of racism and white supremacy that provides the fertile ground for homophobia in African American religious life. He does not address that potential contradiction, opting instead to refute potential philosophical and religious arguments against homosexual orientation and experience.

Griffin addresses particular arguments like appeals to natural law, the notion that homosexual orientation is a choice (and, as Jeremiah Wright notes in his anti-homophobia sermon, "Good News For Homosexuals," a choice of sin), and the notion that homosexual orientation somehow precludes the possibility of procreation. It is interesting that Griffin devotes so much space to attending to these types of arguments, for others have already done that kind of work. However, it is a necessary move as Griffin situates these philosophical and religious arguments in contemporary debates emerging in black communities concerning homosexuality. He takes on these arguments because of emerging antigay activists like Martin Luther King's niece, Alveda King, and Debbie and Angie Winans, and because of coalitions like the one formed by Reverend Clarence James and twenty-nine other ministers. These activists may address black communities, but they base their arguments against same-sex marriage and homosexual identity on the same philosophical and religious grounds as whites.

It is at the midpoint of the book that Griffin shifts away from homophobia and toward attending to the lives and experiences of black gays and lesbians. His fourth chapter is a search for the historical black queer. This move is an important move for Griffin as he endeavors to show the reader that black queers have not only existed in history, but have also played pivotal and heroic roles in African American civic and religious life.

To that end, Griffin posits George Washington Carver and James Cleveland as gay men. He looks for their putative homosexuality in the silent spaces of their respective lives. I shall quote from Griffin at length regarding Carver:

> The two most compelling examples of [George Washington] Carver's homosexuality came from Tuskeegee's administrators, who noted Carver's sexual gestures directed toward male students and his love letters written to males in Alabama. Tuskeegee administrators often were embarrassed because Carver had a "bad habit" of placing his hands on the buttocks of the male students. This evidence, along with his largely young male following (known as Carver's boys) and the erotic letters to young Alabama males veiled in the flowery language of the day, provide insight for us about Carver's sexual identity.[3]

What Griffin has to say about James Cleveland's alleged homosexuality is even less conclusive. His section on Cleveland is a brief biographical sketch and discography. He concludes with:

> Cleveland grew up amidst the homophobia of black churches, and like most homosexuals of his generation, followed the social and religious conventions by getting married. Like so many mixed-sexual-orientation marriages, the marriage ended in divorce.[4]

Griffin tells the reader that George Washington Carver wrote erotic letters to young men and that the erotic nature of those letters was obscured in "flowery language." However, he does not share any of the textual evidence with the reader, forcing the reader to either agree with his assertions or dismiss them outright. His failure to share any of the textual evidence with the reader works to undermine his assumptions concerning Carver's homosexuality. His comments can be dismissed as innuendo as they appear to be thin and unsustained claims. His comments about James Cleveland are even more vague. He assumes that the reader will recognize Cleveland as a homosexual. Yet, as with Carver, Griffin fails to provide the reader any evidence to support his presentation of Cleveland as gay. By failing to point to any concrete evidence of Cleveland or Carver's homosexuality, Griffin leaps to an assumption that is not supported in the text.

The aforementioned critique of Griffin's treatment of Carver and Cleveland is not an argument that either man was heterosexual. Rather, what I am concerned about is the a priori presentation of either person as homosexual in the face of an apparent lack of evidence and what that presentation means for Griffin's overall argument concerning black gay existence and the church. Further, neither of these men speak for themselves. As both Washington and Cleveland are dead, we have to turn to some form of textual evidence in order to categorize them as either hetero- or homosexual (that either man could have been bisexual or even asexual does not appear to enter as a consideration). Griffin takes it upon himself to not only speak for them, but he also imposes upon them his particular understanding of gay identity. In essence, he commits the same error that bell hooks makes when she asserts without any evidence that a schoolteacher in her old Kentucky town was gay. Such a discursive move allows the reader only two options. The reader must either assume that Griffin is correct or the reader must assume that Griffin is wrong.

It appears that proving Carver's and Cleveland's homosexuality is not the point that Griffin wants to make. Rather, Griffin is concerned with the rhetorical effect of presenting these two historical figures as gay. Both Carver and Cleveland have contributed greatly to African American culture and history. George Washington Carver, through his scientific prowess, has put to a lie the assertion that African Americans are not capable of excelling in scientific endeavors. James Cleveland, through his musical prowess, has been credited as being one of the most influential figures in the development of contemporary Gospel music. Thus, both men become paradigmatic figures for Griffin. They are paradigms of not only African American exceptionalism, but also the effects of enforced heteronormativity. What Griffin is arguing in and through his discussion of Carver and Cleveland is that enforced heteronormativity damages black homosexuals. Implicit in his discussion of these men and others is an argument about the deferred potential of these men to have been even greater people, if only the black community had not been homophobic. As paradigms of exceptional blackness and as examples of closeted black gay men, Griffin endeavors to show that black homosexuals harbor deep commitments to black communities and that, unfortunately, the reverse is not true.

Griffin moves on to the near-present. He pays special attention to Tommie Watkins (the first openly gay person to seek ordination in the African Methodist Episcopal Church) and Leonard Patters, a former minister at Ebenezer Baptist Church in Atlanta. He briefly discusses the struggles that the two men faced at their respective congregations and then pointedly states,

> Given their experiences of homophobia and heterosexual supremacy in black churches, black gays recognize that black heterosexuals have been dishonest about the level of opposition and oppression they inflict on gays. Although black gay Christians acknowledge the racism of whites and the homosexual hatred of white heterosexuals, many, such as Jacob, a gay member of a black Southern Baptist church, still feel that on average "the white community is a little more open-minded, even in the South, about homosexuality. With the black community it's more strictly religious as far as our faith and upbringing." Perhaps there is validity to this claim when considering that in the 1990s, two white Southern Baptist churches in North Carolina...ordained an openly gay man and held a wedding for a gay couple, respectively. *No church of any black denomination has demonstrated the gospel message with this level of liberation and religious justice for black lesbian and gay Christians.* (emphasis added)[5]

If Griffin's argument is unclear at the beginning of the text, it becomes crystal clear here. Implicit in the subject of his book and explicit in the above paragraph is Griffin's disappointment with the black church. That disappointment is predicated upon an assumption that the black church is a standard-bearer against oppression. This assumption is not unfounded, as historians, religious scholars, as well as members of black churches have promoted the institution as the "bedrock of the black community."[6]

Griffin's argument is similar to Cone's initial arguments concerning black theology and the black church. Liberation for both Cone and Griffin was and should continue to be the primary mission of the church. Griffin's positioning of black churches (which are supposed to be the articulators of new images and visions of liberation) vis-à-vis white Southern Baptist churches (which have historically been presented as integral parts of racial separatism) is clearly intentional. His judgment of black churches in this matter is equally clear. Black churches have fallen victim to a pernicious form of heterosexism and homophobia that prevents them from being the liberationist institution that they claim to be.

As black churches have fallen victim to this pernicious heterosexist discourse that relegates black homosexuals as deviant, black gays have responded to this by forming their own congregations. He contends that this response has been a necessary move. Some black gays who leave the black church due to its heterosexism and homophobia then affiliate with predominantly white Metropolitan Community churches, "only to be confronted with the racism of white lesbians and gays."[7] The option left to black gays is to form their own churches, as in the case of the late Dr. James Tinney, who founded Faith Temple, or Bishop Carl Bean, who founded the Unity Fellowship church.

Griffin focuses on these churches as models of the type of pastoral care for black homosexuals as he concludes that all black Christian churches require a true liberation theology. He contends that black pastors can be leaders in the fight against homophobia and heterosexuality and can and should divest themselves and their churches of language that marginalizes black gays and lesbians. He urges the black church to "critically engage the relationship between Christianity and homosexuality in the same faithful way that a critical engagement of Christianity and race is offered."[8] As I noted before, Griffin's claim is that black churches have strayed from their own model of liberation. They have become transformed into agents of oppression and demonization and, as such, have precipitated a breaking away of some into smaller, more faithful congregations. Further, the entrenched homophobia within black churches prohibits black pastors from providing the kinds of pastoral care that they should be providing to black gays and lesbians who are struggling to come to terms with their sexual orientation. If the black church is focused on saving black families, Griffin argues, then it ought to focus on saving all forms of black families. Implicit in that argument is the contention that black families are comprised of more than heteronormative, nuclear family units.

Griffin's work is very important, as it is the first sustained critique of the presence of black gays and lesbians in the black church. His attempt to point toward a pastoral theology that liberates black gays and lesbians from the cycles of heterosexist oppression is admirable; however, it is his work in foregrounding the presence and voices of black gays and lesbians that is most helpful for both black religious studies and black theologians. He takes seriously the methodological approach of privileging experience as a means of doing theology. It is this serious approach to black queer experiences that enlivens his work.

However, it is also his approach to black queer experience that poses a particular conceptual problem. As he attempts to make black queer experiences sympathetic to the reader (presumably black heterosexual Christians), he has to valorize the black homosexual. The valorization of the black homosexual in Griffin's work also necessitates the inscription of a heroic narrative on homosexual expression. In other words, sexual and erotic experiences are sanitized in order to make a case for inclusion of black homosexuals in black theological and ecclesiastical discourse. When Griffin speaks of black homosexuals and their sexual selves, he couches these sexual selves and their sexual experiences in an oft-repeated phrase, "love relationships."[9] While Griffin does acknowledge the necessity of affirming black gay sexuality, it is curious that when speaking about black gay sexuality, it is contained within the position of monogamous "loving" relationships. This positioning and policing of black gay sexuality within heteronormative structures not only sanitizes black gay sexuality, it reifies a particular set of sexual relations produced by dominant discourse. In other words, what I read when I see the phrase "love relationships" is a near-apologetic phrase that is designed to "normalize" black gays and lesbians in order to gain the sympathies of black heterosexuals. Potentially for the sake of a presumably heterosexual, Christian audience, Griffin does not delve into the particulars of black gay *sexual* experiences. The use of the phrase "love relationships" and, in one particular instance, the use of the phrase "make love" is a rhetorical move, designed to move heterosexual perceptions away from the stereotype of the lascivious or sexually insatiable homosexual.

It is this rhetorical move that I find problematic. As I mentioned before, the deployment of these terms serves to police black homosexuality. It is policed, redescribed, and repackaged within the boundaries of the same heteronormativity that Griffin seeks to disturb. In order to present an image of black homosexuality that would be palatable to his readers, Griffin has to present black homosexuals as an aggrieved party suffering great injustice at the hands of heterosexual oppressors. In other words, Griffin has to follow the same model presented by Cone and others in the formulation of black liberation theology. As such, the aggrieved black homosexual seeks the goods of connubial bliss, goods that have been cruelly denied them by homophobic black heterosexuals. By describing black homosexuality within a heteronormative framework that works to constrain sexual expressions within the bounds of "love," Griffin can show that the denial of the logical expression of this love (i.e., marriage) constitutes a gross violation of the Christian Gospel. Black homosexuality so contained does not receive the benefit of being subject to the same forms of diversity that Griffin exhorts as being central to African American life. In essence, the sexual diversity present in and through black gay bodies is rendered virtually invisible in favor of a more appealing presentation of black queer monogamy.

Griffin's lack of a sustained critique of the concept of liberation in black liberation theology further limits his argument. While it is clear what liberation might look like for Griffin with regard to black homosexuals, it is not clear how his view of black gay liberation fits into the overall schema of black liberation. He characterizes liberation for black gays and lesbians as the affirmation and appreciation of diversity among black people.[10] It appears that Griffin tacitly agrees that the goal of black liberation theology is the liberation of black peoples from white supremacy and that the liberation of black gays and lesbians is part of this overall trajectory.

Further, Griffin's descriptions of God are quite thin. If I read Griffin correctly and surmise that he is seeking a pastoral theology that not only can accommodate black gays and lesbians but significantly help reshape African American attitudes toward sexual difference, then he needs to present a more sustained description of who God is and how this God functions in his theology. God is constantly and consistently invoked and evoked in the text, but is never explicated. Further, a cursory examination of the text's index yields no reference to God. This appears to be a curious omission that begs a question: to what God is Griffin appealing? Indeed, to what God could black queer theologians appeal?

Victor Anderson

The above question is probably best addressed by Victor Anderson in his works *Beyond Ontological Blackness: An Essay on African American Religious and Cultural Criticism* (1995), the essay "Deadly Silences: Reflections on Homosexuality," which appears in the book *Sexual Orientation and Human Rights in American Religious Discourse* (1998), and his latest book *Creative Exchange: A Pragmatic Theology of African American Experience* (2008). In these works, Anderson attempts to displace the controlling narratives of "blackness" and God-as- anthropomorphized liberator of the oppressed, as presented in black liberation theology. It is his argument that the reification of heroic narratives of black identity are bound up in conceptions of masculinity and femininity that only allow for limited (and stereotypical) descriptions of and conversations concerning black homosexuals. As such, he calls for a revised black theology that is not predicated solely on liberation but oriented toward human fulfillment.

Anderson's critique of black liberation theology is predicated on his commitments to his conception of human flourishing and fulfillment, which are more fully stated in later works. Thus, his arguments are not predicated upon arguments for liberation—at least, not liberation as constructed by black liberation theologians. *Beyond Ontological Blackness* begins with an examination of the "problem" of black identity. Simply put, for Anderson, the problem of black identity is the problem of representation. How are African Americans to construe their identities and their experiences in the face of white supremacy? Anderson argues that African American cultural and religious criticism has reified a black identity that exists in counterpoint to white supremacist descriptions of black identity. Of course, such responses have historically been necessary. Anderson recognizes the historical and philosophical roots of white supremacy and the importance of attempting to subvert racist presentations of African American (or, in this case, African diasporic) identities. However, these responses to what Anderson calls "categorical racism" eventually led to a racial apologetics that inscribed upon the black body a heroic function.[11]

Anderson's argument is not that racial apologetics as it plays out in African American cultural and religious criticism is the problem. Rather, it is the manner in which that apologetics lead to what Anderson calls "ontological blackness" and the manner in which that ontological blackness is deployed in black liberation and womanist theologies. For Anderson, ontological blackness

> ...mirrors categorical racism. It represents categorical ways of transferring negative qualities associated with the group onto others within the group. It creates essential criteria for defining insiders and outsiders within the group. It subjugates the creative, expressive activities of blacks...under the symbolism of black heroic genius... *It makes race identity a totality that subordinates and orders internal differences among blacks, so that gender, social standing, and sexual orientations are secondary to racial identity.*[12] (emphasis mine)

As I argued in the second chapter, black liberation and womanist theologies not only relegate sexual orientation to a secondary status, they syndicate or assimilate it into ontological blackness. Thus, addressing issues of sexuality in African American life are syndicated, or folded into issues concerning combating categorical racism.

I take much of my critical methodology from *Beyond Ontological Blackness*. I find Anderson's explication of the problem of ontological blackness and the manner in which it constrains sexual difference in African American life compelling. I also find his critique of black liberation theology persuasive. He notes that "talk about liberation becomes hard to justify where freedom appears as nothing more than defiant self assertion of a revolutionary racial consciousness that requires for its legitimacy the opposition of white racism."[13] As he goes on to note, the blackness of black liberation theology is a blackness created by whiteness, or, more accurately, white supremacist thought.

It is *Beyond Ontological Blackness* and subsequent essays (some of which later appear in *Creative Exchange*) that build upon his argument that African American religious criticism need not be singularly fixed upon one particular and heroic narrative of black life in America. As Anderson rightly notes, this ontological blackness does not exist solely in black liberation theology. He observes that contemporary African American cultural criticism also relies upon heroic descriptions of black life in order to refute white supremacist assumptions about black inferiority. By drawing on a wide range of philosophical and theological sources, Anderson presents an argument for looking at African American life (indeed, all human life) through the lens of the grotesque as opposed to the heroic. Drawing on British aesthetic theory, Anderson argues that employing the grotesque has several features useful for understanding African American religious and cultural experience:

> First, the grotesque recovers and leaves unresolved prior and basic sensibilities such as attraction/repulsion and pleasure/pain differentials...Second, the nonresolution of the aesthetic and cognitive matrices renders the objects perceived and our apperception of the object confused or ambiguous. Third, these unresolved tensions may leave possibilities open for creative ways of taking an object or subject; for in the grotesque, an object is, at the same time, other than how it appears when one contour or another is attenuated. Fourth, the grotesque disrupts the penchant for cognitive synthesis and the aggrandizing functions of cultural genius and the heroic epic by highlighting the absurd and sincere, the comical and tragic, the estranged and familiar, the satirical and the playful, and normalcy and abnormalcy.[14]

These functions of the grotesque disrupt the stable yet rigid under-standings of African American identity and cultural life. For Anderson, African American cultural life cannot be reduced to simple, heroic binaries. In other words, he argues that African American cultural life and productions should not be presented solely as heroic racial productions designed to subvert or combat white supremacy. There are many areas of black life that cannot be presented as heroic rep-resentations of "the race." To present black life as a unified "heroic" narrative distorts the rich diversity of black life. Such diversity, by nature of human existence, also includes unresolved differentials.

What Anderson sees in African American life are many instances of grotesque existence. By looking at African American neoconser-vative critics, Anderson presents a compelling argument about the richness of black cultural commentary and criticism. However, *Beyond Ontological Blackness* is but a prolegomenon to a larger con-cern about the representations of African American life and religious experience. His later essays and latest work *Creative Exchange* high-light his concerns about the deployment of heroic narratives within African American religious thought and criticism. Here, I wish to turn to his essay "Deadly Silences: Reflections on Homosexuality and Human Rights in the African American Community" and Creative Exchange.

"Deadly Silences" does not attempt to examine the process by which African American religious communities deploy biblical texts in order to support antigay sentiments. He also does not seek to "recount the litany of abuses of black gays and lesbians carried out by the black churches."[15] What is of concern to Anderson in this essay is the manner in which the silences in African American churches disclose a problematic discourse around black gays and lesbians. His argument is, first, that black churches are not silent about gays and lesbians. Rather, the churches speak volumes about sexual difference. However, the negative assessment of sexual difference that constitutes black church discourse on homosexuality causes a deadly silence for black homosexuals. By relating a story about a young man who com-mitted suicide because of this deadly silence surrounding sexual dif-ference, Anderson grounds his argument in the lived experiences of black gays and lesbians.

His second argument is introduced in "Deadly Silences" but will receive greater attention in *Creative Exchange*. For Anderson, the presence and the flourishing of black gay and lesbian individu-als and their relationships "contribute to the flourishing of the black community."[16] Basing this argument on the philosophy of natural goods and natural rights, Anderson argues that the support, care, and nurturing of black gay and lesbian individuals and their relationships are part of an intricate web of interpersonal relationships that include hetero- and homosexual individuals. As such, he relocates the debate about sexual difference away from a thoroughly religious or biblical argument. Simply stated, Anderson argues that African American religious communities have a responsibility to recognize the human rights of black gays and lesbians. He acknowledges that this imperative may come into conflict with the "sexual theologies" promulgated by the churches. However, for Anderson, it is a concern for the well-being of all African Americans (regardless of sexual orientation) that supersedes particular (and possibly flawed) religious readings of black sexual bodies.

It is that same concern for the well-being and flourishing of African Americans that grounds Creative Exchange. Unlike Horace Griffin or Elias Farajaje-Jones (who I discussed briefly in chapter 2), Anderson is not interested in writing an atomized theology that speaks only to one particular subject. *Creative Exchange* represents Anderson's attempt to construct a pragmatic theology that can illuminate the diversity, the richness, and the unresolved ambiguities of African American religious experiences. He acknowledges that African American experience serves as the starting point in both his pragmatic theology as well as in black liberation and womanist theologies. However, he reiterates his concern that those experiences as presented in black liberation and womanist theologies are distorted. His attempt to construct a pragmatic theology of African American experience rests on how he is able to reconfigure God, the black church as a center of human value, and sexual difference in African American life.

As his argument about sexual difference in African American religious life and experience is contingent upon his discussion of God and human experience, I will briefly attend to his theological argument before exploring his argument about sexual difference. Anderson bases his theology upon a wide range of American theologians. James Gustafson, Henry Nelson Wieman, Gordon Kaufman, Josiah Royce, and Howard Thurman all contribute significantly to Anderson's pragmatic approach. As Karl Barth and Paul Tillich influenced James Cone's theological method, so too do these thinkers inform Anderson's theology.

Drawing on their theological and philosophical positions, Anderson presents a different interpretation of God than is typically found in

African American theology. God is not a discrete entity who has a personality such that it is oriented only toward the oppressed and against
the oppressors. Such a description is far too limiting for Anderson.
Rather than construing God as a personal being, Anderson offers the
following descriptions of God:

> However, God is inferentially grasped by reflection on the world, its
> processes, patterns, and powers. God gives meaning and value to the
> whole of human experience in the world, because God transcends
> every particular experience in a unity of experience. The name *God*
> conceptually signifies the unification of every reality, where reality is
> understood as the undifferentiated totality of experience. God signi-
> fies the union of all life in its concrete actuality and ideal potentiality.
> Therefore, God designates the infinite in meaning and value. As Royce
> once proposed, God simply is the World. (Italics author's)[17]

This might appear to be a very large conception of God. However, it
is a minimalist conception of God. By characterizing God as the patterns and processes of the world that bear down upon us for either
our flourishing or our destruction, Anderson posits a "God/World"
that is not maximally powerful. That is to say, God is not an entity
who stands over and against human reality and experience, judging
and siding with humans. Anderson cites Henry Wieman's argument
that God cannot be associated with a person or personality, as personality develops within human society. Rather, God is construed as
"the creative event or creative interchange or interaction."[18]

As the creative event or interchange, God/World is expressed in
the "concrete actuality" of human experience.[19] For Anderson, the
black church functions as one of "two key creative centers of value in
African American religious experience."[20] By that, Anderson means
that the black church functions as a site of creative exchange in which
various goods are exchanged. He agrees with Peter J. Paris and C. Eric
Lincoln's assessment of the black church as a powerful social force
in African American communities. However, he is cautious about a
wholesale acceptance of their assertions about the black church, as he
thinks that a strong reading of black churches as "a surrogate world"
may lead back to the forms of ontological blackness that he finds
problematic in African American cultural and religious thought. By
juxtaposing this assessment of the black church's social standing with
the unresolved ambiguity of the black church's relationship to its gay
and lesbian members, Anderson draws attention to one of the black
church's most problematic areas.

Anderson characterizes the black church's sexual-gender politics as grotesque. In other words, the sexual-gender politics of African American churches are filled with unresolved ambiguities and contestations. The same black churches that affirm the dignity and worth of its black parishioners also has been the site of condemnation with regard to its gay and lesbian members. The same black churches that profit from the talents of its gay and lesbian members characterizes those members as a threat and enforce a silence surrounding sexual difference that, as I mentioned in the discussion of "Deadly Silence," renders black gays and lesbians virtually invisible.

As in "Deadly Silence," *Creative Exchange* does not seek to offer a biblical reinterpretation of human sexuality in relation to the black church. Anderson squarely locates an argument for black gays and lesbians within the realm of human fulfillment and flourishing. I will quote him at length:

> African American gays and lesbians are human beings with rightful claims to the fulfillment and flourishing of their bodily, mental, and spiritual integrity. This recognition is a sufficient basis for the black church to advocate for their protection from bodily harm, threat to life, gay bashing, sexual harassment, and sexual double standards, one for straight members and one for them. As human beings, possessing a natural right to associate, establish friendships, companionships, and families, I see same-sex marriage as entailed in the constellation of natural goods and desires that need no theological justification for their rightness.[21]

While Anderson states that he does not seek to present a theological justification for same-sex marriage, such a justification is present in his pragmatic theology. By construing God as World and not a being of personality, Anderson has subtly removed from black religious discourse a theistic rationale for prohibiting or denouncing same-sex sexual attraction and activity. If, as Anderson posits, God is merely the world and the potentialities contained therein; and if God/World does not have any personality (as human beings understand personality to be constructed vis-à-vis our encounters with other human beings and other processes and patterns), then the theistic claim against homosexual attraction and identity cannot hold. God/World could not be described as being "against" homosexuality nor can God/World be described as being "for" homosexuality, as such a conception does not have a personality that would necessitate taking a particular side or position with regard to human behavior, attractions, and the like.

As such, homosexuality and the attendant physical expressions are part of our taken-for-granted world and do not need to be explained away or justified. Likewise, these physical or emotive expressions of same-sex attraction need not be condemned.

For Anderson, the black church ought to be open enough to celebrate and affirm the lives and relationships of black homosexuals. The creative exchange of which Anderson speaks occurs when individuals in the black church encounter and affirm difference, including sexual difference. However, Anderson veers very closely to construing the presence of black homosexuals in black churches as heroic or salvific. I will highlight two passages that will illustrate my point:

> The presence of same-sex loving members ironically keeps the churches themselves open to the "newness" of life and the creativity it fosters and nourishes. African American same-sex loving members keep the black church itself sexually honest and opens the church to wider worlds of sexual difference because these people are also fellow believers. This is why many do not leave the churches of their youth. For the very black churches that tacitly "accept" their presence without advocating for their sexual loves and practices are also the churches that nurtured their faith...For many, the black church is not only a center of value; it is also their spiritual home.[22]

First, it is not clear what Anderson means here by the phrase "sexually honest." It is an interesting phrase, given the rituals of deception that many African American gays and lesbians engage in, particularly in relation to black churches. By "opening the church to wider worlds of sexual difference," it would follow that these black homosexuals who remain in black churches are entering into some form of discourse with their heterosexual counterparts. This discourse, which would keep the black church sexually honest, requires disclosure. As I read Anderson's argument, such sexual honesty requires black gays and lesbians to be open and honest about who they are and with whom they desire sexual congress. However, as I noted above, many black gays and lesbians do not choose to reveal to their fellow church members their sexual orientations. The pressure to conform to a heteronormative ideal exists in far too many mainstream denominational and nondenominational African American churches to make the kind of exchange that Anderson envisions a present reality.

The very grotesquery of which Anderson speaks, which allows the black church to utilize the talents of black homosexuals while keeping them virtually invisible, works against the church being "open to the

'newness' of life" allegedly fostered by the presence of black gays and
lesbians. That which Anderson speaks about is certainly grotesque.
It is full of unresolved ambiguities and contestations. However, that
does not mean that we as black queer religious scholars leave these
unresolved ambiguities and contestations as they are. In other words,
merely placing it in the realm of the grotesque does not absolve the
black church of culpability in the emotional and psychological destruction of black gays and lesbians or promoting anti-intellectualism
through unreflective appeals to Scripture and tradition.

Anderson mentions the Web site Operation Rebirth as a resource
that combats the homophobia of black churches and advocates for
black gays and lesbians by listing black congregations that affirm sexual difference. While it does indeed provide a list of black churches
that affirm sexual difference, it also has a section titled "What Is
Abuse?" which categorizes some of the forms of discrimination black
gays and lesbians have endured in churches. I will list a few of the
forms of abuse that Operation Rebirth lists:

- Do they make you fearful? (fearful of God, or fearful of their pastoral
  authority)
- Ignoring your presence (speaking against you although you're a part of
  their congregation)
- Name calling (like faggot, sissy, dike, etc.)
- Degrading you or your family
- Laughing in your face (*during their sermon*)
- Refusing to do things with you or for you (denying you a position on
  their staff, in the ministry, or employment)
- Treating you as a child (threatening to discipline or embarrass you if
  you try to leave or speak up)
- Commenting negatively about your physical appearance
- Comparing you unfavorably with other men and women ("Straight"
  Men and "Straight Women" are REAL or GODLY men and women)
- Having a double standard for you (Your pastor does EXACTLY what they
  preach against, but you're the one that's considered the abomination)
- Telling gay-hating jokes
- Withholding means to practice (participate in the church ministries)
- Forcing adherence to a belief system (if you don't believe as they do, or
  believe what they say, you're going to hell, or are threatened with being
  "kicked out" of the church) (Italics author's)[23]

Such abuse is common within black congregations that do not have
favorable attitudes toward homosexuality. As Anderson notes, such
methods of silencing and rendering invisible black gays and lesbians

"vitiate the forms of generative care and creativity" that they bring to black churches and black communities. To Anderson's credit, he does not position homophobia and HIV/AIDS as determinant of the lives of black homosexuals. However, while he acknowledges that "many" black homosexuals remain in the same black churches that vilify their sexuality, he does not address those who choose not to remain in the black church. Anderson does note that many opt to affiliate with affirming congregations such as the Unity Fellowship Church, but that acknowledgment continues to locate African American gays within black Christian traditions. Returning to Operation Rebirth, the Web site owners have a section that points black gays to Hinduism, Buddhism, and Islam.

Another problem with Anderson's argument is that he appears to assign a moralizing function to black gays. In other words, the presence of black homosexuals in black churches has a civilizing function. By the claim that black homosexuals open the church to "wider worlds of sexual difference" and "keep the black church sexually honest," Anderson positions black gays and lesbians as a moralizing force within African American churches. His desire to harmonize his pragmatic theology with the black church's theology and provide an alternative to the church's homophobic practices leads to a diluted and romantic interpretation of black queer experiences. Like Griffin, when speaking of black homosexual experiences he deploys the terms "marriage," "loves," and "same-sex loving." These terms and the manner in which they are deployed constrain black gay and lesbian sexuality within categories established and maintained by heteronormativity. That said, his earlier essay "Deadly Silence" offers a far more explicit approach to black gays themselves than *Creative Exchange* does. Taken together, his later essays and *Creative Exchange* argue for an emancipated black gay and lesbian sexuality that is rooted in the idea of the search for common goods and creative encounters in which human beings acquire a deep appreciation of difference rather than a superficial tolerance (as shown in such statements like "Love the sinner, hate the sin") of difference.

Anderson's pragmatic approach yields a different view of God than is currently offered in black liberation and womanist theology. His view of God as the World offers some intriguing possibilities for theologically exploring sexual difference in African American communities. As I have noted above, God/World does not contain either prohibition or approval of gay and lesbian relationships and sexual activity. For Anderson, the ethical test of the adequacy of either same-sex or heterosexual sexual activity is whether or not these activities contribute to or detract from human flourishing. As human beings, black gays and lesbians have (or should have) access to the same goods that contribute to human flourishing and fulfillment as other kinds of humans.[24]

This, however, leads to another question that I put to Anderson's pragmatic theology. It is not clear what this pragmatic theology means in terms of ethics, particularly for black gays and lesbians and especially for those who choose to remain in black churches that espouse antigay sentiments. There are several factors within Anderson's arguments that lead me to question the potential for ethical action within *Creative Exchange*. First, Anderson's pragmatic theology includes an ethics of openness that is oriented toward expanded conceptions of African American life and experience. Second, Anderson's assertion of the black church's primacy in African American life and his desire to participate in its "moral and social renewal" appear to trump the legitimate concerns surrounding the antigay discourses that emanate from many black churches. Third, his description of black queer experiences are seemingly limited. While he attempts to articulate a theological argument for expanded approaches to difference in African American life, I find his arguments concerning black homosexuality too closely aligned to his conception of the grotesque and too limited.

Conclusion

In returning to black gay male theologians and uncovering their approaches to sexual difference in African American life, we see that the queen indeed does speak. However, what is it that the queen has to say about her subjects? Black gay male theologians engage in a process of retrieval. By that, I mean they work to retrieve black homosexuality from limited and limiting descriptions. They point out and critique the ways in which black gays are marginalized and spoken for by black heterosexuals instead of speaking for themselves. They critique the overwhelming silences that permeate African American religious scholarship.

The work of scholars such as Griffin and Anderson is essential in that it calls African American religious and cultural critics to be mindful of the presence and contributions of black homosexuals. By taking on the task of critiquing black liberation theology and African American cultural criticism, they do point to both the best of our

intellectual traditions, but also admonish African American scholars to push beyond constraining intellectual frameworks. While they
address issues of sexual difference in African American life, they are
not wholly framed by the concerns as posited by heterosexual African
American theologians and cultural critics. They seek to present different ways of viewing God, divine activity in the world, and human
orientation to the divine.

However, the project of retrieving black homosexuality from virtual invisibility falls victim to a lack of clarity concerning just who
God is or what God might be for black homosexuals. In the case
of Farajaje-Jones and Griffin, God remains fairly nebulous and ill-
defined. God simply stands for gays and lesbians. Griffin's assertion
that a *true* liberation theology is one that accepts and celebrates the
diversity of human sexuality makes an implicit claim that the God of
black Christianity is one that liberates. However, the problem that
Griffin has is the problem that Anthony Pinn challenges black liberation theology with having. What can a true liberation theology that
speaks to the sexual diversity of African American life say about the
moments of finitude that confront African American homosexuals?
What can a true liberation theology say about the black transgender
who has been beaten up? What can such a liberation theology say
to the black man who feels he needs to remain "on the down low"
in order to retain his family, his class status, and the like? What can
a true liberation theology that speaks to black gays and lesbians say
about the God who they are supposedly oriented toward? Finally,
what can a true liberation theology say about those black gay and
lesbian, bisexual and transgendered subjects?

The next two chapters will turn to the literary productions of
black gay men. These chapters have two tasks: first, I seek to find
what black gay writers are saying about their experiences in general.
I want to find out how these writers construe black homosexuality
and the relationship between black gay men and a seemingly hostile
black community. Second, I return to these writers in order to understand how they interpret religious experiences as well as the relationship between black queers and the church. I turn to the writings of
black gay men in order to show that there has been a largely untapped
resource for black religious scholars seeking to understand or make
sense of sexual difference in African American life. By merely speaking for black homosexuals instead of paying careful and close attention to the voices of black gays, I find that black religious scholars
essentialize and distort black queer experiences.

4

The Representations of Homosexuality in Black Gay Men's Writing

Introduction

In chapters 1 and 2 I explored representative texts in black religious criticism. I addressed the question of when, where, and how black homosexuals enter into black religious criticism. I argued that black queer identity enters into black religious criticism as a "problem people." The experiences of black queer men are often described only in terms of homophobia and plague. What I find missing in black religious and cultural critics' accounts of black queer life and experience are the voices of black queer men. To be sure, theologians such as Kelly Brown Douglas, and cultural critics such as Michael Eric Dyson, and bell hooks have spoken extensively against homophobia. However, I am concerned that the limited attention to the ways in which black queer men speak of and for themselves distorts our understandings of, and limits the possibilities for, an appreciation of sexual difference in black life. As I argued in chapter 2, the concerns and interests of black queer men are syndicated into a general concern for protecting black communities from the effects of white supremacy. Continuing interest in explicating resistance to white supremacy precludes a fuller reading of the lives of black queers. Mere tolerance of sexual difference fails to present wider understandings of sexual difference in that tolerance is far less concerned with the lived experiences of black queers and more interested in presenting black heterosexuals as needing to tolerate difference as part of a larger agenda concerned with defeating white supremacy and racism. I argued that it is openness to those voices that may enlarge our understandings of sexual difference in black communities. Commitments to the interests of particular black communities might obligate black theologians and cultural critics to gloss over the particularities of black queer experiences. The repeated reference to works of dead writers may show that black theologians and cultural critics have not understood that there are other literary and cultural voices that can illuminate our understandings of sexual difference in black communities. I ended chapter 2 by presenting the possibility that black queer men can, have, and continue to speak for themselves.

This chapter turns to the voices of black queer male writers and their writings. I will look at the ways in which these writers represent sexual difference. The controlling question in this chapter is, "How do black queer writers describe and interpret black queer experience?" Do these writers subordinate sexual difference to racial difference? Further, this chapter explores the ways in which black queer writers describe black queer sexuality. While black queer male writers' representations of homosexuality give a more complete picture of homosexuality in black communities, those representations also subordinate sexual difference to racial difference. Much of the literature written by black queer men appeals to a God who is either for or against homosexual sex and identity. The discussion of black queer writers and religious experience, however, is reserved for chapter 5. Further, this chapter as well as the following chapter will thematize the literary expressions of black queer men. The writings of black queer men are arranged around themes of hunger, estrangement, anxiety, and alienation. As I read black queer literary productions, I find that while these writers critique negative assumptions of black queer identity by heterosexuals, they maintain a tenuous relationship with heterosexual black communities. These writers do not seek to reject black institutions (i.e., the black church) altogether. Rather, they hope that these institutions can enlarge their views of black identity to accommodate and appreciate black queer experience.

This chapter shifts from speaking about black gay men to speaking of black queer men. This shift occurs out of my usage of queer theory. I recognize that the terms gay and queer contain different significations. Annamarie Jargose contends that "queer describes those gestures or analytical models which dramatize incoherencies in the allegedly stable relations between chromosomal sex, gender and sexual desire."[1] The terms gay or lesbian imply fixed sexual orientations and preferences as much as they signify discrete, stable sexual identities.

Black Queer Literary Formation

This chapter and the following chapter argue that the literary expressions of black queer men signify both black queer experience as well as the encounters between black homosexuals and black heterosexuals. This signifying includes a transvaluation of black religious traditions in ways that call into question the rhetoric of tolerance as well as a claiming of voice. By a "claiming of voice," black queer writers dare to "spill the tea" about their own lives, instead of waiting for black religious and cultural critics to speak for them.

In the anthology *Black Like Us: A Century of Lesbian, Gay, and Bisexual African American Fiction*, the editors delineate three eras of black queer writing.[2] Those eras are the Harlem Renaissance (1900–1950), the Protest Era (1950–1980), and the Coming Out Era (1980–2000). The editors' rationale for demarcating black queer fiction in distinct yet interconnected eras is informative and worth quoting at length:

> The methodological approach we take in the introduction is "integrative." That is, each introduction attempts simultaneously to engage black history, women's history, and gay and lesbian history (to employ the conventional identity labels), as well as to illuminate the literary movements of each of the foregoing groups. We adopt this methodology for two principal reasons. The first is to make clear that race, gender, and sexual orientation are interconnected aspects of personhood. The second and related reason is to deliberately complicate our understanding of history, civil rights, and social and literary movements. Typically, we study black history as though it were disconnected from women's history; often we study gay and lesbian history as though it were somehow not a part of women's history; and rarely do we study black history in the context of making sense of gay and lesbian history (or vice versa). The tendency is to study literary movements in the same disaggregated way.[3]

What Carbado et al. seek to do in this collected volume is to ground black queer writing historically. That is, they want to show that black queer writing is as much a part of American history as other literary productions. Further, the editors of this anthology seek to bring black queer literature from the margins of literary discourse and "expand the literary canon of black queer writing."[4]

This chapter and chapter 5 make use of the editors' periodization of black queer writing. However, it is possible that delineating black queer writing into distinct periods might deform understandings of black queer literary production. For example, the editors designate the period from 1950 to 1980 "The Protest Era." While this era describes the period of the modern civil rights movement, it also implies that all black queer writing that appears during these years may be categorized as protest writing. When we compare writers such as Samuel Delany and Essex Hemphill, both of whom have writings that are grouped in this period, we see that their writings are radically different. Delany's science-fiction short stories and novels are general meditations on race, gender, and sexuality, while Hemphill's poetry and critical essays directly confront homophobic expressions within black nationalist thought and other areas of black life. Langston Hughes' short story "Blessed Assurance" is another example of black queer literary productions that falls outside neat temporal categories. Although Langston Hughes is most noted for his writings during the Harlem Renaissance, "Blessed Assurance" appears in the 1960s. However, the story is categorized as part of the Harlem Renaissance, which ended prior to the publication of the story. Further, Essex Hemphill's work is catalogued as part of the Protest Era, but it is evident that Hemphill wrote well past 1980 and into the early 1990s. Despite these concerns, the periodization of black queer literary production in *Black Like Us* is helpful for tracing broad movements in black queer literature and, as such, provides the general framework this book uses for thematizing black queer literary production.

This chapter and the following chapter propose that black queer writers take an approach to black queer experiences of alienation from institutions in black life as "reading." According to the documentary "Paris is Burning," *the read* is a performance that takes place within black queer communities. To *read* someone is to verbally expose that person's lies or hypocrisies. For example, Essex Hemphill describes a scene between two men on a bus in Washington, DC:

You my bitch!

No! Uh uh. *We* are bitches!

No! You listen here. *I* ain't wearing lipstick, *you* are! I ain't no bitch! I fucked *you*! You *my* bitch!

This argument continues without resolution until we arrive at 16th and U Streets. The bus is packed with passengers, and as we approach the stop, I see ten more waiting to board. Just as the first person at the stop steps aboard, a strident, hysterical voice cuts loose from the back:

"I'm a 45-year-old-Black-gay man-who *en-joys* taking dick in his rectum!" SNAP! "I'm not your bitch!" SNAP! "Your bitch is at home with your kids!" SNAP! SNAP! (emphasis author's)[5]

The last statement contains the *read*. The forty-five-year-old black gay man *reads* his companion (Hemphill calls him "Homeboy") for his use of the word "bitch," arguing that both of them are bitches but he is not Homeboy's bitch. The *read* publicly exposes and inflates a person's shortcomings or imperfections. In the case of Hemphill's story, it is Homeboy's classification of his receptive partner as a "bitch" that is *read*. As *reading* evolved from the drag balls in New York City during the 1970s and 1980s, it, like the drag subculture that spawned the practice, is now larger-than-life. As Charles Nero points out, the *read* is a practice that belongs to the rhetorical strategy of signifying.[6] A *read* is performative in the sense that it is a dramatic interpretation of the person (or, in this particular case, institution) being *read*. The reader directly "calls out" the person being read. The reading is not covert. The reader not only brings the person being read into focus but also brings the reader himself or herself into sharp focus.

As black queer writers perform a reading of black experience, they do so in order to bring black queer experience from the periphery of black experience. Black queer writing employs a hermeneutics of retrieval. This hermeneutics is in keeping with the method employed by the writers of the Harlem Renaissance as well as contemporary African American cultural critics. Through this hermeneutics of retrieval, black queer writers seek to also retrieve those voices that have been marginalized within black queer communities. They seek to rescue the voice of the black "sissy," the drag queen, the effeminate black queer. However, by retrieving these voices, black queer writers do not seek to marginalize the voices of the black "butch queen" or the black "trade." By employing this hermeneutical approach, black queer writers create literatures that, as Charles Nero states, validate the lives of black homosexuals.[7]

At the same time as black queer writers retrieve black queer experience from the periphery of black existence, these writers and their literatures also destabilize stable, steady readings of black identity. This reading of black queer literature's destabilizing function is drawn from Annamarie Jargose's deployment of the term "queer" and the development of queer theory. Jargose argues that queer theory "debunk[s] stable sexes, gender and sexualities" and that such a function "develops out of a specifically lesbian and gay reworking of the post-structuralist figuring of identity as a constellation of multiple and unstable positions."[8] I take Jargose's description of this particular claim concerning queer theory and apply it to the literary utterances by black queers and argue that black queer writers "queer" black experience. This queering of black experience means that black identity, black experience, and black culture (including black religious expression) cannot be reduced to neat, distinct, and discrete categories.

Thematizing Black Queer Literature

The Harlem Renaissance may be regarded as the first wave of black queer literature. The Harlem Renaissance gave birth to an era of black artistic production that was to dispel racist myths about black people.[9] For W.E.B. DuBois, those men and women who would produce superior cultural works were distinguished. They would help lift the black masses through their exceptional literary and artistic productions. This "talented tenth" would provide intellectual and moral leadership. Racial pride was a dominant theme during the Harlem Renaissance, and the productions of black queer artists reflected that theme. Carbado and others noted that

> The topic of sexual orientation, however, lacked a forum in early black civil rights activism...Sexual minorities had been silenced out of sham, fear of criminal retribution, and, importantly, a lack of understanding of the inherently political nature of sexual identity...As DuBois's "Talented Tenth" platform placed extreme emphasis on black respectability, the "outlaw" community of homosexuals early in the century, no matter their education or social status, were effectively sidelined.[10]

While the politics of the "New Negro" and the Harlem Renaissance did not specifically address issues of sexual orientation, many of the writings of the period did.

Langston Hughes, one of the most celebrated artists of the period, wrote a short story entitled "Blessed Assurance." In this story, Delmar (shortened to the more "effeminate"-sounding Delly) comes under the homophobic scrutiny of his father John. From the first paragraph, Hughes establishes the "otherness" of being black and gay in American society as well as in the black church. Delly's suspected homosexuality leads to John's "distrust of God."[11]

Hughes' story does not originate from Delmar's point of view. Rather, the story is told from John's perspective. Delmar does not speak for himself. He is presented as a quiet, "sweet boy" who does not get into any trouble and sings in his church's junior choir. As a singer, Delmar is described as having a "sweet high tenor with overtones of Sam Cooke."[12]

Although the story is not told from Delmar's viewpoint, Hughes does indicate that Delmar and Dr. Manley Jaxon, the Minister of Music at Tried Stone Baptist Church, are involved in some form of romantic relationship. Early in the story, the reader finds out that Delmar has gone to New York with the Junior Choir and that "the Minister of Music had taken Delly on a trip to the Village."[13] Hughes appears to leave the reasons for this side trip to the Village up to the reader. However, the interpretation of a romantic affiliation between Jaxon and Delmar is strengthened when the reader sees that Jaxon has written "an original anthem, words and score his own, based on the story of Ruth."[14] The work is dedicated to Delmar. Hughes notes that it would appear, based on the composition, that Ruth's part would be sung by a woman.[15] However, it is Delmar who sings Ruth's part. When Delmar begins singing, Jaxon, playing at the organ, falls off his stool in a "dead faint:"

> The "Papa, what's happening?" of [John's] daughter in the pew beside him made hot saliva rise in his throat—for what suddenly had happened was that as the organ wept and Delmar's voice soared above the choir with all the sweetness of Sam Cooke's tessitura, backwards off the organ stool in a dead faint fell Dr. Manley Jaxon. Not only did Dr. Jaxon fall from the stool, but he rolled limply down the steps from the organ loft like a bag of meal and tumbled prone onto the rostrum, robes and all.[16]

His fall from the stool is dramatic, illustrating the erotic power that Delmar's singing commands. The erotic power of Delmar's voice is confirmed by his sister Arletta, who notes that his voice often makes the girls in the choir and in the church so overcome, they eventually start screaming.[17] Jaxon's dramatic response to Delmar's singing confirms the eroticism between them.

Hughes' story presents black queer men who exist within the black church. Their existence is not an open existence, that is, neither Delmar nor Jaxon appear to have spoken of their sexual orientation to anyone else. Indeed, it appears as if Delmar is not even aware of his transgressions. For his father, Delmar has violated nearly every tenet of black masculinity. Delmar never played sports; he did not even like football, the game his father played in high school.[18] However, Delmar appears comfortable with his sexuality, whatever it might be. Not only has Delmar refused to go to a historically black college, he has decided to study at the Sorbonne, in Paris. Hughes offers the counterpoint that John had gone to Morgan State University, in Baltimore.

John notes that Morgan was a fine institution, but Hughes leaves the reader to question such an assessment with a parenthetical caveat, "in his mind." Delmar's decision to study in Paris is presented as a rejection of his father, and, by extension, a rejection of his blackness.[19]

Despite his dismay at Delmar's decision, John decides to allow Delmar to go to the Sorbonne:

> Normally John would have wanted his boy to go there, yet the day after the Spring Concert he asked Delmar, Son, do you still want to study in France? If you do, maybe—er—I guess I could next fall— Sorbonne. Say, how much is a ticket to Paris?
>
> In October it would be John's turn to host his fraternity brothers at his house. Maybe by then Delmar would—is the Sorbonne like Morgan? Does it have dormitories, a campus? In Paris he had heard they didn't care about such things. Care about such what things didn't care about what? At least no color lines.[20]

John's sudden change in attitude concerning Delmar's desire to go to the Sorbonne occurs following the Spring Concert where Dr. Jaxon faints at the sound of Delmar's voice. At first, Delmar's decision to go to the Sorbonne represents a betrayal of the race, but after the Spring Concert, John appears to no longer be able to tolerate Delmar's transgressive presence. The Spring Concert put on by the Tried Stone church contained an original song—based on the story of Ruth in the Old Testament—written by Dr. Jaxon. The transgressiveness of this song is found not in the song itself, but for whom it was written. Jaxon dedicates the work to Delmar, and assigns the solo lead to Delmar. The solo itself is based upon Ruth's desire to remain with Naomi when she decides to migrate to Moab. The song contains lines derived directly from the first chapter of the book of Ruth:

> Entreat me not to leave thee,
> Neither to go far from thee.
> Whither thou goeth, I will go.
> Always will I be near thee...[21]

The tribute, or gift, that Dr. Jaxon makes of the anthem is presented in the story as a declaration of love. Hughes, through Delmar and Dr. Jaxon, subverts the presumptive heterosexuality of the black church. Further, Jaxon uses the Bible in the form of the story of Ruth to affirm the relationship he has with Delmar.

Hughes presents Delmar as a person who is not bound by rigid definitions. Instead, it is the heterosexual John who is imprisoned by rigid categories of race and masculinity. His adherence to an inflexible code of racial and gendered identity prevents him from fully understanding his son. Further, it is that same inflexibility that leads to his ultimate breakdown. Ironically, it is the church that sets the scene for a transcendent moment between Delmar and Dr. Jaxon. It is the church that also sets the scene for John's apparent breakdown.

John's breakdown and his anxiety about his son's sexuality signify something about John rather than Delmar. Delmar is oblivious to the erotic power he possesses, but his father is acutely aware of the power of sexuality. Perhaps John is not as heterosexual as he would like to appear. John has spent his life attempting to be the acceptable black man by joining the church, by participating in a black fraternity, and by marrying and having children. When Hughes describes Delmar as "a brilliant queer," perhaps the person who is queer is not Delmar, but John. This text is a moment in which he who is queer unknowingly queers the non-queer. John is estranged. He desires to be part of an acceptable black middle class, but his wayward wife (who leaves him for another man) and his sexually ambiguous son threaten to shut him out from among the class of acceptable black persons. Being cast out from among acceptable black society would automatically render John a queer person. As such, John desires to be non-queer. However, his reaction to his son's singing queers him. As his son's singing continues, John becomes visibly upset. Delly's singing and John's reaction to it destabilizes John's neat concepts of acceptable black identity and throws him into confusion about the limits of acceptable black masculine performance.

The figures of Delmar and Dr. Jaxon say less about themselves and far more about black heterosexual men who aspire to be part of the elite. Delmar and Dr. Jaxon unknowingly signify John's anxieties about masculine sexuality. Instead of Delmar and Dr. Jaxon "coming out" and affirming their sexual orientation, it is John who protests what he considers to be a deviant identity. Through his anxiety concerning his son's sexuality, John betrays to the reader an acute unease with difference. During the solo that serves as the climax of the story, the presence of Delly's queerness overwhelms John's taken-for-granted world.

"Blessed Assurance" is an atypical example of writings of the Harlem Renaissance, as it is one of the few literary productions that is explicit about sexual orientation. Much of the literature from the period that is purported to deal with sexual orientation does so through inference. For example, Richard Bruce Nugent's controversial "Smoke, Lillies, and Jade," published in 1925, is a "dreamy, heavily elliptical plot" that revolves around an apparently bisexual artist who is musing about a sexual encounter with a person named Beauty.[22] "Smoke" predates "Blessed Assurance" by over thirty years, and is considered to be the first "explicitly gay story published by an African American writer."[23] Its publication in the short-lived periodical *Fire!!* signaled an end to the racial heroism of the Harlem Renaissance. "Blessed Assurance" may be read as a more explicit dismantling of the racialized assumptions of the Harlem Renaissance by using black masculine anxiety as a means to highlight black heterosexuals' hyper-awareness and intolerance of sexual difference.

The years following the Second World War saw the birth of the modern civil rights movement. The *Brown. v. Board of Education* Supreme Court decision that desegregated public schools marked the beginnings of what Carbado et al. call the Protest Era. During the years from 1950 to 1980, African American people actively worked to dismantle legal systems of segregation and de facto systems of employment and housing discrimination. As the movement grew, questions of leadership and representation surfaced. Younger black people questioned the parochial nature of the Southern leaders of the movement, while black women charged black men with blatant sexism.

Although the literature produced in this period was more diverse than that of the Harlem Renaissance, poetry, short stories, and critical essays formed the dominant literary forms of the period. This period saw greater diversity in the type of literature produced by black queer men. The writing of this period is bolder than much of what preceded it. Many of the pieces I will look at are explicit in their descriptions of gay experience, both sexual and nonsexual. During this period, writers such as Essex Hemphill, Joseph Beam, and Samuel R. Delany emerged. These writers and others were more able to explore the boundaries of race, sexual orientation, and gender than their prede-cessors during the Harlem Renaissance. While not wholly abandoning the racial heroism present in much of the writings of the Renaissance, people such as Hemphill, Beam, and Delany were able to use different genres to tease the limits of sexuality. For example, Delany used the genre of science fiction to write stories and novels that repositioned categories of race, gender, and sexual orientation.

In an essay titled "The Possibility of Possibilities," Samuel Delany and Joseph Beam discuss the contours and possibilities of black queer literature. Both Beam and Delany understand science fiction as a genre in which future visions signify present conditions. When Beam asks about the role of personal vision in the creation of "futuristic cultures and worlds" and the role of queers as society's visionaries and seers, Delany notes that "it's a societal flaw when social forces nudge gay people toward a single (or limited group of) social function(s)...if the choices for gay people is conceived of as singularly limited by the general populace, then none of the three societies provide real freedom."[24]

For Delany, gays should have the same "possibility of possibilities" that are open to heterosexuals. As a literary genre, science fiction proves "mental practice in dealing with a whole *range* of different situations" (emphasis author's).[25] *Tales of Nevèrÿon* is a compilation of short stories located in the ancient (and perhaps mythical) land Nevèrÿon. In the world of Nevèrÿon, race, gender, and sexual orientation are fluid constructs. Gorgik, a former slave-turned-liberator, is a central figure in this world. Through Gorgik, Delany calls notions of a "correct" sexual orientation into question. Gorgik's rise from slavery to become a member of the Child Empress' High Court and then a military captain can be read as a signification on W.E.B. DuBois' notion of the Talented Tenth. Delany describes Gorgik as

> ...a man who was—in his way and for his epoch—the optimum product of his civilization...for the civilization in which he lived, this dark giant, soldier, and adventurer, with desires we've not yet named and dreams we've hardly mentioned, who could speak equally of and to barbarian tavern maids and High Court ladies, flogged slaves lost in the cities and provincial nobles at ease on their country estates, he was a civilized man.[26]

Although Gorgik may be read as a signification on the Talented Tenth, Delany presents Gorgik in other tales in such a way as to simultaneously subvert the racial heroism of the Talented Tenth. Gorgik's relationship with a purchased slave is of special interest here.

His relationship with Small Sarg subverts conventional "sidekick" relationships in fantasy stories. Gorgik and Small Sarg have a sexual relationship. Their sexual relationship is one that challenges contemporary assumptions regarding sexual practices in society. In "The Tale of Dragons and Dreamers," Gorgik and Small Sarg have a revealing conversation with two women. I will quote this conversation at length:

> "I see a bruised and tired slave of middle age," said the woman who wore a mask and who had given her name as Raven... "From that, one assumes that the youngster (Small Sarg) is the owner."
>
> "But the Boy," added the redhead kneeling beside her, who had given her name as Normea, "is a barbarian, and in this time and place it is the southern barbarians who, when they come this far north, usually end up slaves. The older for all his bruises, has the bearing of a Kolhari man, whom you'd expect to be the owner."
>
> Gorgik, sitting with one arm over one knee, said: "We are both free men. For the boy the collar is symbolic—of our mutual affection, our mutual protection. For myself, it is sexual—a necessary part in the pattern that allows both action and orgasm to manifest themselves within the single circle of desire. *For neither of us is its meaning social, save that it shocks, offends, or deceives.*" (emphasis added)[27]

In this passage, Delany deflects our modernist ways of apprehending sexual difference. The collar, a symbol of slavery and oppression in the context of American history, is given new meaning here. Gorgik is aware of the multiple layers of meaning that the collar presents. Delany uses the linguistic conventions in science fiction and fantasy to present possibilities for sexual expression not present in conventional society. In science fiction, or, sci-fi, futuristic and fantastic settings provide a backdrop whereby the writer may make commentary regarding contemporary issues.

As a figure in science fiction who signifies upon the pulp, overtly heterosexual (yet homoerotic) and white figures of Tarzan and Conan the Barbarian, Gorgik has the luxury of criticizing contemporary mores toward sexuality. Gorgik's awareness of the multiple layers of meaning in both the collar and in the sexual activity with Small Sarg signifies on our protestations of having a "contemporary" or "advanced" view of sexual relationships. It is because this story takes place in a time that would, by the standards of modernity, be considered "barbaric" and "uncivilized" that Gorgik's statements concerning sexuality are both powerful and confrontational. Interestingly, Gorgik signifies on other gay literary figures in that neither Gorgik nor Small Sarg express a sense of alienation from their respective cultures. Their status as barbarians and sexual dissidents perplexes those who encounter them, much in the same ways that black homosexuals perplex heterosexuals, both black and white. Further, their status as fantasy heroes perplexes and frustrates the traditional presentation of the pulp, science fiction, or fantasy hero. As I mentioned Tarzan and Conan the Barbarian earlier, these heroes are defined primarily by their whiteness and their heteronormative masculinity. Tarzan's heroic whiteness is displayed in and through his ability to rise above the other "savage" elements of deepest, darkest Africa. He is the noble savage who, though deprived of the accoutrements of "civilized" society, is, through his innate superiority as a white male, able to become "lord of the jungle." Conan the Barbarian as a more accessible pulp figure appeals to the heteronormative sexual fantasy of the muscle-bound warrior who always gets the girl(s) and displays not only his sexual prowess, but also his superior fighting skills. He is a character who is never conquered, and certainly would never submit himself to any form of bondage—not even for sexual pleasure. As disruptive characters, Gorgik and Small Sarg "queer" and "race" those constructions by presenting not only the racially atypical hero-sidekick combinations, but also presenting them as far more sexually fluid than either Tarzan or Conan.

Black queer writers used poetry, short stories, and critical essays to reflect on black queer experience and critique black culture. Writers such as Marlon Riggs and Essex Hemphill did not write in the shaded tones that characterized Delany's sci-fi/fantasy stories. Nor did they write using the type of metaphorical language that is in Hughes' "Blessed Assurance." Rather, they wrote in the clear and powerful protest language that was characteristic of the black power and black arts movements of the 1960s and 1970s. As the literature and other expressive elements of the black arts movement sought to refute white supremacist claims of black inferiority, the literary expressions of Riggs and Hemphill and Beam sought to refute black nationalist claims of black homosexual deviance. Hemphill's essay, "If Freud Had Been a Neurotic Colored Woman: Reading Dr. Frances Cress Welsing," is a refutation of Frances Cress Welsing's claims that homosexuality among black queer men is an effect of white supremacy. In *The Isis Papers*, Cress Welsing contends that white supremacy (the oppression of peoples of color throughout the world) forces homosexuality upon black men. In her view, homosexuality is a sexual identity that is a choice. She alleges "white male and female homosexuality can be viewed as the final expression of their dislike of their genetic albinism in a world numerically dominated by colored people."[28] Welsing argues that homosexuality among black men is a "result of the imposed power and cruelty of the white male and the totality of the white supremacy social and political apparatus that has forced 20 generations of Black males into submission."[29]

Hemphill's essay charges that Welsing's comments regarding the nature of black homosexuality are dangerous. He places Welsing's homophobia in "collusion" with the very same white supremacist forces she claims to agitate against.[30] This essay serves to place black queer men as an integral part of the black liberation struggle. Rather than place, describe, or explain away black queer existence as an aberration that can be eradicated, Hemphill argues that black people cannot achieve liberation without the "unqualified support and participation of Black queers and lesbians."[31]

In addition to combating black nationalist claims against homosexuality, these writers also wanted to draw attention to the AIDS crisis that was devastating black queer men across America. Keith Boykin highlights the impact of the AIDS crisis on black queer literary production when he argues that "the AIDS outbreak had...mobilized a cadre of trailblazing black queer poets, writers, artists, and film makers in the 1980s. Many of these men had already told us about a culture that predated the down low."

For Hemphill, the AIDS crisis forced black heterosexuals to deal with the reality of black queer existence. AIDS highlighted the ways in which black queer men are alienated from both black and gay communities on the basis of sexuality and race, respectively. In short, Hemphill presents a fragile minority-within-a-minority that is in crisis. While Delany's writing plays with the boundaries of sexuality, race, and class, Hemphill's writing is much more serious and much more urgent.

Hemphill's poetry, short stories, and critical essays tend to be thematized around visibility and loss. Consider this excerpt from his poem "Commitments:"

> I will always be there.
> When the silence is exhumed.
> When the photographs are examined
> I will be pictured smiling
> among the siblings, parents,
> nieces and nephews.[32]

This piece is a signification on black peoples' assumptions regarding the presence and visibility of black queer men in families. It is a lamentation, a dirge. The words "exhumed" and "examined" denote a death. In this poem, the existence of the black queer man's sexual identity will be uncovered at a future time.

The remainder of the poem lays out the traditional events that constitute black family life in America. However, in all of these events, the black queer man must keep his identity secret. The phrase "my arms are empty" signifies the loneliness he feels he must endure for the sake of his family. His arms are "so empty, they would break around a lover." In other words, not only are his arms empty, not only has he not been emotionally fulfilled, he has been emotionally starved by his family. His sexual identity dies so that the black family may continue to have gatherings and events undisturbed. Hemphill presents a sexuality that is in need of nourishment, not a depraved sexuality only in search of carnal pleasures. This figure has sacrificed his own happiness and his desire to have a lover for the good of the black family in order to be present for other family members, as he himself recedes into the background and is rendered mute.

For Hemphill, Riggs, Beam, and others, writing black queer literature is to write black queer existence into black history. The process of collecting poetry, short stories, and critical essays and assembling anthologies is intentional. The development of black queer anthologies signifies a collective action. Anthologies suggest a collaborative effort and a community that supports that collaboration. Anthologies of black queer literature suggest an enterprise that represents not only the existence (and, hence, visibility) of black queer men, but also the diversity found among them. Anthologies serve as a signification on the politics of racial identity. They directly challenge the notion of "the black man" as a singular, monolithic concept. The anthologies, the poetry, short stories, and the like exist to name "that inexpressible existence," and give voice to black queer men.[33] Further, the anthologies of poetry and short stories serve as an archival record of the existence and the experiences of black queer men. When Sylvester and Hemphill write that they wish they could have found works about and by black queer men when they were younger or that they were able to find themselves in the pages of the anthologies they had begun to produce, they echo Joseph Beam's statement that "visibility is survival." The AIDS crisis produced an acute crisis of visibility among black queer writers. As they collected anthologies like *In The Life*, they argued that these collections would provide a record of black queer existence that would endure beyond the AIDS crisis.

By bringing visibility to black queer existence, Hemphill, Riggs, Beam, and other black queer writers sought to redefine what it means to be black and gay. Their writings are hermeneutical, existential meditations on black queer experience. The foreword to *In The Life: A Black Gay Anthology* is illustrative:

> Being first black and then gay, these words express things that I have experienced, things found in the black queer culture that are unknown to many. It makes me proud that these writers and artists have found a place to express our feelings and experiences. Many passages were so real to me and will be real to you as well. At times I cried just remembering how it is to be both black and gay during these truly difficult times. But here we are, still proud and living, with a culture all our own.[34]

According to the late disco singer Sylvester, who penned the above foreword, black queer experience is real and in need of serious attention. The desire for attention echoes a desire for belonging. This desire for belonging may be read as desire for reconciliation with the larger black community. However, this reconciliation cannot happen if black queer experience is merely tolerated and addressed only in the service of fighting white supremacy, for black queer life is far more than an endless, heroic struggle against the forces of white racism. Rather, the writers of the 1970s and 1980s, many of whom began facing the HIV/AIDS crisis, saw the tendency in black religious and cultural life to either dismiss black queer experience as antithetical to heroic blackness or marginalize black queer experience as deviant and deserving of divine punishment in the form of plague. They responded by arguing that black queer identity was not a problem that needed to be fixed. I also find this passage in an essay by Daniel Garrett to be provocative:

> It will be important for us to begin to recover black queer history, and not simply the history of the famous or "talented" gays and bisexuals such as Langston Hughes and Bessie Smith, but the black queer postman or teacher or nurse or milkman or parent. It is important to discuss with black queers over 50 the changes they've seen over the years.[35]

What Garrett is proposing is far different from what we see in bell hooks' description of Mr. Richard. As I noted in the chapter 2, if Mr. Richard was indeed gay, he never spoke for himself. He never spoke to his own existence and experience. Garrett suggests that writers pay close attention to the voices of black queer men.

These anthologies of black queer writing in the 1970s and 1980s directly challenge black nationalist assumptions about black masculinity and homosexuality.[36] Not only were black queer writers in the 1970s and 1980s attempting to write themselves into the black literary canon, they were rebelling against nationalist rhetoric that marginalized black queer existence as a by-product of white supremacy. Additionally, these writers, influenced by the radicalism and the confrontational approaches of the black power movement and the sexual revolution, dared to speak the unspeakable by discussing what was at the core of black queer experience. They spoke about black queer sexuality and sexual experience.

The longing that these writers spoke of, this desire for home, also finds expression in a desire for love. These writers are open about a desire for sex, for companionship, for love. In "Isn't It Funny," Hemphill reflects on the irony of a lover's inability to see him as a man. He demands that the lover look at him. Both of them are men, signified by Hemphill's line "with my dick as straight as yours."[37] This passage is a demand. The man voicing this demand commands visibility. He does not desire to have his sexual identity and sexual experience feminized in order to facilitate sexual relations with another man. However, he does acquiesce to his lover's desire to obscure what is real with what is ideal. The lover obscures his sexual activity with another man through the consumption of alcohol and through furtively sneaking "all over town like two damn thieves."[38] Hemphill's protagonist is not in love with his sexual partner. He recognizes that his lover serves the purpose of fulfilling his sexual needs. Despite that, the protagonist desires to be seen. He understands that the lover might assure himself that he is not "gay" if he can be with a man who looks like his current girlfriend.

By invoking the lover's girlfriend, Hemphill acknowledges the queerness of black queer experience. The pervasive repression of black queer sexualities leads black queer men to furtively sneak around, hiding their sexual desires from others, lest they be judged by black nationalists and black preachers as defective and detrimental to "the race." Hemphill calls into question a politics of respectability within black life by explicitly showing the effects of such a politics. This politics forces black queers to hide their erotic relationships and estranges them from a putative "normal" black culture. In this poem, what black queers long for is not tolerance by a paternalistic black heterosexual community. Instead, what they seek is a society that appreciates sexual difference.

In the 1990s, anthologies of black queer writing gave way to novels featuring a single linear narrative. These narratives centered on fictional characters. Writers such as James Earl Hardy and E. Lynn Harris gained wider audiences with their representative novels *B-Boy Blues* and *Invisible Life*. Of the two writers, Harris appears to have acquired greater fame. He has written six novels since *Invisible Life*. His writing has captured the attention of a black mainstream, as he has been featured or profiled in *Ebony* and *Essence* magazines as well as *Black Issues Book Review*. He has been hailed as having brought homosexuality in black communities out of the closet.

I will focus on Harris' first two novels, *Invisible Life* and *Just As I Am*, and highlight his portrayal of black queer life and experience through his protagonists and antagonists. *Invisible Life* introduces the main protagonist, Raymond Tyler, Jr. At the beginning of the novel, Raymond is a college senior at the University of Alabama. He comes from a black middle-class family—his father is a politician and his mother a schoolteacher. Ray aspires to a career in politics or law, and is a highly popular member of a fictional black fraternity, Kappa Alpha Omega. He is also in a steady relationship with Sela, a cheerleader (and, thus, also highly visible) and a member of the nonfictional Delta Sigma Theta sorority. These facets of Ray's life present him as a "normal," desirable black man.

It is Ray's first sexual experience with a man that destroys his "normal" world and introduces him to the apparently abnormal world of homosexuality. Ray's first encounter with gay sex comes in the form of a college football player named Kelvin. Ray first notices Kelvin at a fraternity party. Harris presents Kelvin in a way that signifies him as an ideal masculine type:

> I noticed a tall, muscular guy who seemed to be attracting a lot of attention from all the females. He stood against one of the banisters looking unapproachable, not saying a word. He was dressed in white linen and looked too mature to be a freshman. From his muscular body I could tell he was a jock, but he wasn't with the athletes at the party. Sela and her sorority sisters gathered in a clique, laughing and flirting with the stranger.[39]

Kelvin is presented in such a manner as to ensure that the reader will perceive him as an ideal masculine type. Kelvin's physique, dress, and "unapproachable" pose suggest heterosexuality.

Ray runs into Kelvin a few days later, setting into motion a chain of events that lead to Ray's first sexual encounter with a man. After an excursion to a neighboring town to buy beer, Ray invites Kelvin up to his apartment to drink some of the beers. During their conversation, Kelvin reveals that he is bisexual and inquires about Ray's sex life. In essence, Kelvin, the worldly bisexual (who is also from the more culturally sophisticated North), seduces the innocent Ray:

> I didn't respond, silenced by his stare. His eyes were deep-set and defiant. Then he touched my nose and moved his fingers down to my lips. I don't know why, but I didn't stop him as he cupped my face and suddenly kissed my lips. I couldn't believe it, but it felt so natural. It was the first time I had ever kissed a man. Honest to God. But his kiss. I had never kissed anyone like this, not even Sela. Before I was conscious of it, I was kissing Kelvin back and putting my arms around waist.... What was happening? This sinful, sexual longing. This was wrong. Everything in my head screamed *no*! Yet my body was saying *yes*... (emphasis author's)[40]

Ray's first same-sex experience constitutes a massive disruption in the continuity of his social world. However, the reader is denied information regarding the nature of that experience. From the above passage, and from the passage as it is presented in the book, it may be assumed that Ray and Kelvin only kissed and performed frottage. If these are the only actions that occurred, does this encounter actually constitute sex? The ambiguity of the sexual relationships between Ray and other men persists throughout not only *Invisible Life* but also *Just As I Am*.

The virtual silence surrounding the sexual exploits of Harris' gay characters is not a matter of merely prurient concern. This silence, particularly when juxtaposed with Harris' florid detailing of heterosexual sex, is disturbing. Later in *Invisible Life*, Ray goes home to Alabama for a Christmas visit. During this visit, he has a meeting with Sela, who, at this point, is engaged to a dentist. Not only do they meet, they have sex. Harris details Ray and Sela's sexual encounter in a way that he never does when Ray has sex with another man. The silence regarding homosexual sex continues in *Just As I Am*. In this continuation of *Invisible Life*, the story shifts away from a singular focus on Ray. *Just As I Am* follows both Ray and his ex-girlfriend Nicole Springer, a Broadway singer. Ray becomes involved with Basil Henderson, a closeted, presumably bisexual pro-football player, while Nicole becomes involved with Pierce Gessler, a wealthy Jewish obstetrician. Once again, the erotic encounters between Ray and Basil are only alluded to, while Nicole's sexual activities with men are given far more detail.

Given Harris' description of how he broke onto the writing scene, the marginalization of black queer men's sexuality in *Invisible Life* and *Just As I Am* may be read as intentional. When Harris wrote *Invisible Life*, he failed to interest publishers. He then self-published the book and sold it to beauty salons and book groups in Atlanta's black communities. Word spread among women, who were shocked and compelled by the story line. They bought copies and told friends to do the same, sparking first-time conversations about the possibility that the men in their lives might be bisexual.[41]

It is interesting that the target audience for Harris' writing was not black gay men. Harris' initial audience was black heterosexual women. Indeed, I first encountered Harris's writing when *Essence* magazine published an excerpt of *Just As I Am* in a 1994 issue. Harris presents a sanitized portrayal of the sexual behaviors of his gay/bisexual characters. This sanitized presentation of black gay and bisexual characters is easily packaged and marketable. With the notable exception of Ray's best friend Kyle, all the black queer men in Harris' novels are "unclockable," that is, they present an image of heterosexuality. They are masculine, handsome, dress conservatively, and have prestigious, high-paying jobs. These men lead glamorous lives. Raymond, as the main protagonist in *Invisible Life* and *Just As I Am*, conforms to this masculine ideal. He is a conformist in the sense that he adopts an upper-middle-class status and profession as a lawyer in order to refute white supremacist stereotypes of black men. His character is successful, intelligent, articulate, and deeply concerned with the ways in which his sexual orientation might be perceived by both black and white people.

In Harris' work, those black queer men who do not conform to the idea of a black masculine hero draw either rebuke from Ray or Basil or pay a stiffer penalty for their transgressions. Ray's best friend Kyle is an example of the marginalization of less desirable representations of black homosexuality. Kyle is portrayed as a flamboyant "queen." His language and mannerisms portray him in stark contrast to the more conservative Ray. Kyle's world is filled with men, sex, alcohol, and drama. Kyle's first appearance is, in and of itself, a dramatic entré into the narrative. When Raymond enters into the bar, he sees Kyle sitting "on his regular stool." He has a cigarrette and a drink in his hands and is surrounded by people. According to Raymond, these people are paying close attention to what Kyle is saying.[42]

Kyle's positioning and demeanor are intended to represent sophistication, popularity, and style. His holding "a drink in one hand and a cigarette in the other" is evocative of the ways in which Hollywood actresses like Bette Davis and Joan Crawford presented their characters in movies. This performative gesture signifies a diva-like attitude, in which the person projects an air of urban sophistication. Harris' use of the phrase to describe and define Kyle is no accident. Kyle is presented as "a master at all the wiles and ways of the black queer community."[43] It is Kyle who teaches Ray the linguistic and expressive codes of the black queer community in New York City.[44] Kyle is glamorous but appears to exist in Ray's (and, later, Nicole's) shadow. His honesty about his sexual orientation is nullified by his excessiveness. Indeed, his honesty is portrayed as excessive and undesirable. Where Raymond appears to be extremely selective about his sexual partners, Kyle is portrayed as being quite indiscriminate about his sexual conquests.

Kyle's queerness remains marginal in that Raymond comments negatively on it. Although Ray initially describes Kyle's flamboyance and openness about his sexuality as refreshing, Ray also describes it as trying. However, as I read Kyle's queerness, I find it odd that his queerness leads him repeatedly to unfulfilling relationships, sexual encounters, and, finally, a tragic death from AIDS.

The black queer men presented in Harris' novels are quite different than those in the writings of Hemphill, Riggs, and Beam. Whereas black queer men in their writings protest the silencing of homosexuality in black heterosexual communities by signifying on the hypocrisy of the said communities, the black queer men in Harris' writings have their sexualities bracketed by issues of race and class. The crisis of sexuality, so blatant and urgent in Hemphill's work, appears as a deeply personal and individualistic moment for Harris' protagonists and antagonists.

As an example of the black queer literature that emerged in the 1990s, Harris' novels present a packaged and sanitized portrayal of black queer experience. Using the conventions of soap operas and traditional romance novels, Harris packages his protagonists and antagonists in appealing and desirable forms. While the characters in Harris' novels acknowledge to some extent the alienation of sexual difference in institutions of black life, those forms of alienation recede into the background in favor of presenting more the entertaining drama of boardroom and bedroom machinations.

In the early years of the twenty-first century, black queer literature continues to follow the dramatic, soap-operatic conventions of the 1990s. For example, J.L. King's *On The Down Low: A Journey Into*

The Lives of 'Straight' Black Men Who Sleep With Men is a book that purports to be a factual account of black men who consider themselves heterosexual but have sex with other black men. King claims to illuminate a shadowy area of black life in America by presenting "the down low" as a valid yet predatory sexuality. According to King, the rising number of HIV-positive black women is attributable to black men who conceal from their wives and girlfriends their sexual relationships with other men. These men do not consider themselves to be gay, for, as King argues,

> Gays march in parades, hang out at gay clubs, go to gay beaches. Gay people may even attend gay churches. They may have the gay flag on their homes and cars...Open and out gay men are not confused about their sexuality...These brothers accept their gayness...But they don't enjoy sex with women, because they are *gay*. (emphasis author's)[45]

For King, gay, heterosexual, and bisexual are stable, fixed sexual identities. Bisexual men "want it all" and are honest with their male and female sexual partners. However, men on the down low, or, the DL, are "so undercover, so in denial...that they are *behind* the closet" (emphasis author's).[46] These men are so alienated from acknowledging their own sexual desires that they will not classify sexual activity with other men as being "remotely homosexual."[47]

King presents the DL as a coping mechanism for black men to be able to deal with the fact that they have sex with other men. He describes sexual relations between men as purely predatory and devoid of any emotional attachment. By deifying black women, whom he describes as being the innocent victims of predatory black men, and by vilifying black queers (in which group I include those "on the DL"), King presents black queer sexuality as an internal threat to the life of black communities. In King's estimation, there is no institution in black life that black men who are on the DL do not utilize in order to find other DL black men.

King claims to have written *On the Down Low* in order to save black women from unwittingly being infected with HIV from black men on the down low. In the introduction to the book, King makes it clear that his allegiances are primarily to God, black women, and, by extension, the black community:

> I do this work because I still love my ex-wife, the mother of my children. In high school, she was more than just my girlfriend. After we

married, she was more than a wife. She was my best friend, confidante, and running partner. It's difficult for me to fathom how I lied to her, but I did...I do this work for all of the women who have loved me and who deserve the truth from me during a time that I was unable to give it.[48]

The themes of alienation that Hemphill, Riggs, and other black queer writers evoked in earlier periods appear in King's work. However, King takes the forms of alienation that, in Hemphill's poetic utterances, force black men to conceal their sexual orientation and remain estranged from their families, churches, and friends and positions them as entrances into salacious descriptions of black "Others." Further, he seems to confirm the "love the sinner, hate the sin" position held by Protestant black churches when he argues that the black church should "provide support systems for men who want and need help dealing with homosexual desires."[49] He claims to promote "education, compassion, and understanding," but that compassion seems to be in the service of protecting black heterosexual relationships, not affirming black queer sexuality.

Keith Boykin counters King's assertions about the DL in *Beyond the Down Low: Sex, Lies and Denial in Black America*. Boykin argues that the DL is not a separate sexual orientation, but a slang term that signifies an illicit sexual relationship. He presents a brief history of the down low within black popular culture, arguing that black people, heterosexual and homosexual, have kept sexual secrets. Initially known as "creepin'," the DL simply was when a person kept unfaithful behavior a secret from their boyfriend or girlfriend.[50] Further, Boykin seeks to divest the DL of its primarily racial connotations by invoking the 2004 scandal involving former New Jersey governor Jim McGreevey. He argues that McGreevey's duplicitous behavior and its subsequent national exposure should expose the presentation of the DL as a primarily African American "phenomenon" as a meaningless lie concocted to cast black gay men as a scapegoat for the HIV crisis in black American life. He argues

When black men become involved in fake relationships, we process the issue by ascribing negative characteristics to an entire group of people, and we tend to think in global terms concerning the breakdown of the black family and other such nonsense. When white men become involved in fake relationships, we simply call it what it is and move on. We don't make sweeping generalizations about all white men, and don't try to study the pathology of their behavior.[51]

What Boykin intends in *Beyond the Down Low* is a different presentation and interpretation of black queer existence and experience. He argues that the major institutions in black America must do more than offer empty platitudes in the fight against HIV/AIDS. Boykin offers an eight-page long treatise on practical steps black people can take to prevent HIV infection as well as educate others about the disease. However, his final chapter, entitled "Love and Fear," is a vague, three-page conclusion to the text. It appears to be a critique of what Boykin considers to be a "politics of fear." He argues that "fear paralyzes our productivity by turning our constructive energy into panic and defensiveness."[52] Further, he implies that those who live on the DL and those who are afraid of men on the DL are paralyzed by that fear.[53]

As I read both King and Boykin, their writings are framed by the existential crisis of prejudicial attitudes of heterosexuals and the ongoing HIV/AIDS crisis. King's *On the Down Low* presents black men as sexually confused predators who, due to the prejudicial attitudes of heterosexuals, threaten the integrity of the black community. *On the Down Low* is less an argument for increased understanding of the complexities of black queer life and more an apologetic treatise that seeks to reconcile these defective men on the DL with the more acceptable black heterosexual community. While Boykin's *Beyond the Down Low* seeks to counter the negative assertions about black queer men in King's work, his descriptions of black queer life are often framed between prejudice and plague.

Conclusion

The representations of sexual difference by black queer writers are diverse. Black queer writers have used and continue to use multiple genres and forms to re-present and package experiences of sexual difference. The different moments in black queer writing address the intersections of sexual difference, race, class, religion, and gender.

The black queer literature that emerged prior to and during the civil rights movement saw writers such as Langston Hughes and Samuel Delany using short stories, poetry, and critical essays to explore sexual identities. However, those stories and poetic expressions were not explicit. Hughes' "Blessed Assurance" may be interpreted as a signification on the attitudes of heterosexuals toward homosexuals. Delany's science fiction/fantasy stories, while investigating the possibilities of sexuality, sexual difference, and race, exist on the periphery of even black queer literature. These writings represent less a coherent movement and more individual attempts to call attention to assumptions about sexuality and race.

Those literatures written by people such as Essex Hemphill and Joseph Beam represent a massive shift in descriptions of black queer life. Sexual difference became the primary location from which these writers fashioned their short stories, novels, poetry, and essays. Using the linguistic and stylistic conventions of the black arts/aesthetic movement, Hemphill, Riggs, and Beam portray sexual difference as a category equal to race. That is, the black queer writers of the 1970s and 1980s wrote out of a revolutionary impulse. These writers saw what they perceived to be a crisis. They contended that the institutions of black life (the church, family, educational institutions, etc.) had ignored and vilified the presence of black homosexuals.[54] Hemphill, Riggs, and Beam wrote to counter arguments presented by black nationalists that claimed black masculinity as the province of black heterosexual men.

The popular novels of E. Lynn Harris represent yet another shift in black queer writing. The novel became the primary mode of literary expression for black queer men in the 1990s. This time, black queer literature followed romantic conventions and was far less revolutionary and far more commercial than the writings of Hemphill, Riggs, and Beam. The dramatic and serialized nature of black queer writing in the 1990s made these writings more commercial and marketable to a mass audience. While these writings did, in some instances, reveal some of the complexities of black queer experience, they also present black queer men as heroic exemplars who wish to reconcile their sexual identities with their racial identities.

In this introductory overview of black queer literature, I have found that the majority of the literature explores the intersection of and tension between sexuality and race. I believe that these representative texts enlarge our understandings of the complexities of race and sexuality. I also believe that, though these writings enlarge our understandings of sexual difference among black queer men, these writings are not perfect texts. As they open us up to wider categories of difference, they may also present distorted images of black queer men. The literature of black queer men presents images of black queer identity that are heroic, tragic, comical, and ironic. Through these images, we see that black queer experience in particular, and black experience in general, is diverse and multifaceted.

In the next chapter, I continue my discussion of black queer literature. However, I examine how black queer literature takes hold of religion and religious experience. I am primarily interested in how the literature of black queer men represents the intersections between homosexuality and experiences within black churches as well as the social worlds that are influenced by African American churches. I will investigate the tensions between race, sexuality, and religion that these literary expressions uncover.

5

Religious Experience in Black Gay Men's Writings

Introduction

The previous chapter engages in an introductory analysis of black queer literature. It traced different movements in black queer literature and analyzed the representations of black queer experiences in those literatures. I argued that those literatures signified on conceptions of masculinity and race. I also found that black queer literature serves as a response to negative conceptions of black homosexuality. Black queer literature assumes the task of defending an oppressed minority-within-a-minority from the vicissitudes of white supremacy and black homophobia.

As I noted in chapter 3, black queer men's literature is often organized around themes of alienation and longing, or, a search for home. Black queer writers address this longing and combat alienation by seeking to make the invisible (black queer existence and experience) visible. That is, by writing about black queer experiences and sharing them in anthologies, short stories, poetry, and novels, black queer writers show diversity in black queer life that is often marginalized in more common descriptions of black homosexuality. This chapter engages in an analysis of the ways in which black queer men's literary expressions take hold of religion and religious life. Several questions will guide this chapter. How do black queer men take hold of the black church? How does black queer literature address the black church—if at all? In the literature of black queer men, is the church held accountable for its marginalization of black queer experience? Finally, are black queer men's literary expressions open to categories of transcendence? This chapter proposes that black queer men approach religious life through a variety of strategies. I will show that black queer writers approach religious life in black communities by signifying on major motifs in Christianity, critiquing what they perceive to be deficiencies in black religious life and by presenting revised approaches to religious experience. Further, these writers approach religious life by arguing for using the body and the lived experiences of black gay men as a starting point for reflection.

Black Queer Literature and the Black Church

I begin my examination of black queer men's literary responses to the black church by returning to Langston Hughes' "Blessed Assurance." As noted in chapter 3, Hughes' story acknowledges the existence of black queer men in the church. However, the story portrays that existence as an invisible existence. The parishioners and clergy are seemingly oblivious to the existence of black queer men in their midst.

In the eyes of Delmar's father, John, the black church is an important site that validates middle-class black sensibilities. Delmar's suspected homosexuality causes John embarrassment. Hughes couples John's homophobic fear with his shame at having been abandoned by his wife (for a man who had "racket" connections) and shows that John's "distrust of God" may be less an apostasy and more a fear of how he might be perceived by the members of Tried Stone Baptist Church. John perceives strong pressure from his social world to conform. Those forces occlude his ability to appreciate his son for who he is and what he may be.

Hughes infuses Delmar's climactic solo and Dr. Jaxon's response with sexual tension. Once the voices of the silenced and marginalized are unleashed, they overwhelm the "normative" heterosexuality represented by the traditional conservative services. The traditional offerings of "amens and hallelujahs" that are typically uttered by the elderly members of the church are now supplanted by a desire to shout, and the teenaged women in the church also become caught up in the excitement of the service. The unrestrained voices of the black queer disrupts and brings new vitality to the service to the point that the pastor can no longer contemplate the mundane ritual of the collection.

> "One down, one to go," was all that came to mind. After a series of pastorates in numerous sophisticated cities where Negroes did everything whites do, the Reverend Dr. Greene had seen other choir directors

take the count in various ways with equal drama, though perhaps less physical immediacy.[1]

Delmar and Jaxon's sexual orientation and the public expression of homoerotic passion disrupt the veneer of "sophistication" black churches use to mimic white traditions. This mimicry itself leads to a stagnation within the church, wherein creativity and vitality is smothered under the weight of racial and class obligations. This story serves as a parody that reveals the hypocrisy of middle-class black Christians. John is portrayed as a typical middle-class black Christian who operates out of the racial philosophy of the Talented Tenth. For John, any outward expression or action that does not "uplift the race" may be seen as a blemish upon the race. Hughes portrays John as a man who is concerned only about the superficialities of religious life.

As a parody, "Blessed Assurance" shows how a preoccupation with status and racial obligation blinds homophobic black Christians to the transformative capacities black queer Christians bring to the black church and black communities. The story implies that there is no contradiction in being black, gay, and Christian. However, the character of John represents those who seek to make homosexuality incommensurate with blackness and Christianity. When John screams "Shut up!" at Delmar, he shouts his denial of Delmar's homosexuality as well as shouting his desire for Delmar to fit within the parameters of heroic black masculinity. In the end, it is the proper black citizen in the form of John who transgresses. He transgresses because he is incapable of seeing beyond his narrow conceptions of black identity.

While "Blessed Assurance" deals with black homosexuality and the black church in a comical fashion, Randall Kenan's *A Visitation of Spirits* deals with the intersection of homosexuality, religion, and religious experiences in a more sustained and serious fashion. It follows the struggle of two men, Horace Cross and his cousin James Malachai Greene. Horace is young, black, and gay, while James, or, Jimmy, is a heterosexual minister. The story unfolds over April 29–30, 1984 and December 8, 1985. The temporal situation of this book is important, as it positions Horace's existential crisis and resolution to that crisis as a signifier on the Christian story of Jesus Christ's crucifixion.

Over the course of April 29 and going into April 30, Horace struggles to literally transform himself into an animal.[2] He seeks to become a bird. Keenan tells us why Horace wants to become a bird:

> He wanted to be alone, to think undistracted. But now he was buoyed
> by the realization that he knew how he would spend the rest of his

appointed time on this earth. Not as a tortured human, but as a bird free to swoop and dive, to dip and swerve over the cornfields and tobacco patches he had slaved in for what already seemed decades to his sixteen years. No longer would he be bound by human laws and human rules that he had constantly tripped over and frowned at.[3]

Those "human laws and human rules" impede Horace's ability to fully embrace his sexual orientation. For Horace, the only way to escape from the limiting expectations of his community is to become something altogether different. Failing that, the pressures of trying to reconcile his seemingly contradictory sexual orientation with the expectations of his community drive him to suicide. In a very detailed analysis of *A Visitation of Spirits*, Robert McRuer notes that Henry Louis Gates "praised Kenan's novel...but was nonetheless wary of the suicidal ending." Gates indicated that he would have preferred for Kenan to move Horace from the small North Carolina town of Tims Creek to the "big city."[4] I will quote McRuer at length:

Gates' prescription for Kenan is in many ways predictable; the "migration to the big city" is a widely available trope in contemporary lesbian and gay literature, with a long and illustrious history. And yet I find the need to transport characters like Horace off to the "big city" symptomatic of a regional elision in queer theory generally. What Gates elides in his suggestion to Kenan is the fact that taking Horace to anywhere entails taking him from somewhere. In this case, the unmentioned "somewhere" is the fictional Fundamentalist Christian, rural, African American community of Tims Creek, North Carolina. Not the most conducive atmosphere for the expression of queer desire, certainly; but as liberal lesbian and gay thought likes to remind us, "we are everywhere," and rather than concede that "everywhere" actually means New York and San Francisco, I am interested in the (perhaps more radical) implications of recognizing that "everywhere" includes such an apparently marginal and inhospitable place.[5]

The above quote also can be applied to Hughes' "Blessed Assurance." Hughes "removes" Delmar (albeit temporarily) from his location and places him in the "big city," that is to say, Greenwich Village. The big city represents new (and possibly frightening) ideas as well as a facelessness that allows one the possibility of acting upon previously suppressed urges or feelings. The removal of the black queer man from the small town is a trope. It is a trope that operates as a double signifier, signifying on both the black queer man and the town from which he is removed. The relocation of the black queer man from the small town to the big city continues to render that man invisible insofar as his rural roots are concerned. By relocating to the big city, the black queer man's sexual orientation remains invisible to his home, his church, and his family. This recurrent trope implies that the black queer man has no place in the small town and the only place he can survive is in the faceless "big city." The sundering of his roots by relocating to the big city also renders that person alienated from his or her home. However, Kenan keeps Horace in Tims Creek. He does not "save" him by evacuating him to the large faceless big city. At the end of *Visitation*, Kenan does not save Horace at all. Rather, Horace commits suicide.

According to McRuer, Horace occupies the position of the trickster. Referring to Gates' work in *The Signifying Monkey*, McRuer notes that Horace's presence does the work of double signifying. Horace signifies upon the racial and sexual inflexibility of Tims Creek. McRuer reads Horace's eventual suicide as a transformative moment for the community, akin to Jesus' crucifixion. However, there is no resurrection. There are only James Greene's recollections of his deceased cousin.

McRuer also notes that *A Visitation of Spirits* functions as a signifier on James Baldwin's *Go Tell it on the Mountain*. There are obvious parallels between the two novels. The respective protagonists of both books, Horace Cross and John, struggle with their burgeoning homosexuality. Both seek solace and validation within the framework of black Christian traditions. Both have had expectations placed upon them by their communities. Horace understands that his family, church, and community have placed their hopes in him. That expectation constrains his freedom to explore his sexuality. His cousin, Jimmy Greene, reflects on how that constraint "got to Horace" as he remembers a Thanksgiving meal in which Horace is expelled from the table after his aunts and grandfather see Horace's pierced ear:

> This is what finally got to Horace, isn't it? I keep asking myself. He, just like me, had been created by this society. He was a son of the community, more than most. His reason for existing, it would seem, was for the salvation of his people. But he was flawed as far as the community was concerned. First, he loved men; a simple, normal deviation, but a deviation this community would never accept. And second, he didn't quite know who he was. That, I don't fully understand, for they had told him, taught him from the cradle on.[6]

Despite being told who he was by the community, Horace knows that he is not totally what or who they say he is. The black community is the arbiter of identity. As such, Horace should have bracketed his own desires and acquiesced to the spoken and unspoken demands of a heteronormative community that saw him as a potential leader. Baldwin's John Greene, like Horace, is constrained by the expectations of his religious community. Those salvific expectations conspire to trump John's homosexuality:

> Everyone had always said that John would be a preacher when he grew up, just like his father. It had been said so often that John, without ever thinking about it, had come to believe it himself...Around the time of his fourteenth birthday, with all the pressures of church and home uniting to drive him to the altar, he strove to appear more serious and therefore less conspicuous.[7]

Like Horace, John too has to bracket his desires. The communities that Horace and John inhabit are closed communities and are dominated by the black Christian church. Given particular readings of biblical texts and of African American identity, black churches would value seriousness and conformity to accepted standards of blackness as signs of leadership potential. Although John lives in New York City, his surroundings may be read as rural, just as Horace's world of Tims Creek, North Carolina. John's father (or stepfather) refuses to allow his family to watch television, or go to the movies, or participate in the lived experiences of the rest of New York. Harlem seems to inhabit an entirely different space than the rest of New York, which John identifies as being occupied almost exclusively by white people.[8] Both Horace and John are warned by their families to avoid emulating the ways of white people. Through the eyes of Horace and John, we see that their families and communities construe sexual difference as being part of those "ways" of being white and sinful.[9]

Using their communities as the bases for their ethical analysis, Horace and John come to see their sexuality as sinful, and in need of alteration. The two boys are neither able to reconcile their sexual difference nor their racialized identities. Thus, they employ radical strategies to resolve those identity conflicts. Religion stands in the background in Horace's case and in the extreme foreground in John's case. Horace's decision to kill himself comes after he refuses to "kill" the demons of his past.[10] After John's apocalyptic conversion experience, he figuratively kills his desire and submits to the authority of the church.

The black church in these novels functions as an oppressive institution. In one way, both *A Visitation of Spirits* and *Go Tell It On The Mountain* call into question black liberation theology's assertion that the black church stands as a liberating institution. While Cone, Hopkins, and Douglas recognize that the black church marginalizes some black people, both Kenan's and Baldwin's novels show how stark and potentially devastating that marginalization can be.

The church stands at the center of the black community in Baldwin's and Kenan's works. Baldwin's John does not confront the church's assumptions about homosexuality. Rather, his salvation experience is a capitulation to the oppressive forces of the church's teachings about homosexuality. Horace's suicide can be read as an act of defiance. He knows he cannot exist as he is in the world of Tims Creek. Thus, he seeks transcendence by transforming himself into an animal. He knows he cannot transform the church. In the form of his venerable family, Horace realizes that he cannot force the church to accept his sexual difference. His one act of overt defiance finds him banished from the "community" in the form of the Thanksgiving table.[11]

The dominant theme in black queer literature regarding sexual difference and religious experience is "otherness." The church functions as a totality wherein difference is absorbed or eliminated. In the case of John Grimes, the church, through conversion, absorbs his sexuality. For Horace Cross, he does not allow the church to absorb his homosexuality, and thus, he is cast adrift. The black church in the works of Kenan and Baldwin offers black queer men no tools with which to resolve their identity conflicts. Instead of serving as a harbor or haven for John and Horace, the black church constrains their complex identities and presents them with the notion that it is they who are in need of transformation in order to take their place as heroic black men.

As the church stands as the mediating institution between John's and Horace's respective struggles with their sexualities and their conception of God, neither boy is able to formulate a conception of God that is not punitive and remote. For example, Horace derives his understanding of God from his community as well as his own experiences. He had been told that God answers prayer and that God would "fix" his sexuality.[12] However, he is led to reevaluate the unquestioned goodness of God:

> I remember taking Communion and wondering how the bread was the
> body and the grape juice was the blood and thinking how that made

us all cannibals. I remember worrying that I was not worthy of taking Communion because I was unclean, no matter how much I prayed and asked forgiveness. I remember wondering what God looks like and I remember after a time stopping wondering what he looked like and wondering more who he was, thinking it was surely possible that he did not like some people so much, despite what my grandfather and the Bible said.[13]

Horace is unable to reconcile that which he has been told with what he thinks. His earliest memories show that he has always had difficulty with the theology and liturgy of the church. Through John and Horace, Baldwin and, more pointedly, Kenan suggest that it is not black queer men who require transformation, but the black community vis-à-vis the black church that requires transformation. In Horace's questioning of what God looks like and whether or not God actually likes some people, Kenan is able to point out a theological problem within African American life. Horace signifies on John Greene's belief in God and the transformative power of the church. It is at this point that I agree with McRuer that Horace Cross brings John Greene's more ambiguous sexuality out of the closet. However, Horace goes further in its representations, but is not able to complete his journey as one among the living.

The productions of the protest writers (Hemphill, Riggs, Beam) present the church as one of the chief enemies of black queer men. Their writings decry the black church's silence in the face of the AIDS epidemic, equating that silence with complicity in the deaths of black queer men. Their charges against the church follow the pattern of the rest of their writings in that there is a strong sense of urgency. They want to call attention to the ways in which the church marginalizes, oppresses, and invalidates black queer men.

These writers do not challenge the assertion that the black church stands as a prominent institution in the black community. Rather, they want the black church to accept sexual difference as a part of black identity that need not be apologized for nor demonized. Charles Nero links the black church's resistance to sexual difference with sexism in his essay, "Toward a Black Gay Aesthetic: Signifying in Contemporary Black Gay Literature." Nero notes how the black church is "eager to oppress gay people to prove its worth to the middle classes. For the sake of conformity which, with hope, leads to success, the middle class is willing to oppress its children."[14]

Essex Hemphill's writings are an example of Nero's charge against the black church. In Hemphill's poetry and essays, it is clear that he believes that the black church is a major purveyor of homophobia in the African American community. His poem "Heavy Breathing" excoriates the institutions of black life in America for rendering black queer people invisible. Hemphill questions politics, religion, and middle-class status in black communities. They are all illusory, and do not provide any safety for black queer men. His criticism of the black church is potent:

> I enter the diminishing
> circumstance of prayer.
> Inside a homemade Baptist church
> perched on the edge
> of the voodoo ghetto,
> the murmurs of believers
> rise and fall, exhaled
> from a single spotted lung.
> The congregation sings
> to an out-of-tune piano
> while death is rioting,
> splashing blood about
> like gasoline,
> offering pieces of rock
> in exchange
> for throw-away dreams.[15]

Hemphill suggests that the black church itself is ill. His concerns echo those of Kelly Brown Douglas in *Sexuality and the Black Church*. Like Douglas, Hemphill is confronting the black church's intransigence concerning its members who are suffering. The believers' murmurings come from a "single, spotted lung," signifying that the church as an organism is ailing. This phrase indicates that the church is as ill as the homosexual men it castigates and alienates. The "out-of-tune" piano may serve as a signification on what he would consider to be outdated sermons and messages within the church. The black church's refusal to acknowledge black queer men stands in stark contrast to the reality of the hundreds of thousands of black queer men who suffer from HIV/AIDS. The juxtaposition of the congregation singing "while death is rioting" suggests that the black church has become a shadow of its former self, a hypocritical and myopic institution so enamored with glories past that it cannot adequately address the present crisis.

The black church in Hemphill's poem offers few resources for dealing with the complex realities of black life in America. Hemphill accuses the black church of offering a "pie in the sky" theology while "death is rioting." His accusation is contemporaneous with black liberation theology's criticism of illusory theologies. Hemphill and black liberation theology wants to call attention to the precarious predicament in which black America finds itself.[16] Both Hemphill and black liberation theologians argue that black communities have been ravaged by HIV/AIDS, black-on-black crime, and a general sense of lovelessness. They both see existential crises in black life that demand the black church's attention.

While Hemphill and black liberation theology have similar concerns about existential crises in black life, "Heavy Breathing" does not offer a liberating God who stands with the oppressed as an intellectual salve. What Hemphill turns to is what he perceives as real and apparent. In other words, Hemphill turns to black bodies. He turns specifically to black gay bodies. It is the truths that he uncovers in and through relationships with other black gay men that Hemphill finds relevant in black life—not the proclamations of black churches.

G. Winston James' short story "Church" discloses a more complex and ambiguous relationship between black queer men and the black church. This ambiguity is displayed in the opening sentences of the story:

> Eerie. That's what it was. Eerie walking into that church after all those years. It was like hearing myself say, "Why do I gotta go to church, Mama?" all over again. It was like hoping that it wasn't first Sunday this Sunday and praying that if I had to be there, at least the Gospel Choir would be singing.[17]

The story, told from a first-person perspective, details Langston Ambrose's emotional reconciliation with the church. He goes back home to die after contracting a fatal cancer due to HIV infection. As he stands before his congregation, he appears to be a successful black man. Langston has acquired all the accoutrements of black middle-class status: he has graduated from New York University, has written several books, and has traveled around the world. He has also performed what would be called in the language of the church, missionary work, as he has done work for Save the Children and CARE.[18] Despite that, Ambrose retains an ambiguous relationship with the black church. His reluctance to go to church and hoping that it wasn't a "first Sunday" is probably rooted in the fact that, in many black churches, the first Sunday of the month is a particularly long church

service. It is interesting that what would soothe his reluctant atten-
dance would be the presence of the Gospel Choir. I find that interesting in that it is a signification on the role of Gospel music in the lives
of African American gay men. While I cannot devote much time to
such a connection, I think that it is in the music of the church that
black gay men find a healing counterpoint to the often brutal ways in
which black communities in general and black churches in particular
treat them.

After a lengthy monologue during the church service, Langston
partially discloses his illness. That is to say, he tells the church that
he has cancer and omits the fact that he is HIV-positive. It is his
mother who screams "Can't no AIDS just take my baby!" However,
the significance of that admission appears to be lost in the emotional
tide that sweeps the congregation. During this emotional moment,
Langston realizes that the church is a family that is part of the black
family.[19] He later wishes that he "could believe in more than just gospel music."[20] At the end of the story, Langston questions the nature of
God by wondering whether God is "whatever made you truly happy
in life." If, as Langston believes, God is whatever makes a person
happy, and if being with other men makes Langston happy, then God
cannot be opposed to black queer sexuality. His answer seems to be
an affirmation of his heretofore unspoken sexual orientation.

The difference between James' short story and Hemphill's poem
are stark. Hemphill wants the black church and the black community
to be more than what it appears to be. His writings present a black
church that is disconnected from the lived experiences of black people. This disconnection leads to the impoverishment of the church's
message. Hemphill's poem portrays a church that is ineffectual in
bringing solace or change in the lives of black queer men. James' portrayal is much different, in that the church is portrayed as an integral
part of the black community, and one that can, when pressed, bring
comfort and reconciliation in the lives of black queer men.

Hemphill does not find spiritual fulfillment within the black
church, but within the outcast black queer community. In the arms
of black men, Hemphill finds those "carnal secrets" that are hidden
from those loyal to the cult of black masculinity:

> For my so-called sins against nature and the race, I gain the burden-
> some knowledge of carnal secrets. *It rivals rituals of sacrifice and
> worship, and conjures the same glassy-eyed results—with less blood-
> shed.* A knowledge disquieting and liberating inhabits my soul. It often

comforts me, or at times, is miserably intoxicating with requisite hang-overs and regrets. At other moments it is sacred communion, causing me to moan and tremble and cuss as the Holy Ghost fucks me. It is a knowledge of fire and beauty that I will carry beyond the grave. When I sit in God's final judgment, I will wager this knowledge against my entrance into the Holy Kingdom. There was no other way for me to know the beauty of Earth except through the sexual love of men, men who were often more terrified than I, even as they posed before me, behind flimsy constructions of manhood, mocking me with muscles, erections, and wives. (emphasis mine)[21]

Hemphill categorically rejects the Christian notion that homosexual sex is deviant. Rather, homosexual sex is sacred and represents more than just a union between two men. At times, sex is so transcendent, that Hemphill argues that it reveals knowledge of the world that cannot be attained through Christian piety. Hemphill intimates that homosexual sex is so sacred that it is analogous to being possessed by the Holy Spirit. This possession and this knowledge is even hidden from those with whom Hemphill has sex, for they are more terrified than he is. He argues that Christian piety may even cause more blood-shed than sexual relations between two men.

Black Queer Literature and Religious Experience

Critical essays by black queer men reinforce Hemphill's assertion that black queer men can have valuable religious experiences among each other and, at the same time, transcend the notions of the "Talented Tenth" that straightjacket the African American community as a whole. In *The Greatest Taboo: Homosexuality in Black Communities*, E. Patrick Johnson presents a compelling argument concerning the fusion of the sacred and the spiritual in the black queer club scene. He recognizes that the club is a place that repositions the black queer body and soul. The club is a place that affirms the holiness and sacred-ness of black queer male sexuality.[22] Johnson recognizes the erotically charged moment of black church worship that Michael Eric Dyson recognizes and criticizes in *Race Rules*. However, Johnson wants to critique that moment from a black queer perspective. He notes that while the black church affirms the sexual subtext within worship, the church "holds a contradictory and duplicitous attitude toward sex-uality in regard to its heterosexual members, [and] the same is true for its attitude toward its gay and lesbian members."[23] Here, Johnson is not significantly different from Dyson in his assessment of black church attitudes toward homosexuality. However, Johnson moves beyond criticism and toward an expanded conception of black queer spirituality. Like Hemphill, Johnson recognizes that the black church may not be capable of meeting the spiritual needs of black queer men. Its insistence on re-presenting a "Manichean dualism" regarding the body and sexuality prevents the black church from resolving the tension surrounding sexuality in general, and that surrounding black queer men in particular.[24]

Johnson, in a similar yet different manner than Dyson, turns to the particular experiences that constitute black queer life. It is similar to Dyson's work in *Race Rules* in that Johnson follows Dyson's method of using anecdotes to illuminate certain facets of black experience. However, it is different in that Johnson attends to a particular feature of black queer life that is absent in either Dyson's *Race Rules* or *Open Mike*. Johnson details his experiences at black queer nightclubs. He notes that the culture of black queer clubs in some ways reflects the culture of black churches. The club fuses the carnality of dancing, sweaty bodies with the religious fervor of a Pentecostal church service. The disc jockey's metamorphosis from a mere record spinner into an exhorter transforms him into a worship leader styled in the tradition of black Baptist ministers.

Even Gospel songs are transformed into affirmations of black queer identity. For example, the Shirley Caesar song "Hold My Mule" was transformed into a popular "house" song. The song tells the story of a man named Shoutin' John who belonged to a church that did not "believe in dancing and speaking in tongues." The church did not appreciate John's different manner of worship. Ultimately, the church expels Shoutin' John. However, John's reply to the deacons of the church is "If I can't shout in your church, hold my mule, I'm gonna shout right here!" The house version modifies lyrics like "It's just like fire! Shut up in my bones!" by adding the word "Yes," which is repeated over and over rhythmically in the background. Johnson notes that the song is transvalued from a confirmation of Christian righteousness to an affirmation of the sacredness of black queer sexuality. Johnson argues that the church is repositioned in this song:

> John's relationship with the "dead" church is similar to African American gay men's relationship to the church in general. Despite John's perception that the church is "dead," he decides to join, hoping he might be able to put some "life" into it. But John soon discovers

that the church is not only dead—it is spiritless. Indeed, the members work hard to "quench" the spirit in him and in the church in general…the black church condemns the African American gay male's sexuality, denying him the opportunity to be out within the context of the church.[25]

In this view, the black church quenches black queer men's sexuality, forcing them to find alternative forms of expression of their sexuality. Johnson believes that when black queer men incorporate elements of black Christian worship into the nightclub space, they "forge alternative epistemological frames of reference…they create new ways of understanding the linking of body and soul or sexuality and spirituality."[26]

In this essay, Johnson wants to show that black queer men are not constrained in the ways in which they take hold of their sexuality and spirituality. He argues that the black church constrains black bodies in general. The black queer nightclub allows the black queer body to "affirm both the sexual and the spiritual."[27] This affirmation allows black queer men to claim their sexualities with neither apology nor need for repentance. He follows Dyson's call for a "theology of queerness" in the black church. Supposedly, this theology would build bridges between gay and straight church members. For Johnson, this theology of queerness would "imagine that the same God who can identify with other oppressed groups…can also identify with gays and lesbians."[28] This God affirms black queer men's sexuality.

This open-ended affirmation of black queer men's sexuality is a hallmark of the writings of E. Lynn Harris. However, Harris' characters come to think differently about God and humankind after overcoming tumultuous events in their lives. Sheila Smith McKoy notes that Harris' novels function in the tradition of black Christian morality plays. In these plays, the protagonist, usually a decent black person (often a female), is seduced by the wily ways of either the "big city" itself or a person from the big city. At the end, the protagonist usually finds that he or she should have followed his or her mother's advice regarding fidelity to the church. Harris follows this formula in his novels, with some variations. In Harris' novels *Invisible Life* and *Just As I Am*, Raymond Tyler is presented as a Christian exemplar. In McKoy's essay "Southern Gay Masculinity," she notes that Harris' works are centered on Christian morals as well as black queer identity:

It is worth noting that the contemporary black queer writer most concerned with reforming Christian doctrine and church policies concerning homosexuality is E. Lynn Harris. Harris, whose works are as much gay romance novels as they are novels about Christian morals, is a best-selling author. All except one of his black queer characters, Basil Henderson, are committed homosexuals and Christians. His novels, then, work to develop a Christian theology that validates gay desire.[29]

It is also worth noting that although Christian doctrine, policies, and morals are in the foreground of his novels, Harris does not place any of his characters within a particular church tradition. The presence of a physical church does not figure prominently in Harris' novels. That is to say, not one of his black queer characters holds any sort of office within a church, nor is any of them a regular church attendee. However, the black church is present in the background of his characters' lives. The title of Harris' second novel, *Just As I Am*, itself is a signification on a Christian hymn. The song itself is a hymn about repentance and return to a God who forgives humans of sin. Harris' use of the song as a title for a novel about the lives of black queer men suggests that Harris is repositioning homosexuality as an identity marker that does not require God's forgiveness.

As a novel that is centered on Christian morality, Harris' black queer characters embody three positions with regard to black queer sexuality. His protagonist, Raymond Tyler, is the black Christian moral exemplar. Basil Henderson, the antagonist in both *Invisible Life* and *Just As I Am*, is Raymond's moral opposite. Raymond's friend Kyle is the worldly, amoral "trickster."

As the moral center of *Invisible Life* and *Just As I Am*, Raymond, offers commentary about the moral status of the black community. Unlike E. Patrick Johnson, the fictional character Ray offers a less theological (and far less complimentary) opinion of black queer nightclubs and bars. As he describes his experiences at the Nickel Bar, a popular after-work hangout in New York City, Raymond distinguishes himself from the rest of the patrons both morally and socioeconomically:

> As I sipped my drink, I eavesdropped on the conversation of two men standing close by. "Miss Thing, I can't believe you didn't work that fine man," the guy standing next to me said to his friend in a high-pitched voice. "He wasn't my type, Miss Honey. Did you see those hands? Trust me, he's not the one," the other giggled. I wondered if these guys talked like that most of the time, and if they did, where did they work?[30]

Raymond's comments about other black queer men and the black gay club space serve as moral commentary about black queer men who do not fit into the black masculine ideal. These nameless and virtually faceless black queer men are shallow and obsessed with sexual exploits. Raymond cannot imagine these men having high-paying, successful careers with their overly effeminate behavior and speech patterns. Raymond attaches a moral significance to black queer men's mannerisms.

In Raymond's view of black queer club culture, the music does not serve a liberating function. The black queer nightclub space does not uncover anything more than sexual desire bereft of commitment. The black queer nightclub only foments predatory sexual instincts among black queer men. Raymond's description of the Nickel Bar is not necessarily complimentary. He describes his first time going to the Nickel Bar as a frightening experience and compares it to walking "through a dark tunnel into a secret world."[31] His description of another black queer hangout, Keller's, is even less complimentary. The club space is a place where black queer men meet other black queer men, primarily for the purpose of having sex, something that Raymond claims he does not do.[32]

It is clear that Raymond possesses a moral character that neither Basil nor his friend Kyle possesses. It is that moral character that highlights his ambiguity about his sexual orientation. Raymond claims that the black queer "lifestyle" is an arduous lifestyle. His moral assessment of the lifestyle is not positive. As a person with Christian morals, Raymond sees the black queer lifestyle as one rife with deception and promiscuity. He seems to avoid some of the pitfalls by maintaining some form of moderation when drinking and refraining from one-night stands. He displays a preference and desire for monogamous relationships. Although in *Invisible Life* we see Raymond dating and having sexual relationships with men and women, the reader sees that Raymond possesses a moral consciousness through his conflict about his duplicity. Although it appears that Raymond has accepted his sexual orientation by *Just As I Am*, it is clear that Raymond continues to have problems with self-acceptance and spirituality. Toward the end of the book, it is Kyle's death that serves as the catalyst for Raymond's rebirth as a self-affirming homosexual.

Kyle represents the "typical" amoral black queer man. He drinks, he smokes, and he has multiple one-night stands. Raymond describes Kyle as being averse to commitment.[33] Although Kyle becomes Raymond's best friend and "mentor in terms of teaching [him] about the gay world," Raymond often refers to Kyle with disdain. For example, early in *Invisible Life*, Kyle meets a man named Rock on the same night as Raymond meets Quinn, the married man with whom he subsequently develops a relationship. Raymond's description of Rock is not flattering, nor is his condescension to both Rock and Kyle.[34] Raymond is critical of Kyle's sexual partners, his attitude, and his mannerisms. Raymond's criticism implies that Kyle is less than Raymond on the basis of his overtly effeminate mannerisms and his aesthetic taste in sexual partners.

As noted above, Kyle's death serves as the sacrifice that makes Raymond's self-actualization possible. However, what is it that is said when Kyle dies? It appears that Kyle must die to fulfill a trope in black literature. That trope is the one of the tragic mulatto, or, in this case, the tragic homosexual. Kyle is a "sissy," and, worse, is an unrepentant sissy. Even though Kyle has all the visible accoutrements of middle-class black life (an Ivy League education, and a high-paying-but-undefined occupation), he does not conform or wish to conform to the tenets of heroic black male existence. He does not even pay lip service to the church, preferring to "hold court" in the black queer bars and nightclubs of New York City. As a homosexual, he is the receptive partner ("bottom") and proud of it, unlike his friend Raymond, from whom the reader only gets a vague notion that he even has sex with other men. In *Invisible Life* and *Just As I Am*, Kyle even serves as a form of "gay conscience" to Raymond, chiding him and admonishing him to be as proud of his sexual orientation as he is about his racial identity.[35]

Kyle appears to embody some traits of the African Trickster as explained by Henry Louis Gates in *The Signifying Monkey*. Gates contends that the trickster figure embodies several characteristics. He says "a partial list of these qualities might include individuality, satire, parody, irony, magic, indeterminacy, open-endedness, ambiguity, sexuality, chance, uncertainty, disruption and reconciliation, betrayal and loyalty, closure and disclosure, encasement and rupture."[36] Kyle does not embody all the characteristics of a trickster figure, but, as Gates argues, trickster figures do not have to encompass all of the above characteristics.[37] As Raymond's guide to the black gay community of New York City, Kyle displays an individuality that does not conform to Raymond's expectations of blackness. That is, Kyle does what he wants to do, with whom he wants to, and when he wants to do it. His quick wit, expressive gesturing, and generally "feminine" behavior mock black expectations of macho behavior.

However, Kyle's presence as an unrepentant, unapologetic homo-sexual is presented as problematic. Unlike Raymond, Kyle does not make his racial identity a priority. He did not attend a historically black college, nor does he concern himself with "giving back to the community"—at least, not prior to contracting the AIDS virus. Kyle's expression of his homosexuality is presented as unreflective and excessive. His unreflective and excessive homosexuality as expressed in his alcoholism and promiscuity is presented as immoral, and demands some form of punishment as a consequence. Thus, Kyle not only becomes addicted to crack cocaine in *Invisible Life*, he contracts HIV and subsequently dies from complications as a result of AIDS in *Just As I Am*, thus fulfilling the trope of the tragic homosexual. Kyle's tribulations and death serve as a moral warning to those who would embark upon a "lifestyle" of excess. Kyle functions as a scape-goat, upon whom all the sins of the black queer community are cast. His death is atonement, not for himself, but for Raymond, as demon-strated in the letter he leaves for Ray in the event of his death. Kyle tells Raymond to live the life that he feels most comfortable living and to recognize that if he is a being created in God's image, then he ought not worry about what other human beings think.[38] It is inter-esting that Kyle notes "Christ made you from His own image." At first, it may be read as a mistake or typographical error on Harris' part. However, I read this statement as a repositioning of Christ for black queer men. Jesus Christ and the assumption of the message of the Gospel as a message of love and acceptance become central in the lives of black queer men like Raymond.

John Basil Henderson is decidedly the antagonist in both *Invisible Life* and *Just As I Am*. In the first book, Basil's presence as an antag-onist is almost tertiary. He appears as one of Kyle's clients after Kyle becomes a male escort. Kyle is enamored with Basil's sexual prowess and physical beauty, while Raymond, drawing on his knowledge of professional football, realizes that Basil (using an alias) is actually a player for the fictional New Jersey Warriors. Basil's moral ambigu-ity concerning his sexual orientation does not lead to critical reflec-tion as it does with Raymond. Instead, Basil's ambiguity leads him to unabashed deceit and promiscuity.

Basil is presented as Raymond's opposite number. He is similar to Raymond in physique: both men are tall, muscular, light-skinned, and have light-colored eyes. However, that is where the similarities end. Where Raymond does not consciously use his attractive physical appearance to further his goals, Basil does. Where Raymond some-times goes by "Ray," Basil drops his first name altogether. If Kyle is amoral, then Basil is altogether immoral, exhibiting behaviors that Harris presents to be the worst traits in black queer communities. He is a violent, duplicitous, selfish person driven by his desire for sex. In *Invisible Life* and *Just As I Am*, Basil cannot acknowledge that his desires for sex with men are a part of him and that those desires are acceptable.[39] By the end of *Just As I Am*, Basil has condemned himself to a life of futility by proposing marriage to a woman.

Basil is portrayed as a sexual predator, one who trades on his good looks and his carefully cultivated masculine charm. His per-sonality is a play or a signification on the biblical Scripture that portrays Satan as possessing the capability to transform into an appealing form.[40] Basil is able to use his physical appearance to his benefit, and to the detriment of unsuspecting gay men and hetero-sexual women.

Basil is enslaved to his passions. He is either unwilling to or inca-pable of governing his passions. He is committed to a life of vice, and does not desire the Good—in the case of Harris' novels, the Good can be construed as survival and flourishing of both tra-ditional black nuclear families and nontraditional families, such as gay and lesbian relationships. Unlike Raymond, for Basil homosex-ual sexual practices have no possibility of expressing a deeper emo-tional connection whatsoever, nor should they. Basil views men who express love for other men as weak. For him, sexual relationships between men take on a nakedly aggressive characteristic. He uses other men's bodies as a conduit to his own sexual satisfaction. At the end of *Just As I Am*, Raymond sums up Basil's attitude toward sexual relationships between men by telling him that he no longer can use Raymond for his sexual needs. He acknowledges that he too had used Basil, but his own desire to be a morally upright per-son trumps his transitory lusts. In one sentence, he admonishes Basil to reorient his thinking about sex between men and recognize that there is more to male relationships than just sex.[41] Raymond's admonition to Basil may also be read as an admonition to hetero-sexual black communities. As the morally upright black gay man, Raymond is telling heterosexual black people as well as predatory black queer men that sex and sexuality among and between black queer men does not and should not be perceived as merely the result of animalistic, uncontrolled urges.

Conclusion

Black queer men's literature addresses issues of black queer men's sexuality and spirituality in diverse ways. The various literatures I have examined show the various literary strategies black queer men employ in reconciling their sexual orientation with religion. These strategies include parody and cultural and religious critique. This chapter has also shown that many of these writers call for a theology that is open to sexual difference in black communities.

When approaching religious experience, black queer men's writings are organized around themes of alienation, reconciliation, and revision. The black church as the central religious institution in black life offers little for black queer men. Although it is supposed to be a source of comfort in a hostile world, its members and leaders often prevent black homosexuals from receiving that comfort. Rather, as black queer writers demonstrate, it serves as another source of hostility toward those whom Janet Jakobsen terms "sexual dissidents." The ignominy of having to refer to a deceased lover as merely a "friend" or risk having the church deny that lover the same funeral rites accorded to a heterosexual partner is as demeaning and painful as being refused service in a store on the basis of skin color. Black queer writers show the ways in which black heterosexuals make black homosexuals appear as a threatening Other. What is operative in alienating black homosexuals is the presentation of black homosexuals as immoral and operating outside the bounds of nature. This presentation of black homosexuals as immoral and unnatural is an appeal to standards of biblical morality, and it allows the black church to adopt strategies of minimizing black queer existence and experience. The strategy within black queer writing is to expose these tactics within the black church as antithetical to not only the putative mission of the black church, but damaging to the black community. In his 1996 book *One More River To Cross: Black and Gay in America*, Keith Boykin tells the tale of a black queer man's confrontation with a preacher at a friend's funeral. He also notes that at Essex Hemphill's funeral his accomplishments as an outspoken and prolific black queer writer were minimized.[42] Despite presenting black queer protagonists who lead fabulous lives with six-figure incomes according to soap-operatic conventions, E. Lynn Harris' characters also struggle with their relationship to the black church. Further, as they reconfigure their relationship to the black church, Harris' characters come to realize happiness by making their sexual selves visible to their family and friends instead of allowing themselves to remain marginal in the life of the black community. Whether through fiction or critical essays, black queer writers rebel against alienation through foregrounding black queer experience.

Through foregrounding black queer experience, black queer writers are also able to present revised views of God and human beings. A reimagined vision of God's relationship to the world hints at the possibility for reconciliation of black queers with those black religious communities that had marginalized them. For the protest writers such as Essex Hemphill, the black church stands as an impediment to black queer men's search for a spirituality that affirms their sexuality. Hemphill's literature represents a strand in black queer men's literature that rejects the black church altogether and agitates for a different conception of God. These writers present a God who is open to multiple expressions of sexuality. They lambaste the black church as an institution that prioritizes race to the exclusion of other concerns within black communities. This prioritizing binds the church up in totalities. Writers such as Hemphill occupy what I call a liberal position as it concerns black queer men and the church.

However, other literature by black queer men shows that some black queer men want the black church to change. Using G. Winston James and Randall Kenan as examples, we find that some black queer men identify with traditional black churches. They represent a moderate approach to the black church and black queer men's spirituality. These writers show that the black church, and, by extension, black communities, benefits from the presence of black queer men. They show that sexual difference is not a threat to the existence or integrity of black churches. Rather, they show that the denial and marginalization of black queer men is a detriment to the flourishing of black communities. They present a moderate viewpoint regarding black queer men's sexuality as it intersects the interests of the black church.

E. Lynn Harris' writings represent what I call a conservative position regarding black queer men, their sexuality, and their spirituality. Raymond represents a black queer man who prioritizes the concerns of black community above the concerns of black queer communities. Indeed, it is difficult to find a black queer community in Harris' novels. Black queer men in Harris' novels require religion and spirituality as a civilizing force. As Harris' chief protagonist in several novels, Raymond Tyler represents the black queer man who desires the same goods as other more "normal" black heterosexual people.

Harris' writings represent a conservative approach to the black church and spirituality. While the black church may need to amend

its homophobic ways, the character of Raymond offers an indictment against the politics of black homosexuality. Raymond's critique of black homosexuality may be read as an implicit indictment
of Hemphill's more aggressive politics. While Hemphill rejects the
black church because of its homophobia, Harris' protagonist wants
black queer men to have a place in the life of the church. Raymond
criticizes the black church's homophobia, but does not explicitly hold
the black church accountable for the marginalization of black queer
men. Harris' gay characters assume total responsibility for their moral
choices. For Raymond, morally praiseworthy behavior for black queer
men entails monogamous relationships and fidelity to the interests of
the black middle class. Although Harris reveals in a later novel that
Basil had been molested by an uncle and offers that as a possible
excuse for Basil's promiscuity, it is Basil who has to, as bell hooks
states in Salvation, "deal psychoanalytically with his childhood."

God is repositioned in the literary works of black queer men. God
as presented in much of the literature is open to difference. Sexual
difference is not a threat to God's existence. Black queer writers uniformly call for a theology that does not bind God to limited conceptions of existence and opens God as well as the human being up to
sexual difference and multiple accounts of being in the world.

While these writers call for a theology that is open to sexual difference, their theological frameworks are somewhat unclear. As it is not
the task of black queer novelists to present a clear theological framework, my previous statement is not a criticism, but an observation. I
infer from their writings a desire to present a different conception of
God. Black queer men's writings have shown diversity in approaches
to God, spirituality, and sexuality. However, the theological sources
for those approaches have, at times, been thin and not well sustained.
For example, E. Lynn Harris' characters repeatedly espouse a belief in
a God who loves all God's children, but God retains an aloof presence
that is not immediately accessible to black queer people. Although
Horace Cross in A Visitation of Spirits signifies a call for revision
within black religious communities, it is not clear how black queer
folk are to reconfigure God, if at all.

Despite that critique, and as I noted above, it is not my argument
that reconfiguring God's relationship to black homosexuals is the
work of fiction writers. Black queer novelists, fiction writers, poets,
and the like have, as I outlined in chapter 3 and in the preceding
pages, concerned themselves with black queer visibility. They have
outlined recurring themes and motifs in black queer life in an attempt

to write black queer identity into visibility. Thus, they have been more concerned with black queer experience than doing theological work. However, when I turn to critical essays such as Horace Griffin's "Their Own Received Them Not" or Elias Farajaje-Jones' essay in *Black Theology, A Documentary Witness*, I find their theological formulations lacking in two areas. First, both Griffin and Farajaje-Jones address homophobia as a problem for black religious criticism that requires amelioration. Second, I find that black queer theologians such as Griffin and Farajaje-Jones tend to elide discussions of black sexuality as they discuss black homosexuals as victims of the homophobia present in the black church.

They present a dialectic in black queer life that mirrors black liberation theology's dialectical approach toward black life in general. Whereas the black liberation theologians and other black religious and cultural critics speak primarily about the dialectic of race, Griffin and Farajaje-Jones speak of a dialectic of sexuality. In this dialectic of sexuality in black life, black heterosexuals are charged with being complicit in a program of oppression. As James Cone earlier charged white Christians with complicity in the oppression of black peoples, Griffin asserts that "the question therefore becomes whether African American heterosexuals are going to do justice toward their daughters and sons, sisters and brothers, mothers and fathers, other relatives, friends, colleagues and fellow Christians who are lesbian and gay."[43] Griffin is not speaking about black queer sexuality as much as he is indicting black heterosexuals for having spoken negatively about other black people who happen to be gay.

Griffin's discussion of God is not dissimilar from discussions of God that are present in the writings of heterosexual black religious critics. God is as anthropomorphized in his talk of a "true black liberation theology" as it is in Cone's early texts. God for Griffin is a liberating entity who has positive intentions toward its creations. Like black heterosexuals, God has to take sides in the dialectic between heterosexuality and homosexuality. Since heterosexuals oppress homosexuals, Griffin argues that God can and must stand on the side of the oppressed. Therefore, God cannot help but favor black homosexuals.

As I argued in chapters 1 and 2, such theological discourses need to be revised. As I read black queer writers such as E. Patrick Johnson, who argue for an expanded view of black queer spirituality that draws on the black church but also draws on the lived experiences of black queer people, I believe that it is not efficacious to attempt to graft this form of black queer spirituality onto a monolithic description of God. As I noted in the first chapter, presenting a God who is oriented toward the oppressed keeps black queer people bound in crisis with no hope of transcendence. As I read black queer writers and as they read their existence and experiences and as they *read* those institutions in black life that would exclude them, I find that an expanded, nonanthropomorphic theological formulation that is oriented toward transcendence rather than finitude is capable of speaking not only toward those moments of oppression and finitude but also about the specifics that constitute black queer life and experience.

The previous discussion about black queer men's literary approaches to religion and spirituality lead to more questions. If, as I have shown in this chapter, black queer writers "read" the black church for constraining black queer people's sexuality within the rubric of black heterosexuality and if these writers present a desire to revise descriptions of God and God's relationship to and with human beings, then what should these revised descriptions entail? As black queer novelists and poets are not theologians and ethicists by training, the task falls to the black religious scholar to posit some form of constructive theology and ethics. The next chapter and conclusion suggest that attention to black queer literature as well as the ways in which black gay men construct their identities via the Internet offer black liberation theology and African American cultural criticism resources for a constructive ethics. I call this ethics an ethics of openness. I will argue that the contours of this ethics open our discussions of liberation beyond freedom from white supremacy and move black theological discourse toward critical and creative engagement with the various modes of difference that are present in African American life.

6

Reconstructing Black Gay Male Identity beyond "The DL"

Introduction

As we have seen in previous chapters, the body of black gay men is a problem for black religious scholars. It is even more of a problem when dealt with theologically, for black religious scholars have presented inadequate theological frameworks with which to take hold of black sexual difference. Even African American gay writers approach black gay male bodies as sites wherein a nebulous "God" at best "loves them," but does very little else to work on their behalf. What is curious about these projects is the lack of a constructive move. It is a daunting task, this reconstruction of black male bodies beyond being merely "problematic." These scholars uniformly point to the disruptive power of black male bodies, and urge African American men to construct their masculinities beyond misogyny, homophobia, and heterosexism. However, in the same way that I question black liberation theology's lack of a substantive description of God and liberation, I question whether African American religious and cultural critics are able to present adequate descriptions of what reconstructed black masculinities would look like. Indeed, as I have noted, the purpose of this chapter is to introduce a move toward new ways of viewing black gay men.

The problem of the black gay male persists in African American life, with only minimal substantive response. This is not to say that what these writers have presented is useless. Indeed, the work of black religious and cultural critics has opened up the academy to wider discourse regarding sexuality in African American life. While I have presented strong readings of these critics, I remain indebted to them for their attempts to push beyond monolithic approaches to black identity. Nevertheless, I want to draw attention to the conceptual problem with linking black gay bodies to existential oppression or any particular conceptions of God.

The problem of the black gay male body is situated in the racialized anxiety of African Americans concerning representation, authenticity, and masculinity. We can categorize this under racial/masculine performance. Simply put, race, gender, and sexuality are scripted and performed. Further, these scripts serve to regulate, police, and control race, gender, and sexuality so that they do not threaten the body politic of African Americans. Thus, the dominant representations of black gay male bodies must service a conception of black identity and African American community that does not weaken "black folks" in the eyes of whites.

The problematic nature of the black gay body is best illustrated by the 1978 movie "Car Wash." While some might argue that discourses concerning black homosexuality have clearly advanced since the late 1970s, I contend that, in some ways, the discourse has not moved very much. The movie itself is a comedy focusing on the lives of several people who work at a car wash. One of the people is a homosexual named Lindy, played by Antonio Fargas. To signify his homosexuality, he wears makeup, dresses flamboyantly, and has affected feminine mannerisms. In a particularly memorable scene, Lindy gets into a confrontation with Duane, an Afrocentric coworker played by Bill Duke. During their exchange, Lindy teases and antagonizes Duane.

> [*Duane has just thrown Irwin's book into a bucket of water*]
> *Lindy*: I'm so tired of you running off at your mouth it's getting me down honey. Why don't you just leave? And be an assassin? Or is the only thing you're good at shooting off is your big mouth?
> *Duane*: Will you please get out of my face you sorry looking faggot.
> *Lindy*: Who you calling sorry looking?
> [Everybody laughs]
> *Duane*: Can't ya'll see she ain't funny?
> [Laughter stops]
> *Duane*: She's just another poor example of how the system is destroying our men.
> *Lindy*: Honey, I'm more man than you'll ever be and more woman than you'll ever get.

The exchange, while played for laughs, reflects the kinds of masculine anxiety that are part of African American life. Black homosexuals are treated paradoxically. Lindy's flamboyance is a threat to black heterosexual males; however, it is also nonthreatening. While Duane may be threatened by Lindy, the threat is based on a perception of Lindy's predatory instincts. That threat can be dismissed, as Duane is the more "masculine" of the two, and should Lindy actually make any attempt to accost him, such an attempt could be easily rebuffed. Further, Lindy's homosexuality is interpreted by Duane as an example of how white supremacy (represented by "the system") destroys black masculinity (which is presented as a threat to white supremacy). Lindy, on the other hand, interprets his homosexuality as the best of both worlds. His masculinity is such that his boldness in being "out" is far superior to Duane's macho posturing, and his ability to accept and display his femininity makes him superior to Duane.

This problem of representation finds expression in the stereotypical tropes that have traditionally been associated with black men. However, when these stereotypes are imprinted upon black gay men, they retain their heterosexist templates and further minimize or marginalize black gay men. The Sambo, Coon, and Black Brute are all assumed as heterosexual black bodies. Stereotypical tropes associated with black gay men, however, characterize them as a perverse amalgam of feminine and masculine stereotypes. The black gay man is characterized as cunning, devious, and sexually depraved. His sexual deviance requires that he act in predatory ways upon heterosexual black men. However, since black gay men want to have sex with other men, this requires that they be feminized. This feminization of black gay men also works to trivialize them. While this is not unique to black communities, the racialized dimension of sexual difference leads to characterizations of black gay men as race traitors.[1]

Black gay men enter into African American consciousness in and through AIDS/HIV and through the specter of homophobia. As such, the body of the black gay male is an object to be feared and to be pitied, but, most of all, to be regulated, policed, and controlled. Black liberation and womanist theologies have attempted to take hold of the body of the black homosexual, but have only been able to do so through HIV and homophobia. As I argued in chapter 3, some black gay theologians have attempted to revise God in their approaches to the black gay body, but have left nebulous and inefficacious accounts of God.

The question that forms the basis for this chapter is, "how can we as black religious scholars reconstruct the body of the black gay man?" What resources might be available to black religious scholars endeavoring to push beyond limited, stereotypical constructions of black gay men? Further, given our current obsession with the "down low," how can we construct black gay men's identities beyond it? To answer that question, I return to the black gay club space and E. Patrick Johnson's description of it. The convergence of different types of black gay bodies, sweating, dancing, grinding with each other and by themselves, says something about the myriad ways in which black gay men construct their own identities. However, the black gay club space is quickly giving way to the Internet as a space whereby black gay men meet other men. Further, cyberspace has altered the ways in which black gay men present themselves. I move to this space and examine the ways in which black gay men utilize Internet "hook up" sites such as Manhunt.net and BGCLive in order present themselves to each other and to the world at large. From snapping "queens" to hypermasculine "B-boys," black gay men find alternative ways in which to construct their identities.

Performing Masculinity

A central theory that informs this argument is that black heterosexual men perform their masculinities according to particular scripts. Drawing on those arguments, I argue that black gay men also perform their masculinities according to—and in defiance of—particular scripts. It is that defiance of largely heterosexist scripts that informs drag performance and the creation of forms of dance and speech within black gay communities. While scholars who write concerning black masculine performance and scripting tend to argue that such performances are driven by heterosexism and are problematic, I contend that black gay men's performances may be read as attempts at reconstructive practices that deserve greater examination. Indeed, I read black gay men's performances as significations on black constructions of masculinity. These significations take the form of parody and exaggeration.

Works addressing the construction of black masculinities could be described as a cottage industry in academia. From Phillip Brian Harper, to Michael Eric Dyson to bell hooks, African American cultural critics have produced significant scholarship that has interrogated black masculinity. These studies have often focused on how black heterosexual men have internalized sexist attitudes and reified an exaggerated "machismo." As I noted in a previous chapter, bell hooks attributes a shift in black men's attitudes to the rise of the black power movement and presents an implied argument that, prior to the black power movement, black men did not aggressively construct their masculinities in ways that oppressed women and people with different sexual orientations. Ronald Jackson agrees with hooks as well as a number of other scholars who assert that African American men "have been affected by their own exclusion from the mainstream to the extent that they have constructed their masculinities differently."[2] However, Jackson takes a slightly different approach in his examination of the constructions of black masculine bodies. He argues that black men are not able to "retrieve custody of the meanings associated with blackness and Black males" because American popular media has so thoroughly corrupted black masculinity as a site of "negative inscriptions."[3] Bryant Keith Alexander claims "the black male body is polemical."[4] He argues that the black male body is a site of multiple contestations and "often constrained by…borders that are neither fluid nor flexible."[5] These scholars understand that the bodies of black men in America constitute a problem. Their intellectual projects purport to address this problematic construction of black male bodies.

Alexander's argument is correct. The body of the black man is polemical. As it is presented in popular media and even in African American cultural criticism, the body of black men is usually presented in extremes. The extreme position of the black male in popular media is one of hypermasculinity. The hypermasculine black man is hyper-heterosexual. He asserts his heterosexuality through minimizing or demonizing black women and asserting himself as the epitome of blackness. However, African American cultural critics respond to this extreme position by positing another extreme identity. Black men in African American cultural criticism are positioned as heroic figures. Further, the grotesqueries of black masculinity are merely asserted to be by-products of white supremacy.

As part of an argument about the reconstruction of black gay male identity is an assertion that black men (homo- or heterosexual) perform their sexual identities. Here, I am indebted to Judith Butler's work on performativity. She notes that performativity

> …is not a singular act, but a repetition and a ritual, which achieves its effects through its naturalization in the context of a body understood, in part, as a culturally sustained temporal duration.[6]

Extending this description of performativity to my discussion of black gay male identity, the curious and problematic black gay male body represents a collision of culturally influenced (perhaps even culturally dictated) and sustained representations.

As I argue that black gay men can and do construct their sexualities in a myriad of ways that are not necessarily constrained by homophobia or HIV/AIDS, I also argue that African American men in general construct and perform their genders and sexualities in myriad ways. I contend that there is no such thing as an "authentic" masculine construction. It is all performative. Further, masculine constructions are bricolage—an amalgam of multiple influences. Briefly, we could consider the performances of such putatively heterosexual musical artists such as Prince, Andre 3000 of the group OutKast, or 50 Cent. These artists at times challenge typical constructions of black masculinity. At other times, these artists perform within the confines of heteronormative, heterosexist black male constructions. These black masculine performances are deployed to confront, confound, and subvert white racism; however, they are also deployed in order to reinforce patriarchal positions over and against black women. Like Prince, black masculinities are sometimes deployed in order to play off conventional assertions of black heterosexual masculinity. On the other hand, rap artists such as 50 Cent present a hypermasculine image that conforms to stereotypical presentations of black men as violent, angry, and dangerous.

Black gay male performances are sometimes deployed to confront, confound, and subvert black heterosexist assumptions about black homosexuality; however, these performances may also reify heterosexist and homophobic assertions of gay identity. The point of this chapter is not to present black gay male identity as "heroic" or "salvific." In other words, I am not interested in replicating past projects in African American theological and cultural discourse that describes black folk as "the salt of the earth." There are grotesqueries in African American life that confound such simple presentations. These grotesqueries exist in African American gay communities as well.

The Grotesquery of Black Gay Life

In returning to the black gay club scene, we must find a way to make sense of E. Lynn Harris's somewhat negative portrayals of the club spaces in New York City and E. Patrick Johnson's positive portrayals of the black gay club space. While I criticize Harris for presenting a romanticized, sanitized description of black gay life via Raymond Tyler (his disdain for the black gay club scene immediately creates a dichotomy between "good" black homosexuals versus "bad" black homosexuals), perhaps Harris via Raymond is not totally incorrect. While Johnson sets up the black gay club scene as a space wherein black gay men recover and reaffirm their sexualities and their religious orientations, Harris sees the black gay club space as a space wherein black gay men enact their predatory instincts.

Both Johnson and Harris are right in the assessments of the black gay club space. There are oppositional sensibilities at work in black gay clubs. This is what I would characterize as the grotesquery of the black gay club scene. The religious transgressiveness of the space that Johnson identifies exists at the same time as black gay men seek each other out for sexual encounters. These are unresolved ambiguities that make the black gay club space a unique space in the lives of black gay men.

The task of reconstructing black gay male identities beyond the current fascination and hysteria surrounding the down low requires an embracing of these oppositional sensibilities. Here, I borrow from Victor Anderson's understandings and deployment of the grotesque. He describes his understanding of the grotesque as involving the "unresolved ambiguities" of African American life. These ambiguities are opportunities for interpreters (in this case, African American religious critics) to view these experiences differently. By shifting our focus away from heroic, monolithic narratives, the grotesque in African American life opens black religious scholars up to seeing not only the heroic but the villainous, the comedic and the tragic, the same, and yet different. The opportunity afforded by the grotesque in African American life is one of creativity. This creativity should open religious scholars to deep appreciation of life. However, Anderson argues that the grotesque is often "captured, frozen and domesticated" by traditional discourses on African American religious experience that allow no room for unresolved ambiguities.[7]

In the context of this work, I find Anderson's understanding of the grotesque to be quite fascinating and useful. An argument concerning the reconstruction of black gay men's identities beyond the DL might argue that the down low is the polar opposite of being "out." Further, such an argument might posit being out of the closet as being more desirable than not revealing one's sexual orientation. As an ethicist by training, my own intellectual impulse is to present an argument condemning the down low. However, the concept of the grotesque cautions me against such a rigid argument. I will present a larger argument about the down low in the following chapter, but for now

I will say that the down low functions as part of the construction of black gay men's identities. This book cannot and will not ignore the DL and will not demonize it nor set it up as a binary opposition to being out of the closet. What I think is necessary is close attention to and deeper appreciation of the multiplicity of black gay men's voices.

Attending to the voices of black gay men requires, as I showed in chapters 3 through 5, deep attention to their literary voices. Clearly, this study has not been a complete study of the literary works of black gay men. The purpose of this study has not been to present an exhaustive study of black gay men's writings, but to show how black gay men can and do represent themselves, and to show how such representations can be useful in African American religious thought. In reading such collections as *Black Like Us, The Greatest Taboo* and *Black Queer Studies* (2005), we see that black queer writers have worked to bring black gays and lesbians from the periphery of African American scholarship. As womanist scholars turn to the writings of black women and show convincingly that black women have written themselves into existence, so too do I argue that black gay men have undertaken the task of writing black male homosexuals into existence.

From reading black gay writers, from E. Lynn Harris to James Earl Hardy, to Randal Keenan, we see that black gay life is, like other aspects of human existence, always caught between oppositional sensibilities. Remaining "in the closet" or "on the down low" as opposed to "coming out," being single as opposed to being in a relationship, monogamy versus any other kinds of sexual relationships—these are but a few of the many dichotomies that face black gay men.

The task of reconstructing black gay male identity begins with embracing the queen. Within African American queer communities, there is a perennial tension regarding the presentation of masculinity and femininity. In other words, the anxiety of black masculinity that Phillip Brian Harper notes in black heterosexual communities also exists in African American queer communities. Culturally, we labor under the assumption that heterosexuality and the attendant assertions about masculinity are either correct or the "default" position for African Americans. Further, we labor under the assertion that black men who perform their sexualities differently than the "normal" black heterosexual male are acting abnormally. This abnormal performance—typified by "acting like a woman" or by expressing a sexual desire for other men—engenders an anxiety within black communities.

Black gay men are not exempt from this anxiety and crisis of black masculinity. Such anxiety can be found in perusing male-to-male personal ads on the Internet. I suggest turning to the Internet because there is only so much that relying solely on black gay men's writings can tell us. I am not looking for a "perfect" site from which to cull "definitive" descriptions of black gay men's identities. Instead, I am turning to the Internet as a complementary source, hoping to add to the literary productions that I have examined. I borrow from Dwight McBride's interrogation of the "gay marketplace of desire" that constitutes male-to-male Internet personals. His examination of Internet profiles in *Why I Hate Abercrombie and Fitch: Essays on Race and Sexuality* centered on the ways in which race, racial fetish, and racism function in cyberspace. McBride notes that the Internet has

> Freed us even from the [politically correct] shackles of the gay bar, a place where we no longer even need to patronize some and pretend to others about the often exclusive and predictably hegemonic nature of our desires on the one hand, or about the problematic fetishistic nature of them on the other. For some this might be liberating, a form of ultimate sexual liberation, perhaps. But is that equally so for all of us?[8]

Clearly, McBride approaches the gay marketplace of desire that is the Internet skeptically. He views this marketplace as a site where black gay men conform to white (usually racist) expectations and white males (presumably middle- to upper-middle class) control the discourse of desire.[9] Black gay men are merely commodities or fetishes (like bondage/domination, feet, or spanking) to be consumed at the whim of white gay men.

Sites like Manhunt.net or Gay.com, which cater primarily to white males, tend to confirm McBride's assertions regarding the racially fetishized nature of the Internet. The Internet itself reflects the fragmented and segmented worlds inhabited by gay men of color. The world of Internet chat rooms that McBride argues functions as a fetishistic space controlled by white males reflects the ways in which fetishizing black gay men (as well as other gay men of color) occurs in the "real" world. Gay clubs and bathhouses previously functioned as spaces where race operated as a commodity to be exchanged.[10] Now, the Internet has intervened and transformed the marketplace of desire.

The Internet, with its myriad of chat rooms, personal spaces, and the like, has come close to replacing the black gay club space as a space where black men can meet other black men. Delving into personal ads via the Internet is a challenge. I am not looking at these ads in order to uncover an unalterable, universal "Truth" about black gay men. Given the nature of the Internet, I consider it to be the virtual version of the black gay club scene, layered with the technological advances of the late twentieth century. The black gay club offers the participant a wide range of bodies with which to interact. These bodies are clad (or not clad) in ways that are designed to convey particular messages regarding that person's wealth, physique, and status. However, the black gay club space is not a utopic space, despite the uplifting, transformative, and transgressive interactions of bodies and music. It is a space that houses a constellation of contradictions and contestations. Functioning as a virtual club space, the Internet houses these same contradictions and contestations and, in some ways, magnifies them. The Internet offers the ability to present oneself so that the picture (should one choose to upload a picture) along with the text conveys a message to all who see the profile. The identity of the person with the profile is constructed; the black gay man's Internet profile is now part of the constructed identity.

I turned to the personal advertisements posted on the Web site Manhunt.net, and profiles posted on the Web site BGCLive.com. I narrowed the search to those profiles posted by black men in the cities of Atlanta and Chicago. None of the profiles use the actual names of the users. Often, the profiles are accompanied by at least one picture (the Web site allows users to upload as many as twelve pictures and designate some photos as "private," to be "unlocked" to select viewers at the user's wish). Some of the profiles show faces; however, many do not. I will not correct any typographical errors in the profiles (thanks to the wonders of modern computing, I will "copy" and "paste" the text); what the reader is seeing is the text of the profile as it appears on screen. I will italicize the names of the profiles so that the reader may easily distinguish the profiles. I am not undertaking a complete sociological examination of these profiles. Rather, I want to use these profiles as "snapshots" into how black gay men may be using the Internet as a form of identity construction.

Whitelighter1

Looking for New Friends

African American, Bodybuilder, former Army Officer, Ex-model. Looking for Nice, Professional, Stable, guys to spend time with. Guys not into Clubs and Bars, but prefer Home, Sipping wine and listiening to Music, Dancing, Movies, Travel.

40 I Muscular I Brown / Bald I Top

Checknuout

Are U looking for me?

Masculine, fit, laid back guy 37yrs 6'1 190# looking for other cool guys to chill with. I like dining out, movies, travel, regular stuff. Anything from friends to fuck buds is cool. Sexually into white guys between 35–50. UNLOCK and show me what u workin with. Not into extremely thin skinny body types. LIARS, CRACKHEADS, AND THOSE STANDING WAIST HIGH IN BULLSH*T, STEP!

37 | Athletic | Brown / Black | Top

jump_man06

I want to have carnal knowledge with Dr. Manhattan.

Really don't know what to expect from this site any more. Just looking for chill,

masculine types I can relate to.

Hit me up if you wanna know more.

Sometimes up for CAM

22 | Athletic | Brown / Black | Top/Vers.

Exmilitary2003

Love sex and lies

Millions of men have lived to fight, build palaces and boundaries, shape destinies and societies; but the compelling force of all times has been the force of originality and creation profoundly affecting the roots of human spirit.

Man life is to short to be stupid, not judgmental, but i do like what i like and know what i dont like

get at me and lets see where it goes you never know

Looking for FRIENDS and the last time i checked that was not a code for fuck buddy. lets chill and go from there

PS also looking for a workout partner in the south loop at LA fitness

Sexycubbrutha

Looking around abit....

Laid back and low key. LTR oriented, looking for a laid-back, masculine dude. Tend to get along better with guys that work out or are in shape. RACE DOESN'T MATTER. Me: not much into the gay scene. You: TRULY masculine, vers, a great sense of humor and perhaps more interested in dating/ltr. Later. PLS DON'T UNLOCK YOUR PRIVATE PIX OFF THE BAT B/C I DON'T; LET'S CHAT A MINUTE FIRST.

37 | Muscular | Brown / Shaved | Versatile

WWE1981

Agenda:...

Men with meaty calf muscles and masculine looking hands, definitely say hi =-)

Be emotionally mature, in decent shape, and reasonably intelligent please. Thanks. I can be shy, so say hello =-)

Please note. If you measure your self-worth by the size of your dick, I don't want to know you in any capacity.

27 | Athletic | Brown / Dark Brown | Bottom/Vers.

NorthsideHeadhunter

Go ahead, try it. You just might like it.

I'm looking for regular guys who happen to be gay. NO PNP.

36 | Heavy Set | Brown / Black | Top

The gay marketplace of desire as constructed by these men in these profiles seems to convey a yearning for what Andrew Sullivan might call "virtually normal." Looking for men "who happen to be gay" or are "emotionally mature" signifies a desire for someone who is comfortable with his sexual orientation and does not have significant "emotional baggage." In order to meet such kinds of men, the above profiles appear to take pains to present the seeker as also comfortable with his sexuality.

However, these profiles also might betray a desire to sanitize, or "heterosexualize," gay identity. Sexycubbrutha's profile makes a point of presenting a desire for a "TRULY masculine" man. In other words, Sexycubbrutha's venture into this gay marketplace of desire seeks an authentically masculine person, which also acknowledges the ephemeral nature of Internet profiles. All of the above profiles tacitly acknowledge the problematic nature of meeting other black men (or, in many of these cases, men of other races) via the Internet. Simply, the profiles that appear on the Internet are advertisements, and the phrase "caveat emptor" applies. The profiles I have noted above profess a desire for black men who are not bound by one particular narrative of sexual difference. However, these desires are also oriented toward one particular narrative of masculinity. Effeminate black men need not apply, unless they are also searching for a masculine black man.

The above profiles were collected from Manhunt.net. As a dear friend and colleague noted when I asked him which sites were most popular among black gay men, Manhunt.net might cater to a particular demographic, while BGCLive (which he characterized as being "number two" in popularity among black gay men, with Adam4Adam. com being number one in his estimation) would cater to a different demographic. The Web site is far more explicit concerning its serving a niche audience. From the Web site homepage, BGCLive describes itself in this way:

> BGCLive.com is the largest gay/bi/trans social network where members communicate with Black and Latino Brothas/Sistas. BGC welcomes all members of the LGB&T community, including the Black Brothas/Sistas, Our Latino Brothas/Sistas, Our White Cousins and Our Far East Coast Cousins from China and India, we are all One Big Family. Anyone who thinks otherwise does not belong here.[11]

BGCLive is clearly a different Web site than Manhunt, even though both Web sites exist primarily to facilitate men "hooking up" with other men for sexual encounters. Whereas Manhunt does not explicitly state that it caters largely to white men, BGCLive makes it clear that its function is to service queer communities of color. The language of the profiles is markedly different. Indeed, the general "feel" of BGCLive is quite different than Manhunt.net. The site presents clear racial boundaries, characterized in familial language. Although the site claims that homosexuals comprise "One Big Family," it is clear that African Americans and Latinos occupy a different familial space than do whites and Asians. Manhunt.net's racial constituency is denoted largely by the images of bodies that greet people who log in to the site. The site always has a picture of a well-built man with no shirt on. Usually, the man is a white man; occasionally, the man greeting site visitors is African American. However, I have noted that there is variety in the white males presented on the site's homepage, while there is only one African American man who occasionally appears on the homepage.

BGCLive further distinguishes itself from Manhunt.net as an Internet community through the use of language. The Web site itself utilizes common vernacular in order to present itself as a site devoted primarily to African American and Latino gays. The spelling of the terms "brothers" and "sisters" as "brothas" and "sistas" is a clear signifier, informing visitors that this site is geared toward African Americans. As I examined a few of the over two thousand profiles in the Atlanta area, I noted that many of them eschewed formal English in favor of slang and vernacular. The reading that I bring to this difference is that these profiles written in slang and vernacular connote a desire to present oneself as "real" or "authentic." BGCLive offers many more options to describe oneself than does Manhunt.net. In other words, the profiles below have more "categories" that can be filled out than does Manhunt.net. In the interest of conserving space, I have deleted much of the descriptive data and concentrated on the statements that the users make in the "Who I Am" portion of the profile.

sxympr

Age: 28

I am looking for a cool, mature, sexy, muscular, masculine, spiritual Black man to get to know and see what happens.

I am a cool laid back good hearted guy. I enjoy movies working-out going to sporting events, church and just hanging out with a good person. I am a very spiritual person I attend church regularly I don't drink, smoke, club or do any kind of drugs, not into the gay scene more of a homebody.

lookin_4_more

Age: 31

A hubby material type guy. A man who knows what he wants, and has no issues expressing it, and going after it. A man who means what he says, and says what he means. I can't stand dudes who paint these pictures of who they are, and in reality they are nothing like they described. What's the reason in lying, as if in time the truth won't come out about you. I am using this as an outlet to meet someone, however that does not mean that I cannot get off here, once I meet someone cool. If this, or any other site is your favorite past time, we will not get along so hitting me up will be a waste of both our time. I am into guy's who are about my height, maybe a little taller than me. Dudes who have a thick, or medium build, not the new fat! Solid built guy's only. No uncut, bottom, fem, or old dudes. Also not into guy's who smoke cigs, or do drugs. If you are emotionally, or mentally unavailable. Do not hit me up. If you hit me up, your pics need to be unlocked, as mine will be if I hit you. I can't stand liars, and in my last sitaution I allowed myself to overlook a lot of shit, because I wanted to believe that he was the man he so convincingly said he was. No bullshit ass niggas!

I am not looking for sex, and will not respond to those type of hits. Nor will I respond to ads that are geared towards that. I am not interested in seeing anyone's dick or ass. I am intrested in your heart, and your mind. I am very str8 forward, and I don't cut corners or bite my tounge. I believe in treating people how I want to be treated, and not

doing anything to someone I don't want done to me. Many people claim
to have morales, but very seldom do they exercise who they say they
are. I am not looking to trick, or mislead anyone, and I won't tolerate
it being done to me. Lastly I am not a internet junky, If I meet someone
cool, I can leave this shit ALONE! If you cannot say the same, I don't
expect to hear from you. I don't compete with internet chat sites!

mrc

Age: 37

Like having fun with the one I'm with. So I'm open for more than
the NORM....can you say and use the word (Partner) Brotha here
ready for that one on one connections/relationship. Yeah Really Kinda
Hombody type guy here, but when I hang out I like to enjoy myself
with movies, plays, running, sightseeing, traveling a bit when I can,
visiting family and friends, usually do things by myself, I'm a very easy
going guy I can't be around drama really I can't and shy away from it
at all times, I am a great listener so they say. Well don't be afraid to ask
me any question.

These profiles are not dissimilar from the ones presented on Manhunt.
net. Indeed, the ones presented on BGCLive have a commonality with
the ones on Manhunt.net in that these black gay men are clear about
desiring a "masculine" man. Phillip Brian Harper's concern about
masculine anxiety in African American life seems crystallized in the
form of these Internet profiles. The masculine ideal is accentuated by
a preoccupation with physical characteristics. In many of the profiles
I reviewed, the text was accompanied by pictures of naked, muscular
torsos. In some cases, the profile described the user as muscular, but
the accompanying picture does not correspond to the description.

The physical representation of the masculine ideal is accompanied by presentations of affective representations. In other words, it
is not enough to "look" masculine (i.e., be in possession of a muscular body); the desired black man must "act" masculine. As many
of the profiles I examined expressed a desire for a man who was
either "drama-free" or "low key," I assert that the construction of
masculinity as presented in these profiles is coded via these terms.
The opposite—to be "full of drama" or to not be low key—is to be
feminine, and thus, not the object of desire. This assertion flies in
the face of BGCLive's own apparent commitment to openness to different forms of sexuality among black gays. The site clearly makes
space for transgendered people in the form of asking if the user has
any interest in transgendered folk. Of course, such a question singles

transgendered people out and makes them an outcast subject within queer communities. That is a problem in both African American and white queer communities that requires far more attention than I am able to provide in this study.

In examining these profiles, I am not saying that these need be instructive in constructing black gay men's identities beyond the DL. Indeed, some of these profiles seem to be constrained by the notion of the DL and also by HIV/AIDS. Further, it might appear futile to examine male-to-male profiles, as one might find nothing theologically useful in them. However, I think that these profiles are useful in that they point to the all-too-human activity of self- and community construction. To which communities are these profiles written? Do the photos included say anything about the men, other than what we might consider to be "obvious"?

I infer that Manhunt.net caters to a different clientele than does BGCLive. Excluding a targeted search such as the one that comprised the data in this chapter, the profiles featured on Manhunt.net are predominantly those of white men seeking other white men. At first glance, the profiles on Manhunt.net indicate that the men who utilize this site might consider themselves to be middle class. The clientele of BGCLive is predominantly African American. While such an assertion is not clearly stated by the Web site, there are clear indicators that white males are not the target audience. Class distinctions are also evident on BGCLive, as many of the profiles I found endeavor to show that the person in question is educated, has a job, and is self-sufficient.

The Internet provides compelling examples of the performance of black gay masculinities. There are those who embrace their alternative constructions of black gay male identity; some revel in their difference, while others attempt to "mainstream" their sexual orientation. These profiles tell stories. Some of these profiles tell larger stories than others. This can reflect how "users" (a term that denotes computer users) view their participation in Internet sites devoted to meeting other men. Clearly, some users view their profiles in a minimalist fashion—a picture, "stats" that give the basics, and possibly a line or two about what they're "looking for" may be sufficient. However, I have focused on the profiles that provide a bit more. The Internet provides us with windows into the ongoing process of constructing black gay male identities beyond the current hype and hysteria surrounding the down low.

Conclusion

It is my argument that reconstructing black gay male identity requires something more than a mere recognition that black gay men are diverse. What is helpful and necessary for reconstructing black gay male identity is a deep appreciation of difference. Given my previous discussion concerning the preoccupation with body image, I think it is necessary to argue that reconstructing black gay male identity beyond the down low also requires moving beyond societal pressures to conform to rigid constructions of masculinity. Part of the "problem" of the down low is its linkage to a hegemonic discourse surrounding masculinity and the construction of gay bodies. A "gay" (and thus, non-masculine) body is alleged to be easily recognizable, in that the gay man is supposed to adopt feminine characteristics. A "masculine" or "down low" man is one who eschews feminine characteristics. Indeed, the body itself becomes a site wherein the "down low" or the "masculine" man is realized. By spending hours in the gym, and eventually developing the ideal masculine body, black gay men can also avoid the stigma of being feminine.

Reconstructing black gay men's identities requires moving beyond such rigid formulations. Such moves require the engagement of minds that are willing to imagine black gay lives beyond typically narrow and unhelpful constructions of sexuality. It is interesting that a Web site like BGCLive appears to attempt a move beyond inflexible articulations of black gay identity. However, with the advent of the Internet in general and chat/dating/hookup Web sites as well as individual weblogs ("blogs") in particular, black gay men are capable of re-presenting black gay identities beyond straitjacketed formulations of black homosexuality. As I read blogs like Rod 2.0 and defunct blogs like Old Gold Soul, I see a concerted effort—primarily by younger black gay men—to move past the heteronormative configurations of black homosexuality and toward configurations that celebrate the diversity within African American life.

Conclusion: Toward an Ethics of Openness

Introduction

The previous chapters of this book have been an attempt to address a deficiency within African American religious and cultural discourse and to highlight the efficacy of using black queer literature as a mirror that reflects the experiences of African American gays and lesbians. Looking into the mirror of diverse black experiences, we see more than just our individual selves. We see more than the problems of HIV/AIDS and homophobia. While we may see these moments as problematic, the task is then to correct these problems. Continuing with the metaphor of the mirror, we see these moments as imperfections in the black body politic and work to resolve those problems. While we work to correct problems, we do not reify those problems as being constitutive of the body. Further, we do not focus on the object in the mirror to the exclusion of all other possibilities. These possibilities and realities are not always flattering. Mirrors do not often show us what we want to see. Instead, mirrors offer us the opportunity for self-reflection, examination, and correction.

In preparing to write this book, I had often been asked, "What is your constructive move?" In other words, in the context of this book the question is, "What has the previous chapters led us to?" What does the mirror of black gay men's literature reflect and how do we go about fixing what we see? In other terms, what do the previous chapters mean for theological and ethical reflections on African American life?

What this work suggests is an ethics of openness. In looking at and critically evaluating black gay men's literature not as perfect, complete representations in and of themselves, but as mirrors reflecting the diversity of black experiences, it has been my task to argue that difference is constitutive of human experience. By focusing on the particular experiences of black gay men in and through their literary productions, we see black communities differently. This text has been and is an invitation to see African American life differently.

In seeing African American life differently through an ethics of openness, I am suggesting that black liberation theology no longer provides sufficient responses or theological resources in understanding African American life. As I posited in chapter 2, black liberation theology presents strong readings of race, class, and gender, but falls quite short when discussing other areas of African American life. This book has been an exploration of black liberation theology and African American cultural criticism's failure to address one particular area of African American life. I have argued that what accounts for that failure is a particularly narrow view of both African American life and experience as well as a particularly narrow view of theology and ethics.

When theology and ethics are offered as a remedy for totalitarian or oppressive conditions and situations, it must be made clear that the particular theology and ethics is itself predicated upon those totalitarian or oppressive conditions. In other words, there is no theology or ethics that remains static, unchanging, and unalterable. However, the theologians I have examined in this work have construed black life in the United States (and indeed, globally) to be a life fraught with unending oppression. Thus, any other area of African American life is then thrust into this matrix of racial oppression. Other forms of difference in African American life are strip-mined to be used as rhetorical resources in the continuing fight against white supremacy. Thus, sexuality in general and homosexuality in particular are colored by essentialized readings of race. Interestingly enough, God and theology seem to drop out of the discussion altogether in favor of tepid protestations against homophobia, a phenomenon that itself gets read in terms of racial oppression. If I read Kelly Brown Douglas and bell hooks correctly, homophobia would or could not exist within black communities without white supremacy.

Such a fallacious argument only serves to prove Victor Anderson's assertion that black liberation theology's presentation of the binary polarities of race "admit(s) no possibility of transcendence or mediation."[1] If black liberation and womanist theologians link homophobia and other antigay discourses to white supremacy and yet cannot imagine black life beyond white supremacist oppression, then it does not appear that, by extension, homophobia can ever be eliminated.

By extension, liberation from white supremacist oppression (and, by inference, homophobia) does not appear possible. Further, as I mentioned before in chapter 2, the linking of homophobia with white supremacy allows black liberation and womanist theologians to neatly elide black gay experiences in favor of self-congratulatory discourse on the evils of homophobia while retaining black audiences. By blaming homophobia on white supremacy, the black "folk" who perpetuate antigay rhetoric and discourse can now say: "It is not my fault; my homophobia is the result of my indoctrination into American life by whiteness." In the final analysis then, homophobia and other antigay discourses are not taken up seriously and are relegated as secondary or tertiary "issues" in African American life. Further, black liberation and womanist theologies do not appear to be able to say anything substantive concerning the relationship between God and oppressed humans other than to say that God stands in solidarity with the oppressed. While this book does not seek to engage in a detailed analysis of the existence of God and the problem of evil and suffering, I contend that there may be another path open to us, one that allows for far greater diversity in African American lives without necessarily appealing to a deity as the source for that allowance.

As I noted in chapter 4, black queer writers do not present a systematic theology that can be appropriated in defense of homosexuality. Indeed, as I have shown, some writers attempt to reconcile their sexual orientations with traditional African American Christian structures, while some critique those structures as being oppressive, non-liberating, and, thus, an impediment to the flourishing of African American gays and lesbians. However, black liberation and womanist theologies have substantively little to offer black queers other than a rhetoric of mere tolerance. My suspicion concerning black liberation and womanist theology's failure to consider in depth the experiences of black queers is that these theologians have not been able to consistently or stringently critique black notions of God.

Conversely, black queer religious scholars such as Victor Anderson and Horace Griffin have sought alternative avenues for addressing sexual difference in black communities. These religious scholars do focus on human potentialities as well as human shortcomings. They point to the successes as well as the failures of black religious communities regarding sexual difference. Further, they argue convincingly for these communities to change the ways in which they speak to and about black gays and lesbians. While Anderson and Griffin respectively pursue either pragmatic or pastoral theological approaches, these approaches remain firmly rooted in conceptions of God that would or could be amenable or commensurate with African American churches.

As Anthony Pinn points out, black liberation and womanist theologies have been concerned with describing human (in this case, black) experiences in light of divine revelation and existence. What Pinn calls "traditional black theology" and what Frederick Ware calls the hermeneutical school of black theology presupposes the existence of God and the breaking in of God in human affairs. Indeed, many of the black gay writers I have highlighted also presuppose the existence of a Christian God who stands on the side of the oppressed and downtrodden. However, I wish to emphasize that these writers also focus on human activity, human shortcomings, and human possibilities.

Black churches and other institutions that fail to affirm black gay and lesbians, while doing so out of a peculiar notion of divine command, nonetheless are institutions comprised of human beings acting upon other human beings. Black theologies that fail to take seriously queer experiences as part of the spectrum of black experiences are written and promoted by human beings to other human beings. In other words, the black theological enterprise is, at its root, a human endeavor designed to provide for other human beings descriptive frameworks for understanding the world in which we as human beings exist and those human-constructed frameworks will likely be deficient in some way. As an ethicist and scholar of African American religious traditions, history, and culture, I am concerned primarily with commenting on those human endeavors.

I agree with Pinn when he says "there is nothing behind the symbol God and, furthermore, this symbol is inadequate in light of African American history and current needs."[2] Those current needs to which Pinn refers include a need in African American communities to move beyond our current understandings (and misunderstandings) of sexual difference. For black gays and lesbians, current needs may be construed as an emancipation from narratives that place them at the epicenter of crisis and contamination. Despite moves from groups within black queer communities that have attempted to reimagine and reconceptualize God as a being of love who loves all its creation, I think that those moves have not been sufficient. Certainly, they have not been adequate to the task of subverting or overcoming antigay rhetoric within other black churches. Indeed, owing to a view that God is the arbiter of morality, and the effective case of existence, some black churches would not even countenance a discussion of God as either merely the world or as a being who loves those who have, in their view, violated the natural order. Conservative African American Christians will continue to view homosexuality as a "sin" rooted in choice. Arguments about homosexuality being natural and part of a divine creation are not likely to sway those who believe in a God who created a heteronormative social order.

The Contours of an Ethics of Openness

As this book has been primarily concerned with the representations of black gays and lesbians in African American theological and cultural discourses, I contend that a constructive ethical move for black intellectuals begins with a move away from traditional and rigid theological formulations and toward more expansive descriptions and critiques of human activity in the world. As I have noted before, an ethics of openness goes beyond mere tolerance and involves a deep appreciation for difference in human life and activity. Note that I have not given to this ethics of openness a racial or sexual characterization, even though I am using sexual orientation in African American life as an example of the usefulness of such an ethics. Further, I have not given this ethics a theistic orientation. When this book was a dissertation project, I began thinking of a theological ethics of openness, predicated upon a pragmatic naturalist reading of God. Based upon my reading of Jerome Stone's *The Minimalist Vision of Transcendence* and Robert S. Corrington's *Nature and Spirit*, I had attempted to graft onto black liberation and womanist theologies a re-presentation of God as simply being the world and the patterns and processes contained therein. However, the problem with such an attempt is that it results in a distortion of the God-symbol such that it would hardly fit within the theological formulations presented by black and womanist theologians.

Further, the problem with such a theological description is one of reductivism. If God can be described as I mentioned above, then what is the usefulness of the God-symbol? Are we not then simply talking about the world as we perceive and understand it? To describe God as God-as-World to me seems unnecessary. If religious scholars are talking about the world, then let us be clear: we are talking about the world and that which happens within it. We are talking about human activity, endeavors, hopes, wishes, fears, dreams, and the like. What I take from pragmatic naturalism and what I find central to black liberationist thought is the primacy of human action. Thus, I locate my ethics of openness in human activity without an appeal to divinity.

Of course, this begs a question. What, then, is particularly religious about this work? If an ethics of openness is predicated on a deep appreciation of human life, worth, and activity, then what is the scholar or reader of religion to take away from this work? I propose three areas in which a humanist ethics of openness can be considered to be a religious ethics.

First, an ethics of openness draws on both the philosophical and religious understandings of ethics as primarily a human endeavor. Ethics is human reflection on moral choices within the realms of human conduct. Further, ethical reflection as an intellectual discipline focuses on theorizing about the causes, means, and ends of ethics. At the end of the day, religious scholars are concerned primarily with human endeavors and strivings.

Second, I suggest that an ethics of openness that relies on a deep appreciation of human worth, value, and action is religious in that it draws on those categories of human experience that humans hold sacred and of deep and abiding value and meaning. Again, I draw on Anthony Pinn's work in establishing African American humanism as a form of religious thought. As he points out, religion is a "general quest for complex subjectivity...a recovery from...absurdity and the finding of one's full value and meaning."[3] Such a broadly conceived view of religion allows for black religious scholars to consider humanism alongside theistic religious expressions.

Third, an ethics of openness may be considered a religious ethics as it is centered on the human being and human flourishing as a matter of ultimate concern. However, this concern is not utterly narcissistic, as it acknowledges that there have been moments in which humans have failed to take into consideration the well-being of the world in which we abide. However, this ethics of openness is not based upon a narrow reading of human flourishing. Rather, this ethics is based upon an awareness that for all humans to flourish, the world that surrounds us and sustains us must flourish as well.

Thus, an ethics of openness that draws on human activity, possibilities, and flourishing is a positive ethics. That is to say, this is an ethics that is not preoccupied with proscribing behavior, but, instead, is concerned with positive commendations. Nor is this ethics of openness concerned with condemning any particular culture (however conceived) as "oppressive." One of the problems with black liberation theology and contemporary African American cultural criticism is that both of these discourses have been presented as reactions against white supremacy. As long as these cultural and religious discourses have white supremacy to react against, they will always posit African American life in all its diversity as existing in spite of white supremacy. However, I contend that the task of religious and cultural criticism is to point humankind toward some positive ends. As a positive ethics, an ethics of openness is concerned with the question, "What makes for human happiness and fulfillment?" I reformulate the question in light of African American queer experience: "What makes for happiness and fulfillment for black gays and lesbians?"

Victor Anderson provides a partial response in his essay, "The Black Church and the Curious Body of the Black Homosexual." He says, "I do not require [the Black Church] to be an advocate of our sexual freedom. I only ask that it not hate us when we advocate for ourselves sexual liberty. I want it to be a refuge for us as it is for all its other members."[4] Anderson here is asking that the traditional black church not be a roadblock (or, should I say, a stumbling block) placed in the way of African American gays' and lesbians' quest for human fulfillment in the form of healthy actualization of their sexualities. He asks that the black church not to use interpretations (and misinterpretations) of biblical texts as well as racial reasoning in order to condemn gays and lesbians outright. Here, Anderson trades upon an assertion that the black church has historically been a "refuge" for black peoples. Further, he trades upon an assumption that the majority of black gays and lesbians, like their heterosexual counterparts, desire to retain some affiliation with the traditional black church and, further, seek to make the black church a refuge for them as well.

What makes for fulfillment for Anderson is the freedom to pursue sexual liberty without interference from religious authorities and institutions. Further, part of human fulfillment for Anderson is the ability to seek refuge in other human institutions without barrier or impediment. I want to go further than Anderson does in that essay and explicitly state that an ethics of openness is not to be found in a "liberation theology," for an ethics predicated upon a concept of liberation requires both oppression and a liberating agent in order to exist. As with black liberation theology, white supremacy and God-as-liberator are necessary for there to be a liberation theology. Thus, as I noted at length in previous chapters, other forms of difference within African American communities become assimilated into the framework or logic of black liberation theology.

Fulfillment and flourishing for African American homosexuals cannot be found in an atomized theology that promises liberation, yet requires continued oppression and narrow constructions of oppressed identity in order to perpetuate itself. Simply put, an attempt to construct a "black gay liberation theology" along the lines of black liberation and womanist theologies would be an intellectual folly, as such a liberation theology would require the Christian God to somehow elect black homosexuals as chosen. However, for this God to show African American gays and lesbians favor, they would have to be continually oppressed. Also, a black gay liberation theology would have to construe black gay identity as monolithic and caught in a titanic struggle against both racist whites and homophobic blacks without possibility of transcendence.

Human fulfillment and flourishing is to be found in the recognition and appreciation of human difference. A criticism of this approach would likely take the form of a moralist question: "What then, is the standard, or the norm of your ethics, if it is not an appeal to a divine entity?" Again, I find Anthony Pinn and Victor Anderson helpful here. While they might approach this question from different perspectives (Pinn as a humanist and Anderson as a pragmatic naturalist who maintains a belief in a god), they both agree that it is the black body that is the site of both flourishing and declining. Both want black theology to broaden its scope and maintain an explicit affirmation of human diversity.

However, as I read Anderson, I find a question important to pose: what of black folks (including gays and lesbians) who do not wish to retain an affiliation with the black church? What of those who, after having come to terms with their sexual orientation, find that not even a black Christian theology that holds liberation as its central concern is sufficient? While a turn to black gay bodies and their quests for fulfillment is essential to our understandings of sexuality in African American life, to locate those bodies and their quests solely within the framework of black Christian experience and expression begs a question: must black homosexuals be Christian?

Implications for Black Liberation and Womanist Theologies

As I have pointed out, one of the problems with black liberation theology in relation to descriptions and discussions of African American life in general and black gays and lesbians in particular is that this theology is rooted to rigid (yet nebulous) descriptions of God as well as rigid descriptions of black life. Also, I have attempted to present an ethics of openness that moves beyond limited presentations of black gays. As I have articulated this ethics, it poses challenges to black liberation and womanist theologies. I will first list the challenges posed to this theological discourse and then elaborate on the implications of those questions.

First, an ethics of openness that is not predicated upon a rigid (or necessary) description of God calls into question the efficacy of black theology's insistence upon particular readings, interpretations, and presentations of God, especially in light of African American experiences. In some sense, this is a tangential response to the question put forward by one of Kelly Brown Douglas's students when she asked her how could a black woman remain Christian, especially in light of the ways in which the black church has contributed to the oppression of African American women. Douglas's initial response is telling, so I will quote her at length:

> I replied that I am a Christian because my grandmothers were, and it was their Christian faith that helped them to survive the harsh realities of what it meant to be poor black women in America. I went on to tell Gabrielle that my grandmothers were Christian because their mothers and grandmothers were Christian. Indeed, it was a Christian faith that allowed their mothers and grandmothers to survive the brutality of the slavery into which they were born. I am Christian, I elaborated, because it was the God of Jesus Christ that my enslaved forebears witnessed to. It was this God about whom they testified as being with them in their suffering, providing for them in their need, affirming their humanity, and eventually setting them free. I am Christian because my grandmothers, who knew not the slavery of their mothers and grandmothers, were certain that it was the God of Jesus Christ who had "brought them a mighty long way" into freedom.[5]

As Douglas later points out, Gabrielle did not find the response sufficient. Further, the dialogue with the student led to the book, *What's Faith Got To Do With It?* and Douglas's attempt to "assess theologically the feasibility of the black Christian tradition."[6] Douglas, like other black liberation and womanist theologians, begins with the intersection of Christianity and African diasporic experiences in an effort to make sense of black Christianity. However, Douglas replicates the primary conceptual problem of the primacy of Christianity (and, by extension, the primacy of a Christian God) in black liberation theology. I contend that Douglas may have missed one of the underlying points of her interlocutor's objection to Christianity. That is to say, not all African Americans retain a loyalty to the black church, or to a particular conception of God. Further, given a history of oppression based partially upon constructions of "God" as a supreme being responsible for creating humanity (and showing favoritism to select groups of its creation), Douglas's interlocutor might have been challenging the very theistic assumptions upon which a black or womanist theology rests. As I conceive of a humanist ethics of openness, human flourishing does not require a rejection of a god, nor is it dependent upon one.

A second challenge is the challenge of future directions in theological discourse. What is this "liberation" in black liberation theology? An ethics of openness that seeks deeper appreciation of difference might not be concerned with liberation—at least, not liberation as presented by black liberation theology. This ethics is more concerned with providing resources for people to think critically about what constitutes fulfillment in this life. Black and womanist theologians perhaps need to begin rethinking their theological approaches to African American life in general. As I engage younger and younger African American students, most of whom have never known de facto or de jure segregation, and as many of them read the traditional and classical black liberationist texts, I find that they are less concerned with concepts of "liberation" and are more concerned with finding ways to achieve success and security in this world. They are more concerned with taking hold of those goods that we in the United States believe to be common to all humankind. An ethics of openness rooted in a humanist reading of black queer lives does not focus on the notion of liberation, but focuses on human flourishing and human fulfillment. Both flourishing and fulfillment rest with human beings working actively against totalitarian discourses and emphasizing the possibilities of human experience. Borrowing from Pinn, the locus of an ethics of openness is the human body. In the case of this study, the locus of an ethics of openness is the black queer body.

Third, an ethics of openness moves the subject from the periphery and displaces the heteronormative, stereotypical gaze upon the black queer body. It is the heteronormative gaze by heterosexuals toward homosexuals that allows for the development and deployment of narrow discourses concerning homosexuals. The heteronormative gaze is, to borrow from Foucault, a form of panopticon.

In this sexual panopticon, it is the black heterosexual who stands in the guard tower and polices the various sexualities in African American life, lest they become unruly and threaten the integrity of a constructed and performed "blackness."

*   *   *

The goal of this book has been to explore black liberation theology and African American cultural criticisms' descriptions of black queer experience. This book has addressed what I perceive to be a problem within these critical discourses, namely, the marginalization of black queer experience and the syndication of black queer experiences into larger racial concerns. I have asked where, when, and how does homosexuality in black life appear in black liberation theology and African American cultural criticism, and have found that homosexuality appears in and through homophobia and plague. By presenting black queer experience and identities as subject to the vicissitudes of homophobia and the HIV/AIDS crisis, black theologians and cultural critics facilitate a discussion about black queers that does not actually attend to the particulars of black queer experience. To be sure, black queers do experience the alienating effects of homophobic discourse and the fear surrounding HIV/AIDS and they attend to homophobia and fear of plague in black communities in their writings, but black queer writers also concern themselves with the representations of black queer experience and identity.

I characterize such descriptions of black queer life by black liberation theologians and African American cultural critics as problem and plague. The problem of homophobia in black communities somehow leads black queers to engage in destructive lifestyles (such as the DL), and, in turn, leads to the spread of plague in otherwise "normal" black heterosexual communities. As I read black liberation theologians' and African American cultural critics' discussions of black sexual difference as a problem that fosters the spread of plague, I cannot find much hope for black queers. It appears as if the only hope available to black queers is to have "tolerant" black heterosexuals "embrace" their wayward "gayness." However, such a tolerant embrace is vulgarly pragmatic, since African American cultural critics and black theologians argue that failure to tolerate homosexuals in black communities and in the black church is derived from white supremacist notions concerning black sexuality. Thus, if black heterosexuals do not want to be perceived as negatively as those who perpetuate white supremacy, then, according to black theologians such as Kelly Brown Douglas and cultural critics such as bell hooks and Michael Eric Dyson, black heterosexuals would do well to eschew homophobia.

However, I have argued that black theologians and African American cultural critics should pay greater attention to the black queer subject. As black liberation theologians and African American cultural critics argue that difference in America matters, I contend that speaking about black sexual difference requires adequate attention to the subject. To that end, I turned to black queer literature. My examination of black queer literature was guided by several questions. First, what are black queers saying about themselves? How are they constructing their identities as black, as queer? Further, how do black queers attend to their religious experiences? My reading of black queer literature in chapters 3 and 4 argues that black queer writers seek to not only write themselves into black experience, but also to describe their experiences and revise critical approaches to sexual difference in black life and black religion. These literatures call attention to what Victor Anderson calls the "curious body of the black homosexual." When Anderson speaks of this curious body, he echoes the literary works of the writers invoked in chapters 3 and 4. I quote him at length:

> Looking at social and cultural reality, if we get past stereotyping the poor sissy choir director and organist or the butch-dyke truck driver, we Black queers and lesbians are the Black Church's fathers and mothers, its sisters and brothers, uncles, aunts and cousins. In the Black community, we nurture Black youth as their teachers from pre-school till college. We are Sunday school teachers and preachers, deacons, ushers, and trustees, not just church musicians and choir directors. We also not only play the worship instruments, we also write the hymns and songs that feed Black heterosexual members' souls Sunday after Sunday and throughout the week, even in the darkest hours of their despairs. Seen from social and cultural reality, the Black homosexual's bodily presence both in the Black community and church calls into question the very idea of a "homosexual lifestyle." In both the church and the Black community, the everyday, ordinary existence of Black queers and lesbians at work and play, in family life and in the pews, fosters and nourishes forms of generative care and creativity that keep Black culture and the Black Church themselves open to novelty and creativity.[7]

Anderson's statement that black queer people are present and visible in the life of the black church calls to mind Essex Hemphill's statement in his short essay "Does Your Mama Know About Me?" that "our communities are waiting for us," and again in his poem "Commitments" when he states that "I will always be there."[8] The problem of visibility in the black church, in black life, and in black religious criticism has not been the absence of black homosexuals. Rather, the problem has been how black heterosexuals speak about black queer presence. By evoking a previous generation of black queer writers, Anderson signifies on black religious criticism's tendency to reduce black queer presence to a problem that needs to be corrected. Anderson and other black queer writers are asking the same question that serves as the organizing question of this book, namely, when and where does the black homosexual enter into black religious criticism?

I argue that the black homosexual enters into black religious criticism in and through black queer literature. Through fiction, poetry, and critical essays, black queer writers write black queer experience into existence, foreground sexual difference, and offer possibilities for transcending fixed representations of black sexuality. The writings of black queer men and the characters, situations, and metaphors contained therein not only speak to these possibilities, they represent black queer people speaking for themselves, rather than being spoken for. The task of the black queer religious critic as represented by these literatures is not to present an idealized, heroic black homosexual. Rather, by speaking the unspeakable (to borrow from Toni Morrison), by illuminating those areas of black life that are not wholly positive but also not wholly negative, and by presenting visions of difference and appreciation, black queer writers as religious critics enliven theological and ethical discourse beyond mere suppositions of a mythical "tolerant" black America. They enliven and enrich theological and ethical discourse by calling into question assumptions about what it means to be human and in relationship with God. As womanist scholars have done, I contend that black queer writers step beyond the physical confines of the black church in constructing black queer religious discourse.

Although Randall Kenan's Horace Cross may be read as a tragic figure, I believe that Horace may also be read as a figure that is a critic of a society that renders him invisible. While his suicide takes him from this mortal coil, he finally acquires the visibility that had been denied him. As a signification on the passion narrative in the synoptic gospels, Horace's final hours, his final battle with the world around him before his suicide is a call for a revision of the ways in which black people take hold of sexual difference. All the markers of difference that make Horace stand out in his community also call into question the assumptions black folk make about black identity. However, while Horace was alive, it was easier for his community to dismiss his difference, his queerness. However, his sacrificial suicide does not serve solely as a moment of finitude for black people in Tims Creek. Despite his failure to transform himself into an animal, he does succeed in transforming not only himself but his community as well. Horace does fulfill his purpose, albeit in ways that his community has not been prepared to accept. His suicide shows the black community that mere tolerance does not lead to cultural fulfillment for black queers.[9]

While this book has been focused on using black queer men's literature as a source for theological and cultural reflection on the lives of black queer people, I do not wish to privilege such cultural productions over and against other forms of black queer cultural expression. For example, the statement that "black men loving black men is the revolutionary act" evokes Sylvester's song "You Make Me Feel (Mighty Real)" in which the late singer sings of how another man makes him feel. He sings of a passion that is typically invoked only in pop or rhythm and blues songs that are oriented toward heterosexual relationships. This song emphasizes a relationship that is not only balanced and mutual, but is also visible. In extolling the qualities of his lover, Sylvester foregrounds something that appears to recede into the background in black religious criticisms' discussions of black sexual difference. He foregrounds the intersubjective relationships between black queer men, instead of focusing on the objectifying gaze of homophobia. What Riggs and Sylvester do in and through their respective statements is expand our appreciation of homosexual relationships. In his essay "Constructing a Doctrine for the Ecclesia *Militans*," Michael Joseph Brown argues for the importance of revising black religious criticism in order to facilitate an appreciation of African American sexual relationships. He states:

> As a complement to the rather disconnected notion of agape, the intensity that characterizes most understandings of eros balances and humanizes the Christian appreciation for, and appropriation of, love. *For example, the idea of sex as an expression of generosity rarely arises in African American religious discourse. As a consequence, predatory or mercenary orientations dominate popular African American discourse on sex.* Love, as a balanced transcendent experience that encompasses sex, is frequently diminished to a relationship that functions primarily as an exchange for sexual and material goods (e.g., the song "Bills, bills, bills" by Destiny's Child). Eros, if deeply appreciated,

can expand and complexify the representation of human relationships in African American culture.[10] (emphasis mine)

To extend Brown's critique to discussions and debates surrounding homosexuality in African American life, it is as though we cannot imagine black gays in general and black gay men in particular as anything other than a subgrouping of problematic people who negatively challenge dominant narratives about black life. While I understand that African American religious discourses seek to highlight and address crises in black life in America, I am concerned that when discussing black queers, black religious critics have presented them as a problem to be fixed. If we as black religious scholars and if we as members of African American communities cannot imagine black life differently, and if we cannot view African Americans as individuals who may and do possess different commitments and different sexual orientations, we will forever be stuck within narratives of crisis and contamination, problem and plague.

The current debates surrounding gay marriage, along with the increasing political conservatism within the black church, will present serious intellectual challenges to black theologians and cultural critics. The 2004 American presidential election and statements concerning gay marriage by black preachers such as Eddie Long show that there is not a singular black community that is solely preoccupied with white racism. Thus, casting homophobia in black communities as a function of white racism is likely to be met with resistance by many black people. African Americans who are opposed to legalizing gay marriage are likely to argue that they are following their moral convictions independent of any overriding white influence.

What can black queer literature offer black theology and African American cultural criticism? I contend that black queer literature offers these critical discourses a different way of viewing black queer identity and a different way of describing God and God's activity in the world. As African American cultural criticism and black liberation theology draw on the experiences of black people, I have found that, within these discourses, the voices of black queers become muted. By that I mean it is odd that black theologians and African American cultural critics who draw heavily on black men's and women's literature suddenly fail to draw substantively on black queer literature when discussing black queer experiences. To be sure, they do refer to Audre Lorde, James Baldwin, and Marlon Riggs and Essex Hemphill. However, those references are fleeting and only employed in the service of refuting white claims of black inferiority. Further, black theologians and African American cultural critics do not survey the contemporary literatures of black queers.

I will briefly return to my discussion of James Baldwin and Randall Kenan's respective literary works. Their literary productions take sexual difference in black life seriously and seek to present alternate visions of black queer life. Further, both Baldwin and Kenan present different conceptions of God and spirituality that are open rather than closed. Unlike Keith Boykin and E. Lynn Harris, these black queer writers present literatures that dare to call into question the presumptive goodness of God and the efficacy of the black church in ameliorating crises in black sexual identity. Where Boykin and Harris seek a God that will affirm black homosexuality, Baldwin and Kenan wrestle with, as Anthony Pinn describes it, the "nitty-gritty" moments in black life. To simply say "God loves everyone" and construct black male characters as being able to "pass in and out of the heterosexual world" is not a sufficient response in the face of the enduring questions about black queer sexuality. Further, such statements obscure the particularities of black sexual experiences.

I began this book project hoping to find a theologically critical voice in black queer literature. What I found were moments where black queer writers engaged in critical reflections on God and black queer sexuality. Those moments in black queer writing appear to have been disrupted by a turn toward popular black queer literatures that are easily accessible to the masses and easily digested by them. Contemporary popular black queer writings do not radically shift black religious understandings of God and black queer sexuality. Rather, they seek to reconcile black queers to a predominantly heterosexual black community by adhering to a politics of respectability that promotes the formation of monogamous, heterosexual black nuclear families and recommends a minimal tolerance of homosexuality as a way of distinguishing black communities from a presumptively homophobic white community.

In examining the experiences and narratives of black queers, black liberation theologians and African American cultural critics and black queer writers must remain vigilant and resist predicating their analyses of black queer lives upon the acceptance of a heterosexual superiority. By encouraging heterosexual blacks to "embrace" an elusive and often ill-defined "gayness," black theologians and cultural critics subordinate sexual difference to a conception of normative heterosexuality. This normative heterosexuality in black communities functions to inscribe an inferior status upon black queer bodies and renders any work on black queers apologetic.

This ethics of openness I suggest in this study makes a constructive contribution to black liberation theology by critiquing the content of liberation for African Americans. As I follow Robert S. Corrington's and Jerome Stone's discussions of transcendence and openness in their respective works, *Nature and Spirit* (1992) and *The Minimalist Vision of Transcendence* (1992), an ethics of openness is oriented toward openness instead of toward closure, and to the possibilities of transcendence instead of to the limitations imposed by finitude. As I relate an ethics of openness that encourages creative exchanges and encounters between black people of different genders, sexualities, and the like, this ethics reconfigures liberation so that it is not merely the rhetorical response to white domination but a practical reality in black life. As part of this constructive move, I argue that such an ethics is open to the multiplicity of possibilities in black life. That is, black life in America is not necessarily framed and determined by white supremacy.

To be sure, racism and white supremacy and their effects are very real possibilities and bear the potential to diminish the flourishing of African Americans. However, such an ethics recognizes such possibilities as possibilities that exist in the world and need not be reified as the main problem facing African Americans. Such an orientation makes liberation predicated upon the cessation of racist discourse and behavior by whites. Further, an ethics of openness as predicated upon a view toward openness and transcendence brings the black church into the conversation. As I envision this ethics, I contend that this ethics of openness fully and creatively engages all the sources that inform black life in America. Part of this creative engagement involves serious and sustained conversation with black churches. As an institution that is deeply involved with the practical realities of black life in America, the black church offers black theology and African American cultural criticism much more than a sentimental site of a nostalgic blackness. What the black church offers is a site of critical discourse concerning the cleavages within black life. For an ethics of openness to be more than an academic reflection on black identity, it must acknowledge and fully engage the black church as a site of moral discourse.

This ethics does not ignore that within black churches there are doctrinal and denominational commitments that would preclude such churches from affirming sexual difference as normative in black communities, nor does it suggest that discussions surrounding sexual difference in black life would be without contention. This ethics does not suggest a normative turn toward sexual difference. By that I mean this ethics does not, nor should it, seek to make homosexuality normative in black life. Further, this ethics does not, nor should it, seek to make heterosexuality normative in black life. What this ethics seeks is a re-presentation of the Golden Rule that Jesus Christ made as a maxim for his followers as the beginnings of a reinterpretation of black experiences. By treating people as we would wish to be treated, we become open to difference, for it requires a vulnerability, an openness to others. Treating others as we would wish to be treated requires deep appreciation of the intrinsic value that humans possess. As African Americans encounter people of different sexualities, religious faiths, and other socioeconomic locations, an ethics of openness that is based upon the various traditions that have framed black life requires close attention to difference not solely for the sake of vanquishing racism and white supremacy, but for the sake of bringing about the community that Martin Luther King called the Beloved Community.

Afterword

As I was writing this book, voters here in the United States elected Barack Obama as the first African American US President. On that same day, voters in the state of California passed an amendment to the state constitution that defined marriage as the union of a man and a woman. Despite the jubilation among Obama supporters, those who opposed Proposition 8 were quite disappointed, in some cases, bitterly so. Exit polls showed that 72 percent of African American voters voted in favor of the proposition, leading to a missive penned by sex-advice and occasional political pundit Dan Savage and published in the Seattle-based newspaper *Slog* that claimed black homophobia was a greater "threat" than racism among white gays.[1] I will quote most of Savage's comments here:

> I'm thrilled that we've just elected our first African-American president. I wept last night. I wept reading the papers this morning. But I can't help but feeling hurt that the love and support aren't mutual.
>
> I do know this, though: I'm done pretending that the handful of racist gay white men out there—and they're out there, and I think they're *scum*—are a bigger problem for African Americans, gay and straight, than the huge numbers of homophobic African Americans are for gay Americans, whatever their color.
>
> This will get my name scratched of the invite list of the National Gay and Lesbian Task Force, which is famous for its anti-racist-training seminars, but whatever.
>
> Finally, I'm searching for some exit poll data from California. I'll eat my shorts if gay and lesbian voters went for McCain at anything approaching the rate that black voters went for Prop 8. (emphasis author's)[2]

There are a number of things that I find noteworthy and problematic about the above quote. I find the near-total erasure of black gays quite interesting. Savage situates "black" homophobia as a threat to all gays, "whatever their color." By this juxtaposition, and by his claim that the numbers of white gays who are racist constitute a "handful," Savage presents an image that black homophobes constitute a horde that easily outnumbers white gay racists. Savage attempts to provide his nonracist bona fides by saying that he does think that white gay racists are "scum," but immediately trivializes the existence of white gay racists by focusing on the apparent multitude of black homophobes. He concludes his tirade by asserting that gay and lesbian voters did not vote for John McCain in the same manner as blacks voted for the passage of Proposition 8. As such, Savage dismisses racism in white gay communities and essentializes African Americans as uniformly homophobic.

Further, the equivocation of gay and lesbian voters voting for John McCain with black voters voting for Proposition 8 is troubling and reduces both gays and lesbians and black communities to one-issue communities without any political or social complexity. I find his minimizing racism that comes from white gay communities while attempting to present so-called "black homophobia" as a form of great oppression while juxtaposing that assertion with an implicit assertion that African Americans (presumably the heterosexual African Americans) owe him (and presumably other white gays) a quid pro quo in light of Obama's win to be not only an egregious assertion of white male middle-class privilege, but also an instructive example of the manner in which black gays and lesbians in particular are minimized, trivialized, or, in this case, made to be virtually invisible in light of allegedly larger issues. In other words, I read the above comments about African Americans made by Savage in the same way in which I read the presentation of black gays in black liberation and womanist theologies. Savage syndicates black interests into the interests he claims to represent, while failing to acknowledge the complexity of the interests of queer communities and black communities. Most problematic is his failure to acknowledge that queer and black communities have members who occupy multiple subject positions. There are black gays and lesbians who move fluidly between queer communities, black communities, black queer communities, and the like. That Savage cannot seem to imagine the complexity of the lives of African Americans and the complexity of the issues of the day signals a failure of our ethics and a failure of our theological and political discourses.

Reading such comments as the ones mentioned above highlights the necessity of moving beyond rigid, dichotomized portrayals of difference in American life. These problems are not solely the province of black liberation and womanist theologians and African American cultural critics. It is apparent that the failure of our ethics, and the failure of our theological and political discourses, is partially due to the manner in which "identity politics" has come to dominate both political and academic discussions. Identity politics as seen in contemporary political and academic debates typically represent a set of binary oppositions (gay/straight, black/white, male/female, rich/poor). The oppressed group is characterized both internally and externally as a monolithic collective. As such, the politics of the monolithic collective can be represented and dominated by single-issue concerns.

This kind of single-issue politics has come to dominate the gay rights movement. For example, Andrew Sullivan's *Virtually Normal* (1995) posits marriage as the centerpiece of a new politics that would ensure equality for gays.[3] Sullivan, a conservative political commentator, argues that marriage would serve as an "unqualified social good for homosexuals." His argument, one that has seemingly been embraced wholeheartedly by LGBT organizations, is rooted in a form of sexual apologetics. Sullivan notes,

> [Same-sex marriage] provides role models for young gay people, who, after the exhilaration of coming out, can easily lapse into short-term relationships and insecurity with no tangible goal in sight. My own guess is that most homosexuals would embrace such a goal with as much (if not more) commitment as homosexuals...Legal gay marriage could also help bridge the gulf often found between homosexuals and their parents. It could bring the essence of gay life—a gay couple—into the heart of the traditional family in a way the family can most understand and the gay offspring can most easily acknowledge. It could do more to heal the gay-straight rift than any amount of gay rights legislation.[4]

Sullivan's argument here places a great deal of power in a heteronormative ideal of marriage. Concomitant with Sullivan's argument that same-sex marriage would "civilize" gays and lesbians is his argument that legal recognition of gay marriage would eradicate homophobia. In a sense, gay marriage would minimize if not eliminate altogether homophobia and HIV/AIDS. If Sullivan's thesis is correct and embracing same-sex marriage is a means by which gays and lesbians gain respectability in the eyes of heterosexuals as well as regulating their own sexual drives, then the men profiled in this piece may serve as the data that proves his argument. At first, it might appear that

Sullivan is indeed correct about his assertions. For example, the *New York Times Magazine* featured a cover story on young gay couples for its April 27, 2008 issue.[5] The couples profiled were all white, college-educated, upper middle-class males under the age of thirty. The ways in which these men spoke about marriage as well as the manner in which the magazine itself photographed them (while doing various domestic chores) posited marriage as that institution that would somehow corral the baser instincts of gay men and lead them to become respectable citizens.

However, between the publication of *Virtually Normal* and the piece in the *New York Times Magazine*, many states have enacted laws and passed constitutional amendments that ban same-sex marriage. Further, some states, like Arkansas, have also restricted access to adoption, making it available only to heterosexual married couples. The passage of Proposition 8 as well as the organization of the Yes on Prop 8 supporters appeared to surprise many LGBT activists. As Dan Savage's blog post indicates, LGBT activists and supporters attempted to come to terms with this defeat. I submit that what we saw with the passage of Proposition 8 was just another in a series of restrictive legislative and governmental acts that highlights the inadequacy of the so-called "marriage equality movement." This movement has privileged a heteronormative construction of queer relationships, while marginalizing if not altogether dismissing other forms of family. As a result, the movement has posited marriage equality as the only matter of concern for all lesbians and gays. However, the positioning of marriage equality as the only concern has precipitated a backlash.

As Nancy Polikoff notes in *Beyond (Straight and Gay) Marriage* (2008), the critical error of LGBT organizations has been to reify marriage as a panacea for queer concerns. Such a move led to responses by right-wing religious organizations such as Jerry Falwell's Moral Majority and Pat Robertson's Christian Broadcasting Network. As early as the 1970s, religious groups mobilized to combat attempts to legalize gay and lesbian relationships. Anita Bryant's movement along with Phyllis Schlafly's antifeminist Eagle Forum pushed back against both gay and feminist initiatives.[6] Into the 1990s, the Religious Right took up same-sex marriage as the "cornerstone of their platforms."[7] However, Tina Fetner notes that not all lesbians and gays think of same-sex marriage as a political or social priority:

> Many in the lesbian and gay community oppose same-sex marriage as a patriarchal, heterosexual institution and point to the success of

lesbian and gay communities in establishing a diverse array of relationship types precisely because they do not view their lives through the
lens of marriage...From this perspective, a lesbian and gay movement
that fights for same-sex marriage would be inherently assimilationist,
doing more harm than good to lesbian and gay communities.[8]

The tension concerning assimilation versus separation within queer
communities mirrors that of black communities. For some queers,
marriage is little more than an assimilationist move designed to erase
or elide that which is distinctive about gay and lesbian culture and
identity. Others argue that marriage is not, nor should it be, constitutive of LGBT activism and advocacy. Indeed, in 2006, a group
of LGBT activists joined together to form an advocacy group that
seeks more than marriage. "The April Working Group" started
BeyondMarriage.org and released a statement in July of 2006 that
articulates the group's goals. In the "About Us" section of the website,
the group notes

> We offer this statement as a way to challenge ourselves and our allies
> working across race, class, gender and issue lines to frame and broaden
> community dialogues, to shape alternative policy solutions and to
> inform organizing strategies around marriage politics to include the
> broadest definitions of relationship and family.[9]

While this book has focused primarily on African American sexual
orientation and its representations (and lack thereof) in black liberation and womanist theologies and has offered a humanist ethics
of openness as an alternative approach, I find myself wondering if a
humanist ethics of openness is a way forward for gays and lesbians
in America in general. Both the April Working Group and Nancy
Polikoff's arguments concerning same-sex marriage are oriented
around an openness to viewing and appreciating forms of difference.
In this case, these groups and individuals are offering revised ways of
looking at the construction of families. If gay rights groups uncritically focus on marriage as though it is the only avenue by which gays
can achieve equality, I am concerned that we may be opening ourselves up to yet another form of discrimination within gay communities and creating narrower and narrower forms of "being" gay.

Notes

Introduction

1. My use of the term "same-gender loving" instead of "homosexual" here connotes how I approached the issue of nomenclature for gays and lesbians in the 1990s. Cleo Manago is credited with proposing the term "same-gender loving" instead of "gay" or "homosexual," because such terminology was, respectively, either rooted in white privilege or far too clinical to be of use for African Americans.
2. Southern Poverty Law Center, "Intelligence Report," available online at http://www.splcenter.org/intel/intelreport/article.jsp?sid=409.
3. http://unityfellowshipchurch.org/mainsite/?page_id=10
4. Victor Anderson, *Creative Exchange: A Constructive Theology of African American Religious Experience* (Minneapolis: Fortress Books, 2008), 5.
5. http://www.covenantwithblackamerica.com/background/
6. Goss notes, "If Jesus the Christ is not queer, then his *basileia* message of solidarity and justice is irrelevant. If the Christ is not queer, then the gospel is no longer good news but oppressive news for queers." Robert Goss, *Jesus Acted Up: A Gay And Lesbian Manifesto* (San Francisco: Harper, 1993), 85.
7. John J. McNeill, *The Church and the Homosexual* (Boston: Beacon Press, 1993), 137.

Black Liberation Theology, Cultural Criticism, and the Problem of Homosexuality

1. Cornel West, *Race Matters* (New York: Vintage Books, 1994), 10.
2. I draw heavily on Frederick Ware's *Methodologies of Black Theology*, James Cone and Gayraud Wilmore's *Black Theology: A Documentary History, Volumes I and II*, as well as Cone's original works, *Black Theology and Black Power*, *A Black Theology of Liberation*, and *God of the Oppressed*, and the work of Dwight Hopkins, Jacquelyn Grant, Delores Williams, and Kelly Brown Douglas. As I discuss black cultural criticism, I draw on the works of cultural critics such as Michael Eric Dyson, bell hooks, and Cornel West. These figures write extensively about black religious life in the United States and present concerns similar to those in black liberation theology. In this

chapter, I turn to Dyson's *Race Rules*, and *The Michael Eric Dyson Reader*, hooks' *Black Looks: Race and Representation* and *Salvation: Black People and Love*, and Cornel West's *Keeping Faith, Race Matters*, and *The Cornel West Reader*.

3. James H. Cone, *Risks of Faith* (Maryknoll, NY: Orbis Book, 1999), 76.
4. http://www.americanrhetoric.com/speeches/stokelycarmichaelblackpower.html
5. Rhonda Y. Williams, "Black Women, Urban Politics, and Engendering Black Power," in *The Black Power Movement: Rethinking the Civil Rights-Black Power Era*, edited by Peniel E. Joseph (New York: Routledge, 2006), 83, 84.
6. Jeffrey O.G. Ogbar, *Black Power: Radical Politics and African American Identity* (Baltimore: The Johns Hopkins University Press, 2004), 60, 61.
7. Ibid., 66.
8. Gayraud S. Wilmore, "Introduction," in *Black Theology: A Documentary History, Volume I: 1966–1979*, edited by James H. Cone and Gayraud S. Wilmore (Maryknoll, NY: Orbis Books, 1993), 15–16.
9. "The Black Manifesto," in *Black Theology, A Documentary History, Vol. I*, 30–31.
10. Ibid., 31.
11. Joseph R. Washington, Jr., *Black Religion: The Negro and Christianity in the United States* (Lanham, MD: University Press of America, 1984), vii.
12. Ibid., 33.
13. Ibid., 42ff.
14. Ibid., xvi.
15. Ibid., xvii, 251, 261ff.
16. Ibid., 261–262.
17. Paul Tillich, *Systematic Theology, Volume I: Reason and Revelation, Being and God* (Chicago: The University of Chicago Press, 1951), 62.
18. James H. Cone, *Risks of Faith: The Emergence of a Black Theology of Liberation, 1968–1998* (Boston: Beacon Press, 1999), xvi.
19. Ibid., 100–102.
20. James H. Cone, *A Theology of Black Liberation, Twentieth Anniversary Edition* (Maryknoll, NY: Orbis Books, 1990), 17.
21. Ibid., 23.
22. Cornel West, *Race Matters* (New York: Vintage Books, 1994), 23.
23. bell hooks, *Salvation: Black People and Love* (New York: Harper Collins Publishers, 2001), xxiv.
24. Ibid., 25.
25. Don Lee, as quoted in *Black Theology of Liberation*, 29.
26. Cone, *Black Theology of Liberation*, 25.
27. Cornel West, "Subversive Joy and Revolutionary Patience in Black Christianity," in *The Cornel West Reader* (New York: Basic Civitas Books, 1999), 436.
28. John Fiske, "Popular Culture," in *Critical Terms for Literary Study*, 2nd Edition, edited by Frank Lentricchia and Thomas McLaughlin (Chicago: The University of Chicago Press, 1995), 327.

29. Stuart Hall, "What Is This 'Black' In Black Popular Culture?" *in Black Popular Culture, A Project By Michele Wallace*, edited by Gina Dent (New York: The New Press, 1998), 26.
30. James Cone, *The Spirituals and the Blues: An Interpretation* (Westport, CT: Greenwood Press, 1972) 32–33.
31. Ibid.
32. Ibid., 35–39.
33. James H. Cone, *Black Theology and Black Power* (Maryknoll, NY: Orbis Books, 1997) 6–7, 42.
34. Cone, *Black Theology of Liberation*, 58, 63.
35. Ibid, 70–74.
36. Ibid, 73.
37. James H. Cone, *Risks of Faith: The Emergence of a Black Theology of Liberation, 1968–1998* (Boston: Beacon Press, 1999), 9.
38. James Cone and William Hordern, "Dialogue on Black Theology: An Interview with James Cone," *Christian Century* (September 15, 1971), 1085.
39. Eldridge Cleaver, *Soul on Ice* (New York: Delta Books, 1968), 33.
40. Delores S. Williams, *Sisters in the Wilderness: The Challenge of Womanist God-Talk* (Maryknoll, NY: Orbis Books, 1993), 1.
41. Jacquelyn Grant, "Black Theology and the Black Woman," in *Black Theology, A Documentary History, Volume One: 1966–1979* (Maryknoll, NY: Orbis Books, 1993), 325.
42. Alice Walker, *In Search of Our Mothers' Gardens: Womanist Prose*, as quoted in *Katie's Canon: Womanism and the Soul of the Black Community* by Katie Cannon (New York: Continuum Press, 1995), 22.
43. Ibid., 23.
44. Anonymous, "Jamaica, A Poem, in Three Parts," as quoted in *White Over Black*, 150.
45. Stephanie Y. Mitchem, *Introducing Womanist Theology* (Maryknoll, NY: Orbis Books, 2002), 8–9.
46. Cone, "Introduction," *Black Theology, A Documentary History, Volume II*, 257.
47. James H. Cone and Gayraud S. Wilmore, eds., *Black Theology: A Documentary History, Volume II: 1980–1992* (Maryknoll, NY: Orbis Books, 1993), 257.
48. Delores S. Williams, "Womanist Theology: Black Women's Voices," chapter in *Black Theology: A Documentary History, Volume II*, 265.
49. Delores Williams, *Sisters in the Wilderness* (Maryknoll, NY: Orbis Books, 1993), 205.
50. Ibid.
51. Katie G. Cannon, *Katie's Canon: Womanism and the Soul of the Black Community* (New York: Continuum Publishing Company, 1995), 124.
52. Delores S. Williams, "Womanist Theology: Black Women's Voices," in *Black Theology, A Documentary History*, 267.
53. Emilie Townes, *In A Blaze of Glory: Womanist Spirituality as Social Witness* (Nashville: Abingdon Press, 1995), 36.

54. Ibid.
55. Cone, *Risks of Faith*, 118.
56. Robert Joseph Taylor, Linda M. Chatters, and Jeff Levin, *Religion in the Lives of African Americans: Social, Psychological, and Health Perspectives* (Thousand Oaks, CA: Sage Publications, 2004), xii.
57. Ibid.
58. Emilie M. Townes, *Womanist Ethics and the Cultural Production of Evil* (New York: Palgrave Macmillan, 2006), 3.
59. Ibid.
60. bell hooks, *Black Looks: Race and Representation* (Boston: South End Press, 1992), 74.
61. Ibid., 76.
62. Renee Hill, "Who Are For Each Other?" in *Black Theology, A Documentary History: Volume II*, 347.
63. Winthrop D. Jordan, *White Over Black: American Attitudes Toward the Negro, 1550–1812* (New York: W.W. Norton and Company, 1968) 33–34.
64. Patricia Hill Collins, *Black Sexual Politics* (New York: Routledge, 2004), 27.
65. Michael Eric Dyson, *Between God and Gangsta Rap: Bearing Witness to Black Culture* (New York: Oxford University Press, 1996), 34.
66. Horace Griffin, "Their Own Received Them Not: African American Lesbians and Gays in Black Churches," *Theology and Sexuality*, 12 (2000): 88–100.
67. Lisa Bennett, "Mixed Blessings: Organized Religion and Gay and Lesbian Americans in 1998," published by the Human Rights Campaign Foundation. Available online at www.hrc.org.
68. Victor Anderson, "The Curious Body of the Black Homosexual," in *Loving the Body: Black Religious Studies and the Erotic*, edited by Anthony B. Pinn and Dwight N. Hopkins (New York: Palgrave Macmillan, 2004), 297–301.
69. Jeremiah A. Wright Jr., *Good News: Sermons of Hope for Today's Families*, edited by Jini Kilgore Ross (Valley Forge, PA: Judson Press, 1995), 83.
70. Toward the end of the "Good News for Homosexuals" sermon, Wright argues that "whoremongers" cannot separate gay people from the love of God. His use of the term whoremonger appears curious. However, earlier in the sermon, Wright relays a story wherein he engaged in a debate with an adulterous heterosexual preacher about affirming homosexual people. According to Wright, when the preacher voiced his objections about gay people, he responded with "I just wonder why you don't have a problem with being married and sleeping with women other than your wife." Ibid., 74.
71. Dwight N. Hopkins, *Introducing Black Theology of Liberation* (Maryknoll, NY: Orbis Books, 1999), 11.
72. Ibid., 199.
73. Ibid.
74. Ibid.
75. Wright, *Good News*, 80.
76. Ibid., 85.
77. Anderson, *Beyond Ontological Blackness*, 65.

Black Religious Criticism and Representations of Homosexuality

1. William Bennett, "Leave Marriage Alone," *Newsweek*, June 3, 1996.
2. Bishop John Shelby Spong, "Blessing Gay and Lesbian Commitments," in *Same-Sex Marriage: Pro and Con, A Reader*, edited by Andrew Sullivan (New York: Vintage Books, 1997), 67.
3. Keith Boykin, *One More River To Cross: Black and Gay in America* (New York: Anchor Books, 1996), 48.
4. Horace Griffin, *Their Own Receive Them Not*, 17.
5. Kelly Brown Douglas, *Sexuality and the Black Church: A Womanist Perspective* (Maryknoll, NY: Orbis Books, 1999), 89.
6. "Religious Beliefs Underpin Opposition to Homosexuality," Pew Forum on Religion and Public Life Study, 4.
7. Jacqueline L. Salmon, "Rift Over Gay Unions Reflects Battle New To Black Churches," *Washington Post*, Sunday, August 19, 2007.
8. Ibid.
9. Dwight N. Hopkins, *Introducing Black Theology of Liberation* (Maryknoll, NY: Orbis Books, 1999), 11–12.
10. Elias Farajaje-Jones, "Breaking Silence: Toward An In-The-Life Theology," in *Black Theology, A Documentary History, Volume II: 1980–1992*, edited by James H. Cone and Gayraud S. Wilmore (Maryknoll, NY: Orbis Books, 1993), 143.
11. Ibid., 152–154, 158.
12. Ibid., 140.
13. Joseph Beam, *In The Life, A Black Gay Anthology* (Boston: Alyson Publications, 1986), 12.
14. Ibid., 146.
15. Ibid., 152.
16. Renee L. Hill, "Who Are We For Each Other?: Sexism, Sexuality, and Womanist Theology," in *Black Theology, A Documentary History, Volume II: 1980–1992*, edited by James H. Cone and Gayraud S. Wilmore (Maryknoll, NY: Orbis Books, 1993), 346.
17. Ibid., 349.
18. Douglas, *Sexuality and the Black Church*, 1.
19. Cheryl J. Sanders, "Christian Ethics and Theology in Womanist Perspective," in *Black Theology, A Documentary History*, 342.
20. Cheryl J. Sanders, *Saints In Exile: The Holiness-Pentecostal Experience in African American Religion and Culture* (New York: Oxford University Press, 1996), 132.
21. Cheryl J. Sanders, "Sexual Orientation and Human Rights Discourse in the African-American Churches," in *Sexual Orientation and Human Rights in American Religious Discourse*, edited by Saul M. Olyan and Martha C. Nussbaum (New York: Oxford University Press, 1998), 182.
22. Kelly Brown Douglas, *Sexuality and the Black Church*, 106.
23. Ibid., 85.

24. Ibid., 91.
25. Ibid., 97.
26. Ibid., 96.
27. Ibid.
28. Jordan, *White Over Black*, 30–31.
29. Jordan, as quoted in *Sexuality and the Black Church*, 33.
30. Douglas, *Sexuality and the Black Church*, 67–68.
31. Ibid., 106.
32. Ibid.
33. Ibid., 107.
34. Sylvester A. Johnson, review of *Sexuality and the Black Church: A Womanist Perspective*, by Kelly Brown Douglas, in *The Journal of Religion* 81, 1 (January 2001): 141.
35. Douglas, *Sexuality and the Black Church*, 89.
36. Ibid., 107.
37. Ibid., 142.
38. Ibid.
39. Cornel West, "The New Cultural Politics of Difference," in *Keeping Faith: Philosophy and Race in America* (New York: Routledge, 1993), 4.
40. Ibid., 18.
41. Ibid., 17.
42. Ibid.
43. Ibid., 24.
44. Ibid.
45. bell hooks, *Black Looks: Race and Representation* (Boston: South End Press, 1992), 7–8.
46. Ibid., 7.
47. West, "The New Cultural Politics of Difference," in *The Cornel West Reader*, 133.
48. bell hooks, *Yearning: Race, Gender, and Cultural Politics* (Toronto: Between the Lines, 1990), 196–201; *Black Looks: Race and Representation* (Boston: South End Press, 1992), 112–113.
49. Michael Eric Dyson, *Race Rules: Navigating the Color Line* (Reading, MA: Addison-Wesley Publishing Company, 1996), 78.
50. Ibid., 80.
51. Ibid., 83–85.
52. Ibid., 86.
53. Ibid., 93.
54. Ibid., 106.
55. Ibid., 104–105.
56. "Homotextualities: The Bible, Sexual Ethics, and the Theology of Homoeroticism," interview with Kevin LaGrange, in *Open Mike: Reflections on Philosophy, Race, Sex, Culture and Religion*, by Michael Eric Dyson (New York: Basic Civitas Books, 2003), 360.
57. Ibid., 362.
58. bell hooks, *Salvation: Black People and Love* (New York: Harper Collins, 2001), 189–190.

59. Ibid., 189.
60. Ibid., 193.
61. Ibid., 196–197.
62. Ibid., 198.
63. Ibid., 204.
64. Audre Lorde, "The Master's Tools Will Never Dismantle The Master's House," in *Sister Outsider: Essays and Speeches by Audre Lorde* (Freedom, CA: The Crossing Press, 1984), 112.
65. Henry Louis Gates, Jr., *Loose Canons: Notes on the Culture Wars* (New York: Oxford University Press, 1992), 38.
66. See hooks, "Homophobia in Black Communities," in *Talking Back* (Boston: South End Press, 1989), 121.
67. Janet R. Jakobsen, *Working Alliances and the Politics of Difference* (Bloomington: Indiana University Press, 1998), p. 167.
68. Janet R. Jakobsen and Ann Pellegrini, *Love The Sin: Sexual Regulation and the Limits of Religious Tolerance* (New York: New York University Press, 2003), 50–58.
69. "The War Over Gays," *Time*, October 26, 1998.
70. Jakobsen and Pellegrini, *Love The Sin*, 55.
71. Ibid., 56.

Black Theology and Homosexuality Revisited: Black Queer Theologians Respond

1. Horace Griffin, *Their Own Receive Them Not: African American Lesbians and Gays in Black Churches* (Cleveland: The Pilgrim Press, 2006), 7.
2. Ibid., 18.
3. Ibid., 116.
4. Ibid., 117.
5. Ibid., 127.
6. For a sociological interpretation of the black church as a bedrock institution in African American communities, see C. Eric Lincoln and Lawrence H. Mamiya's *The Black Church in the African American Experience* (Durham, NC: Duke University Press, 199).
7. Ibid., 187.
8. Ibid., 223.
9. Ibid., 60, 108.
10. Ibid., 225.
11. Victor Anderson, *Beyond Ontological Blackness: An Essay on African American Religious and Cultural Criticism* (New York: Continuum Press, 1995), 78.
12. Ibid., 85.
13. Ibid., 117.
14. Ibid., 129.
15. Victor Anderson, "Deadly Silence: Reflections on Homosexuality and Human Rights," in *Sexual Orientation and Human Rights In American*

Religious Discourse, edited by Saul M. Olyan and Martha C. Nussbaum (New York: Oxford University Press, 1998), 194.

16. Ibid., 195.
17. Victor Anderson, *Creative Exchange: A Constructive Theology of African American Religious Experience* (Minneapolis: Fortress Press, 2008), 132.
18. Ibid., 130.
19. Ibid., 144.
20. Ibid.
21. Ibid., 167.
22. Ibid., 160.
23. http://operationrebirth.com/abuse.html
24. Anderson, *Creative Exchange*, 167.

The Representations of Homosexuality in Black Gay Men's Writing

1. Annamarie Jargose, *Queer Theory: An Introduction* (New York: New York University Press, 1996), 3.
2. Devon W. Carbado, Dwight A. McBride, and Donald Weise, eds, *Black Like Us: A Century of Lesbian, Gay, and Bisexual African American Fiction* (San Francisco: Cleis Press, 2002), xvi.
3. Ibid., xvii.
4. Ibid.
5. Essex Hemphill, *Ceremonies* (San Francisco: Cleis Press, 1992), 84–85.
6. Charles I. Nero, "Toward a Black Gay Aesthetic: Signifying in Contemporary Black Gay Literature," in *African American Literary Theory, A Reader,* edited by Winston Napier (New York: New York University Press, 2000), 400.
7. Ibid., 415.
8. Jargose, *Queer Theory*, 3.
9. Devon W. Carbado, *Black Like Us*, 1.
10. Ibid., 9.
11. Ibid., 58.
12. Ibid., 59.
13. Ibid.
14. Ibid., 60.
15. Ibid.
16. Ibid., 61.
17. Ibid.
18. Ibid., 58.
19. Ibid.
20. Ibid.
21. Ibid.
22. Ibid., 72–73.
23. Ibid., 73.
24. Samuel R. Delany and Joseph Beam, "The Possibility of Possibilities," in *In the Life: A Black Gay Anthology* (Boston: Alyson Publications, 1986), 200–201.

25. Ibid., 202.
26. Samuel R. Delany, *Tales of Nevèrÿon* (Hanover: University Press of New England, 1993), 77–78.
27. Ibid., 238–239.
28. Frances Cress Welsing, *The Isis Papers* (Chicago: Third World Press, 1991), 86.
29. Ibid.
30. Hemphill, *Ceremonies*, 60.
31. Ibid., 64.
32. Essex Hemphill, *Ceremonies* (San Francisco: Cleis Press, 1992), 55.
33. Douglas Steward, "Saint's Progeny: Assotto Saint, Gay Black Poets, and Poetic Agency in the Field of the Queer Symbolic," *African American Review* (Terre Haute) 33, 3 (Fall 1999): 515.
34. "Foreword," in *In the Life: A Black Gay Anthology*, edited by Joseph Beam (Boston: Alyson Publications, Inc., 1986), 11.
35. Daniel Garrett, "Creating Ourselves: An Open Letter," in *In the Life*, 96
36. Essex Hemphill, "I Am A Homosexual," in *Fighting Words: Personal Essays by Black Gay Men*, edited by Charles Michael Smith (New York: Avon Books, 1999), 150–151.
37. Essex Hemphill, "Isn't It Funny," in *In The Life*, 108.
38. Ibid.
39. E. Lynn Harris, *Invisible Life* (New York: Anchor Books, 1994), 7.
40. Ibid., 16–17.
41. Theoloa S. Labbe, "E. Lynn Harris: Black, Male, Out And On Top," *Publishers Weekly* (New York) 248, 31 (2001): 54.
42. Harris, *Invisible Life*, 42–43.
43. Ibid., 48.
44. Ibid.
45. J.L. King, with Karen Hunter, *On The Down Low: A Journey Into The Lives Of 'Straight' Black Men Who Sleep With Men* (New York: Broadway Books, 2004), 19–20.
46. Ibid., 20.
47. Ibid., 21.
48. Ibid., xv–xvi.
49. Ibid., 84.
50. Keith Boykin, *Beyond the Down Low: Sex, Lies, and Denial in Black America* (New York: Carroll and Graf Publishers, 2005), 39–60.
51. Ibid., 72.
52. Ibid., 286.
53. Ibid., 287.
54. Hemphill, "I Am A Homosexual," 151–152.

Religious Experience in Black Gay Men's Writings

1. Devon W. Carbado, *Black Like Us*, 61.
2. Randall Kenan, *A Visitation of Spirits* (New York: Vintage Books, 1989), 11–15.
3. Ibid., 12.

4. Robert McRuer, *The Queer Renaissance: Contemporary American Literature and the Reinvention of Lesbian and Gay Identities* (New York: New York University Press, 1997), 69.
5. Ibid.
6. Kenan, *A Visitation of Spirits*, 188.
7. James Baldwin, *Go Tell it on the Mountain* (New York: Dell Publishing, 1981), 11, 13.
8. Ibid., 36.
9. Kenan, *A Visitation of Spirits*, 186, 187.
10. Ibid., 81.
11. Ibid., 181–188.
12. Ibid., 110–114.
13. Ibid., 251.
14. Charles I. Nero, "Toward A Black Gay Aesthetic: Signifying in Contemporary Black Gay Literature," in *Brother To Brother: Collected Writings by Black Gay Men* (Los Angeles, CA: Alyson Publications, Inc., 1991), 241.
15. Essex Hemphill, *Ceremonies* (San Francisco: Cleis Press, 1992), 19–20.
16. James H. Cone, *A Black Theology of Liberation*, xix, xx, 24–27, Essex Hemphill, *Ceremonies*, 189.
17. G. Winston James, "Church," in *Shade: An Anthology of Fiction by Gay Men of African Descent*, edited by Bruce Morrow and Charles H. Rowell (New York: Avon Books, 1996), 91.
18. Ibid., 96.
19. Ibid., 101.
20. Ibid.
21. Essex Hemphill, "Introduction," in *Brother To Brother: Collected Writings by Black Gay Men*, Essex Hemphill (Los Angeles: Alyson Publications, 1991), xxviii.
22. E. Patrick Johnson, "Feeling the Spirit in the Dark: Expanding Notions of the Sacred in the African American Gay Community," in *The Greatest Taboo: Homosexuality in Black Communities*, edited by Delroy Constantine-Simms (Los Angeles: Alyson Publications, 2000), 89.
23. Ibid., 95.
24. Ibid., 90–95, Dyson, *Race Rules* 83–95.
25. Ibid., 104.
26. Ibid.
27. Ibid., 105.
28. Ibid., 108.
29. Sheila Smith McKoy, "Rescuing the Black Homosexual Lambs: Randall Kenan and the Reconstruction of Southern Gay Masculinity," in *Contemporary Black Men's Fiction and Drama*, edited by Keith Clark (Urbana, IL: University of Illinois Press, 2001), 34n.
30. E. Lynn Harris, *Invisible Life* (New York: Anchor Books, 1994), 44–45.
31. Ibid., 45.
32. Ibid., 68.
33. Ibid., 74–75.
34. Ibid., 50–51.

35. Ibid., 51, *Just As I Am*, 89–91.

36. Henry Louis Gates, *The Signifying Monkey: A Theory of African American Literary Criticism* (New York: Oxford University Press, 1988), 6.

37. Ibid.

38. Harris, *Just As I Am*, 306.

39. In later works, Harris seems to take bell hooks' advice concerning black men dealing psychoanalytically with their childhoods seriously. Harris creates a backstory for Basil that explains away his intemperate sexual lifestyle. In *Not A Day Goes By*, Harris reveals that Basil had been sexually molested by his uncle. This molestation, apparently, serves as the precursor to Basil's later promiscuity.

40. 2 Corinthians 11:14, *New Oxford Annotated Bible, Third Edition, New Revised Standard Version* (New York: Oxford University Press, 2001).

41. Harris, *Just As I Am*, 345.

42. Keith Boykin, *One More River To Cross: Black and Gay in America* (New York: Anchor Books, 1996), 123–125.

43. Horace Griffin, "Their Own Received Them Not," 100.

Reconstructing Black Gay Male Identity beyond "The DL"

1. Phillip Brian Harper, *Are We Not Men?: Masculine Anxiety and the Problem of African-American Identity* (New York: Oxford University Press, 1996), 11.

2. Ronald L. Jackson, II. *Scripting the Black Masculine Body: Identity, Discourse, and Racial Politics in Popular Media* (Albany, NY: State University of New York Press, 2006), 128–129.

3. Ibid., 2.

4. Bryant Keith Alexander, *Performing Black Masculinity: Race, Culture, and Queer Identity* (Lanham, MD: AltaMira Press, 2006), 74

5. Ibid., 75.

6. Judith Butler, *Gender Trouble: Feminism and the Subversion of Identity* (New York: Routledge Classics, 1990), xv.

7. Victor Anderson, *Creative Exchange*, 11.

8. Dwight A. McBride, *Why I Hate Abercrombie and Fitch: Essays on Race and Sexuality* (New York: New York University Press, 2005), 112.

9. Ibid., 123.

10. Essex Hemphill, "Does Your Mama Know About Me?" in *Ceremonies* (San Francisco: Cleis Press, 1992), 44–45.

11. http://bgclive.com/index.php.

Conclusion: Toward an Ethics of Openness

1. Victor Anderson, *Beyond Ontological Blackness* (New York: Continuum Books, 1995), 14.

2. Anthony B. Pinn, *African American Humanist Principles: Living and Thinking Like The Children of Nimrod* (New York: Palgrave Macmillan, 2004), 104.

3. Ibid., 66.

4. Victor Anderson, "The Black Church and the Curious Body of the Black Homosexual," in *Loving the Body: Black Religious Studies and the Erotic*, edited by Anthony B. Pinn and Dwight N. Hopkins (New York: Palgrave Macmillan, 2004), 311.

5. Kelly Brown Douglas, *What's Faith Got To Do With It?: Black Bodies, Christian Souls* (Maryknoll, NY: Orbis Books, 2005), xi–xii.

6. Ibid., xiii.

7. Anderson, "The Black Church and the Curious Body of the Black Homosexual," 310.

8. Essex Hemphill, "Does Your Mama Know About Me?" and "Commitments," in *Ceremonies* (San Francisco: Cleis Press, 1992), 46 and 55.

9. In using the term "cultural fulfillment," I draw on Victor Anderson's use of the term in *Beyond Ontological Blackness*. He defines cultural fulfillment as "the satisfaction of categorical and reflexive goods." Drawing on Jurgen Habermas and Germain Grisez, Joseph Boyle and John Finnis, Anderson reads cultural fulfillment as satisfying both those needs that are constitutive of and necessary for human existence: "life, safety, work, leisure, knowledge, and the like." Cultural fulfillment also satisfies those other needs that "[assure] subjective meaning and [alleviate] alienation." 26–27.

10. Michael Joseph Brown, "Constructing a Doctrine for the Ecclesia *Militans*," in *Loving the Body: Black Religious Studies and the Erotic*, edited by Anthony B. Pinn and Dwight N. Hopkins (New York: Palgrave Macmillan, 2004), 68.

Afterword

1. http://latimesblogs.latimes.com/lanow/2008/11/70-of-african-a.html.

2. http://slog.thestranger.com/2008/11/black_homophobia, posted by Dan Savage on November 5, 2008.

3. Andrew Sullivan, *Virtually Normal: An Argument About Homosexuality* (New York: Vintage Books, 1995), 178.

4. Ibid., 183, 184.

5. Benoit Denizet-Louis, "Young Gay Rites," *New York Times Magazine*, April 27, 2008.

6. Tina Fetner, *How the Religious Right Shaped Lesbian and Gay Activisim* (Minneapolis: University of Minnesota Press, 2008), 23–25.

7. Ibid., 110.

8. Ibid., 111.

9. http://www.beyondmarriage.org/about.html.

Bibliography

Adorno, Theodor W. *The Culture Industry: Selected Essays on Mass Culture.* Ed. J.M. Bernstein. London: Routledge, 1991.

Alexander Bryant Keith. *Performing Black Masculinity: Race, Culture, and Queer Identity.* Lanham, MD: AltaMira Press, 2006.

Anderson,Victor. *Beyond Ontological Blackness: An Essay on African American Religious and Cultural Criticism.* New York: Continuum Publishing Co., 1995.

———. "A Relational Concept of Race in African American Religious Thought." *Nova Religio* (2003): 7.

———. *Creative Exchange: A Constructive Theology of African American Religious Experience.* Minneapolis: Fortress Press, 2008.

Arato, Andrew and Eike Gebhardt, eds. *The Essential Frankfurt School Reader.* New York: Continuum Publishing Company, 2000.

Aristotle, *Politics,* Bk. I Ch. 13, 10–15.

Arnold, Matthew. *Culture and Anarchy.* New Haven: Yale University Press, 1994.

Asante, Molefi Kete. *Afrocentricity: The Theory of Social Change, Revised and Expanded.* Chicago: African-American Images, 2003.

Back, Les and John Solomos, eds. *Theories of Race and Racism: A Reader.* London: Routledge, 2000.

Baldwin, James. *Go Tell It On The Mountain.* New York: Dell Publishing, 1981.

Bates, Karen Grigsby. "Review of *Losing the Race: Self-Sabotage in Black America,* by John McWhorter." *The Journal of Blacks in Higher Education* 29 (October 31, 2000): 136.

Bennett, William. "Leave Marriage Alone." *Newsweek,* June 3, 1996.

Boykin, Keith. *One More River To Cross: Black and Gay in America.* New York: Anchor Books, 1996.

———. *Beyond the Down Low: Sex, Lies, and Denial in Black America.* New York: Carroll and Graf Publishers, 2005.

Butler, Judith. *Gender Trouble: Feminism and the Subversion of Identity.* New York: Routledge Classics, 1990.

Bynum, Bill. "Discarded Diagnoses: Homosexuality." *The Lancet* 359 (June 29, 2002): 2284.

Cannon, Katie Geneva. *Katie's Canon: Womanism and the Soul of the Black Community*. New York: Continuum Publishing, 1995.

Carbado, Devon W., Dwight A. McBride, and Donald Weise, eds. *Black Like Us: A Century of Lesbian, Gay, and Bisexual African American Fiction*. San Francisco: Cleis Press, 2002.

Clark, Keith, ed. *Contemporary Black Men's Fiction and Drama*. Urbana, IL: University of Illinois Press, 2001.

Cleaver, Eldridge. *Soul on Ice*. New York: McGraw-Hill Book Company, 1968.

Coleman, Monica A. "Must I Be A Womanist?" *Journal of Feminist Studies in Religion* 22.1 (2006).

Cone, James H. *Black Theology and Black Power*. San Francisco, Harper and Row, 1969.

———. *A Black Theology of Liberation, 20th Anniversary Edition*. Maryknoll, NY: Orbis Books, 1990.

Cone, James H and Gayraud S. Wilmore, eds. *Black Theology: A Documentary History, Volume I: 1966–1979*. Maryknoll, NY: Orbis Books, 1993.

———. *Black Theology: A Documentary History, Volume II: 1980–1992*. Maryknoll, NY: Orbis Books, 1993.

———. *Risks of Faith: The Emergence of a Black Theology of Liberation, 1968–1998*. Boston: Beacon Press, 1999.

Corrington, Robert S. *Nature and Spirit: An Essay in Ecstatic Naturalism*. New York: Fordham University Press, 1992.

Delany, Samuel. *Tales of Nevèrÿon*. Hanover: University Press of New England, 1993.

Dickerson, Debra J. *The End of Blackness: Returning the Souls of Black Folk To Their Rightful Owners*. New York: Pantheon Books, 2004.

Douglas, Kelly Brown. *Sexuality and the Black Church: A Womanist Perspective*. Maryknoll, NY: Orbis Books, 1999.

———. *What's Faith Got To Do With It?: Black Bodies/Christian Souls*. Maryknoll. New York: Orbis Books, 2005.

Dubey, Madhu. *Black Women Novelists and the Nationalist Aesthetic*. Bloomington, IN: Indiana University Press, 1994.

DuBois, W.E.B. *The Souls of Black Folk*. New York: Signet Classics, 1995.

Dyson, Michael Eric. *Race Rules: Navigating the Color Line*. Reading, MA: Addison-Wesley Publishing Company, 1996.

———. *Open Mike: Reflections on Philosophy, Race, Sex, Culture and Religion*. New York: Basic Civitas Books, 2003.

Eagleton, Terry. *The Idea of Culture*. Oxford: Blackwell Publishers, 2000.

———. *Literary Theory: An Introduction, 2nd Edition*. Oxford: Blackwell Publishers Ltd., 1996.

Edgar, Andrew and Peter Sedgwick, eds. *Key Concepts in Cultural Theory*. London: Routledge, 1999.

Fetner, Tina. *How the Religious Right Shaped Lesbian and Gay Activism*. Minneapolis: University of Minnesota Press, 2008.

Foucault, Michel. *The History of Sexuality, An Introduction: Volume I*. New York: Vintage Books, 1990.

Gates, Henry Louis. *The Signifying Monkey: A Theory of African American Literary Criticism*. New York: Oxford University Press, 1988.

Geertz, Clifford. *The Interpretation of Cultures*. New York: Basic Books, Inc., 1973.

Gilroy, Paul. *Against Race: Imagining Political Culture Beyond the Color Line*. Cambridge: Belknap Press, 2000.

Grant, Jacquelyn. *White Women's Christ and Black Women's Jesus: Feminist Christology and Womanist Response*. Atlanta: Scholars Press, 1989.

Green, Michael. "Cultural Studies." In *A Dictionary of Cultural and Critical Theory*, edited by Michael Payne. Oxford: Blackwell Reference, 1996. 124–128.

Griffin, Horace. *Their Own Receive Them Not: African American Lesbians and Gays in Black Churches*. Cleveland: The Pilgrim Press, 2006.

Hall, Stuart, ed. *Representation: Cultural Representations and Signifying Practices*. London: Sage Publications, 1997.

Hamer, Dean and Peter Copeland. *The Science of Desire: The Search for the Gay Gene and the Biology of Behavior*. New York: Simon and Schuster, 1994.

Harper, Phillip Brian. *Are We Not Men?: Masculine Anxiety and the Problem of African American Identity*. New York: Oxford University Press, 1998.

Hegel, Georg Wilhelm Friedrich. *Lectures on the Philosophy of World History, Introduction: Reason in History*. Cambridge: Cambridge University Press, 1975.

Hemphill, Essex. *Brother To Brother: Collected Writings by Black Gay Men*. Los Angeles: Alyson Publications, 1991.

———. *Ceremonies*. San Francisco: Cleis Press, 1992.

Higginbotham, A. Leon, Jr. *In the Matter of Color: Race and the American Legal Process, the Colonial Period*. New York: Oxford University Press, 1978.

Higgins, John, ed. *The Raymond Williams Reader*. Oxford: Blackwell Publishers, Ltd., 2001.

hooks, bell. *Black Looks: Race and Representation*. Boston: South End Press, 1992.

———. *Salvation: Black People and Love*. New York: Harper Collins, 2001.

Hopkins, Dwight N. *Introducing Black Theology of Liberation*. Maryknoll, NY: Orbis Books, 1999.

Huggins, Nathan Irvin, ed. *Voices From the Harlem Renaissance*. New York: Oxford University Press, 1995.

Jackson, Ronald L., II. *Scripting the Black Masculine Body: Identity, Discourse, and Racial Politics in Popular Media*. Albany, NY: State University of New York Press, 2006.

Jakobsen, Janet R. *Working Alliances and the Politics of Difference*. Bloomington: Indiana University Press, 1998.

Jakobsen, Janet R and Ann Pellegrini. *Love the Sin: Sexual Regulation and the Limits of Religious Tolerance*. New York: New York University Press, 2003.

Jargose, Annamarie. *Queer Theory: An Introduction*. New York: New York University Press, 1996.

Jordan, Winthrop. *White Over Black: American Attitudes Toward the Negro, 1550–1812*. New York: W.W. Norton and Company, 1977.

Kant, Immanuel. *Observations on the Feeling of the Beautiful and Sublime.* Berkeley: University of California Press, 1960.

Kellner, Douglas. "The Frankfurt School," available online at http://www.gseis. ucla.edu/faculty/kellner/papers/fs.htm, pg. 1.

Kenan, Randall. *A Visitation of Spirits.* New York: Vintage Books, 1989.

King, J.L, with Karen Hunter. *On the Down Low: A Journey into the Lives of 'Straight' Black men Who Sleep With Men.* New York: Broadway Books, 2004.

————. *Coming Up From the Down Low: The Journey to Acceptance, Healing, and Honest Love.* New York: Crown Publishers, 2005.

Kirsch, Max H. *Queer Theory and Social Change.* London: Routledge. 2000.

Labbe, Theoloa S. "E. Lynn Harris: Black, Male, Out And On Top." *Publishers Weekly* (New York) 248. 31 (July 30, 2001).

Macey, David. *The Penguin Dictionary of Critical Theory.* London: Penguin Books, 2000.

Markley, Robert. "British Theory and Criticism, Early Eighteenth Century," available online at http://www.press.jhu.edu/books/hopkins_guide_to_literary_ theory/entries/british_theory_and_criticism-_1.html.

McBride, Dwight A. *Why I Hate Abercrombie and Fitch: Essays on Race and Sexuality.* New York: New York University Press, 2005.

McRuer, Robert. *The Queer Renaissance: Contemporary American Literature and the Reinivention of Lesbian and Gay Identities.* New York: New York University Press, 1997.

Midgley, Mary. *Beast and Man: The Roots of Human Nature.* Ithaca, NY: Cornell University Press.

Miles, Robert. *Racism and Immigrant Labour.* London: Routledge and Kegan Paul, 1982.

Mondimore, Francis Mark. *A Natural History of Homosexuality.* Baltimore: The Johns Hopkins University Press, 1996.

Morgan, Robert. "The 'Great Emancipator' and the Issue of Race." *The Journal of Historical Review,* available online at http://www.ihr.org/jhr/v13/ v13n5p-4_Morgan.html.

Morrison, Toni. *Playing in the Dark: Whiteness and the Literary Imagination.* Cambridge, MA: Harvard University Press, 1992.

Murray, Stephen O. and Will Roscoe, eds. *Boy-Wives and Female Husbands: Studies of African Homosexualities.* New York: St. Martin's Press, 1998.

Napier, Winston, ed. *African American Literary Theory: A Reader.* New York: New York University Press, 2000.

New Oxford Annotated Bible, Third Edition, New Revised Standard Version. New York: Oxford University Press, 2001.

Outlaw, Lucius T. Jr. *On Race and Philosophy.* New York: Routledge, 1996.

Payne, Michael, ed. *A Dictionary of Cultural and Critical Theory.* Cambridge, MA: Blackwell Reference, 1996.

Pew Forum on Religion and Public Life Study. "Religious Beliefs Underpin Opposition to Homosexuality." November 18, 2003.

Pinn, Anthony B. *Why Lord?: Suffering and Evil in Black Theology.* New York: Continuum Publishing Co., 1995.

————. *African American Humanist Principles: Living and Thinking Like the Children of Nimrod*. New York: Palgrave Macmillan. 2004.

Polikoff, Nancy D. *Beyond (Straight and Gay) Marriage: Valuing All Families Under the Law*. Boston: Beacon Press, 2008.

Richards, David A. *Identity and the Case for Gay Rights: Race, Gender, Religion As Analogies*. Chicago: University of Chicago Press, 1999.

Said, Edward. *Orientalism*. New York: Vintage Books, 1979.

Sanders, Cheryl J. *Saints In Exile: The Holiness-Pentecostal Experience in African American Religion and Culture*. New York: Oxford University Press, 1996.

Smith, Charles Michael. *Fighting Words: Personal Essays by Black Gay Men*. New York: Avon Books, 1999.

Steward, Douglas. "Saint's Progeny: Assotto Saint, Gay Black Poets, and Poetic Agency in the Field of the Queer Symbolic." *African American Review* (Terre Haute) 33. 3 (Fall 1999).

Stone, Jerome. *The Minimalist Vision of Transcendence: A Naturalist Philosophy of Religion*. Albany: State University of New York Press, 1992.

Sullivan, Andrew. *Virtually Normal: An Argument About Homosexuality*. New York: Vintage Books, 1995.

Taylor, Mark C., ed. *Critical Terms for Religious Studies*. Chicago: University of Chicago Press, 1998.

Teal, Donn. *The Gay Militants*. New York: Stein and Day Publishers, 1971.

Tudor, Andrew. *Decoding Culture: Theory and Method in Cultural Studies*. London: Sage Publications, 1999.

Ware, Frederick L. *Methodologies of Black Theology*. Cleveland, OH: The Pilgrim Press, 2002.

Warner, Michael. *The Trouble With Normal: Sex, Politics, and the Ethics of Queer Life*. New York: The Free Press, 1999.

Washington, Joseph R. Jr. *Black Religion: The Negro and Christianity in the United States*. Lanham, MD: University Press of America, 1984.

Welsing, Frances Cress. *The Isis Papers: The Keys to the Colors*. Chicago: Third World Press, 1991.

West, Cornel. *Keeping Faith: Philosophy and Race in America*. New York: Routledge, 1993.

————. *The Cornel West Reader*. New York: Basic Civitas Books, 2000.

Williams, Delores S. *Sisters in the Wilderness: The Challenge of Womanist God-Talk*. Maryknoll, NY: Orbis Books, 1993.

Williams, Raymond. *The Sociology of Culture*. Chicago: The University of Chicago Press, 1981.

Wilson, William Julius. *The Declining Significance of Race: Blacks and Changing American Institutions*, 2nd Edition. Chicago: The University of Chicago Press, 1980.

Index